ISLAM AND ROMANTIC ORIENTALISM

ISLAM AND ROMANTIC ORIENTALISM
Literary Encounters with the Orient

MOHAMMED SHARAFUDDIN

I.B.TAURIS PUBLISHERS
LONDON · NEW YORK

Published in 1994 by
I.B.Tauris & Co Ltd
45 Bloomsbury Square
London WC1A 2HY

Paperback edition 1996

175 Fifth Avenue
New York
NY 10010

In the United States of America
and Canada distributed by
St Martin's Press
175 Fifth Avenue
New York
NY 10010

A full CIP record for this book is available from the British Library

A full CIP record for this book is available from the Library of Congress

ISBN 1-86064-026-5

Typeset by The Midlands Book Typesetting Co.
Printed and bound in Great Britain by
WBC Ltd, Bridgend, Mid Glamorgan

Contents

Preface

A WORD about my purpose in this book may be helpful. I intend to demonstrate the implications of the key phrase, realistic orientalism. As we shall see, the phrase implies a paradox, or even an oxymoron, in that it links together two disparate ideas: the idea of imaginative escape and libidinous investment contained in the notion of orientalism, and the idea of a body knowledge outside the self and independent of the subjective desire contained in the notion of realism. The longing for an exotic and alluring alternative — one that was free of politics — to the predictabilities of everyday life, produced, insofar as these poets at least are concerned, a detachment from the home values that opened a space for the recognition of Islam as a unique form of life, as worthy of respect as the home culture.

There are, however, several points that require our attention. Most modern critics, especially those working in the field of intercultural relations, have studied previous writers from strictly modern viewpoints, using new concepts and judgements that seem to exceed the limits of literary and critical appreciation. Constantly searching for ideological formations and political classifications, they are concerned mainly with what makes people conform, what entraps them in their existing attitudes, in society as a closed system of interrelated values. My own interests lie elsewhere: in the way in which a society — any society — renews itself, not in how it remains static and enslaved by its perceptions and dogmatic conventions; in the way ideologies transcend themselves, not in how they determine consciousness; and in the way in which the practice of poetry can become (as Byron himself would put it quite polemically) a process of discovering and learning, not merely one of repetition and reassurance.

I have chosen to emphasize neutrality and objectivity as qualities that contribute (as they have in most world literatures) to the making of a genuine and revealing literature. In fact, the examples I have chosen in this book show that poets are not politicians, in the common sense of the word, and cannot be viewed only as such. Being different from those working in the spurious world of political agendas and conspiracies, with some obvious exceptions on both sides, poets and other creative writers should not be limited to one mode of perception by their readers, nor to one single ideological interpretation. Beckford, Byron, Conrad and Kipling, among others, were products of their imperialist culture, as Edward Said brilliantly demonstrates in his recent book *Culture and Imperialism* and its more important precursor *Orientalism*; but if we judge them to be no more than that, then we have condemned an important segment of society as a bunch of authors who were misguided by their age's ambitions and imperial conspiracies. This accusation, attractive as it is to modern audiences concerned mainly with change and radical opposition, is not only faulty but also misleading, as it obliterates certain important aspects of authors who would otherwise be viewed as rebels against their age's prejudices and blindness to other cultures.

This, as I try to show, is true in the case of Lord Byron, whom Edward Said counts among the Romantics who misrepresented and 'restructured' the Orient and were not 'guided' by their dealings and interaction with it. This, in my opinion, is a limited view of literature as a creative progress towards the discovery of truth and not merely a reflection of the age's social and political tendencies. Unfortunately, Said has cast the shadow of his own scepticism, both political and spiritual, over the possibility that some conscientious and high-minded writers may be born out of a society that has been defined as imperial. On the other hand, my aim is not so much to defend imperial inclinations, but rather to rethink the context and purpose of a given text and what it aims to achieve in its audience before we condemn its author as a partaker of his age's ignorance and blindness.

The second point I would like to stress is the profoundly political nature of 'realistic orientalism' as exhibited in the examples I have chosen. While not denying Said's argument that orientalism served as a political ideology to make the orient unreal, and therefore open to Western exploitation and control, I have focused on a contrary strand that affected a minority (although a very influential one): namely that orientalism which, because it proved receptive to the radical energies liberated by the French Revolution, offered an effective vantage point from which to condemn the reactionary forces at home and the prevailing spirit of intolerance reflected in relations with a culture such as that of Islam. In fact, Islam was the only alternative civilization powerful enough and sufficiently close to the West to invite such positive reception: Japan was not sufficiently known, China was too distant, and the indigenous populations of Africa and Latin America too alien and too localized. Moreover, modern critics have been tempted to examine authors as products of their own cultural and social milieus, while somewhat ignoring the personal side of these authors. I wish to stress this point, for it was indeed their individual singularity and particular personality that was the prime instigator of their interest in other cultures. This is a unique characteristic that seems to link all these authors.

At the end of the eighteenth century a close association developed between two young writers, Landor and Southey, who became fast friends, both of them British, both starting life as 'Jacobin' radicals, and both turning fairly quickly to conservatism. Early in the second decade of the following century a similar association was formed between Byron and Moore. Both were members of the fashionable world, both distanced themselves from English values (though for different reasons), and both were capable of the playfulness and wit born of self-confidence and leisure. For all four poets orientalism marked a point of departure in their poetic careers and, indeed, in the whole perception of Islam and the orient in England.

My third point bears on my fundamental purpose in this book, where I try to conduct an analysis of culture at the crossroads of poetry, politics, religion and sexuality. The approach I have adopted is intended to highlight, rather than overlook, those elements which promote genuine interchange between cultures, and promote the sort of understanding that effects a change in the perception of others, but without giving justification to whatever is defined as wrong in the relationship between the perceiving and the perceived cultures. Despite the difficulty of this approach, I believe it is a worthwhile task, especially in this difficult age of strained relations between nations, to demonstrate that every society is capable of producing in its literature positive elements that enhance the promotion of human knowledge and universal truth.

* * *

I should like, lastly, to acknowledge my gratitude to Professor Jacques Berthoud, Chair of the Department of English, University of York, for the unlimited support and encouragement he gave me during my years of study for my PhD, which I earned under his supervision. I am particularly indebted to him for his valuable comments, linguistic and otherwise, which proved essential in the final presentation of the material. I also wish to express my thanks to several individuals who provided valuable assistance and moral support from the early stages of this book's writing and publication: Professor F. T. Prince (Southampton), Jennifer Kay Hullinger (Cincinnati), the late James Sweid Nesteby (Illinois), Professor Ryan and Carol LaHurd (Minneapolis), Gabrielle Van Bruck (London), Abdulmalik N. Eagle (London), Jonathan Wordsworth (Grasmere), Anna Enayat (London) and Helen Simpson (London). Many thanks are also due to the administrators of the British Council (Sana'a and London) for granting me the scholarship to finish my studies.

Introduction

THE relation between Islam and the English literature is basically a relation between two cultures and between two political and religious systems conditioned by historical and geographical factors. Any study of this topic is therefore bound to be multilayered. Edward Said, however, has shown in his book *Orientalism* (1978 — the most significant recent contribution to the subject) that the relationship between Islam and Christianity, or East and West, has been essentially *political* from its earliest beginning. Ever since the encounter between the Greeks and the Persians in the fifth century BC, the East has always been represented by the West in hostile terms. Said argues that the literature of the West has served to define, formulate and indeed enhance this hostile relationship throughout. The literature of Greece, for example, represented Persia as a despotic power that needed to be curbed and eventually subdued. Even then, information was not neutral, but sought to enforce itself and to shape men's minds. This relationship between knowledge and power Said developed from Michel Foucault's analysis of cultural systems, as conducted in his *The Archaeology of Knowledge* and *Discipline and Punish*.

My aim is not to expose the political implications of Said's book, or to argue for or against the ideology it advances. It is rather to explore the development of orientalism — the image of Islam in the West — in English Romantic narratives. But a brief discussion of Said's book will help to alert us to the polemical nature of this topic.

In his introduction, Said defines orientalism as a system invented by the West on the assumption of a strong distinction between East and West. Europe as represented by orientalism has usually looked at the Orient as a place of romance inhabited by exotic human beings and filled with haunting memories and landscapes. Said takes the late 18th century as an approximate starting point for western orientalism, which he describes as 'the corporate institution for dealing with the Orient — dealing with it by making statements about it, authorizing views of it, describing it, by teaching it, settling it, ruling over it: in short, Orientalism as a Western style for dominating, restructuring and having authority over the Orient'.[1] To Said, orientalism does not study the Orient for the sake of establishing the truth of what it describes, and it possesses no disinterested view of the object of its preoccupation. Said's criticism of orientalism reaches a climax when it deals with a work that acquired unchallenged authority as a source of information about the Orient: William Lanes's *Modern Egyptians*, which in the 19th century virtually replaced the reality of the Orient itself as a criterion of truth about the Orient. As an example, Said refers to Nerval, for whom, when he 'borrows passages verbatim from *Modern Egyptians*, it is to use Lanes's authority to assist him in describing village scenes in Syria, not Egypt'.[2]

Said powerfully sums up this kind of discourse with the maxim: 'Orientalism overrode the Orient.'[3] Things about the orient 'always rose from the specifically human detail to the general transhuman one; an observation about a 10th-century Arab poet multiplied itself into a policy towards (and about) the Oriental mentality in Egypt, Iraq, or Arabia. Similarly a verse from the Koran would be considered the best evidence of an incredible Muslim sensuality.'[4] This process of falsification is precisely what made the Orient remote and seductively exotic to the western mind. And therefore, as Europe exercised more and more power over the Middle East, the Orient itself, in Said's striking phrase, became 'orientalized by Orientalism'.

The pervasive misrepresentation of the East in orientalism, even at its most scholarly phase, has its source not only in power relations but also in history. According to Said, European response to Islamic hegemony over a large part of the world at the start of the 14th century produced 'a lasting trauma'.[5] As early as the 11th century, Erchembert, a cleric of Monte Cassino, had described the Muslim armies as 'a swarm of bees, but with a heavy hand . . . they devastated everything'.[6] Such ideas as that of terror, devastation and voluptuousness became inextricably associated with Muslims. After the Crusades, no real communication took place between the two civilizations, no genuine translation of major Islamic texts was encouraged. For Said, what was said about Islam 'comes not so much for the sake of Islam in itself as to represent it for the medieval Christian'.[7] Misconceptions of Muhammad as an Antichrist impostor and Muslims as pagans flourished during this period.

These misconceptions were institutionalized in the West in terms of a superiority–inferiority distinction. By the 19th century, they conditioned foreign policy, as the statements of such important figures as Napoleon, Balfour and Cromer indicate. Napoleon's expedition to Egypt, for example, was motivated by the declared principle of 'saving it from barbarity'. But in this Napoleon simply repeated the views of his countryman Volney, who was in turn merely representing a whole cultural orientation. Not even Karl Marx was free from this pervasive bias. His denunciation of 'Oriental despotism' in *Surveys from Exile* sought to justify England's occupation of Hindustan: 'whatever have been the crimes of England she was the unconscious tool of history in bringing about that revolution' essential to the social state of Asia.[8]

For Said, then, 'Orientalism is a discursive phenomenon, internally consistent and self-perpetuating in virtual insulation from any correspondence with a "real Orient".'[9] This 'real Orient' is not only ignored or avoided by orientalists: it is not even perceived by them. In short, orientalism is an ideology, the purpose of which aimed covertly to nourish the political domination of the West. He sums up this view by comparing orientalism to a drama and the orientalist to a dramatist:

> In the depths of this Oriental Stage stands a prodigious cultural repertoire whose individual items evoke a fabulously rich world: the Sphinx, Cleopatra, Eden, Troy, Sodom and Gomorrah, Astarte, Isis and Osiris, Sheba, Babylon, the Ginii, the Magi, Nineveh, Prester John, Mahomet, and dozens more; settings, in some cases names only, half-imagined, half-known; monsters, devils, heroes; terrors, pleasures, desires.[10]

Said's analysis of orientalism is a powerful one, and any serious study of the subject has to take it on board. It is, however, not without its difficulties. First it suffers from a disease not unlike the one it seeks to diagnose, which may be called 'anti-Orientalism'. For Said the West is so systematically prejudiced that it distorts everything. Said tries to expose distortions, but he does this so systematically that he falls into the same trap. (Several reviews of his book suggested how cavalier he can be with evidence.) But secondly, his argument wavers between two extreme positions without ever facing both of them at the same time. The idea of a perspective, or ideology, or discursive system, or (to quote the term of Foucault, Said's strongest influence) *épistéme*, is in radical conflict with the idea of evidence, or truth, or justice, or 'the real Orient'. Said wants to eat his cake and have it: for him, orientalism is at once an autonomous cultural system (which presumably can only be changed by political or military defeat, and not by reason — not, for example, by books like his own) and also a form of deliberate prejudice against an ascertainable objective reality outside the system. For all its strength and moral importance, Said's study is empirically suspect and methodologically contradictory.

Yet, as I have said, my purpose is not to endorse or refute Said's position, but to define my own by comparison and contrast — to study a determinate literary phenomenon as a stage in a developing intercultural relationship. It is therefore essential to account for ideological and historical change within a given society, but this I cannot do on the basis of Foucault's *épistéme*, or of ideology in a hard sense. I do not believe that the thought of *all* western writers was *wholly* conditioned by an all-enveloping cultural grid, nor that they were the inevitable product of their age's imperialist and political ideologies. Insofar as they were part of their period (a period which contained the American and French revolutions), they had available to them its innovative as well as its conservative tendencies. We need to keep in mind that the Romantic movement emerged as resistance to massive despotism, and that its writers were reacting against political and cultural centralization. It was possible for a genuine interest in other countries and cultures to develop.

The examples I have chosen for special study are Landor, Southey, Moore and Byron; the last two of whom Said himself includes, along with Beckford and Goethe, as contributing to what he called the 'restructuring' and 'orientalization' of the Orient.[11] Any attempt to examine a process of historical development must be historically realistic; that is to say, it must take into account *what was possible in the age*. Historical progress is not achieved by one leap from darkness to light and from prejudice to truth, but *progressively*, as a gradual advance *towards* true understanding. Each period allows only a certain latitude of free play: one must therefore acknowledge partial contributions (such as those made by the writers examined) as notable achievements, and not repudiate them as compromised and incomplete. In my opinion all four narrative verse texts I have chosen to examine — *Gebir* (1798), *Thalaba* (1801), *Lalla Rookh* (1817) and the so-called 'Turkish Tales' (1813–16) — mark an advance in the understanding of and sympathy with the Orient, and therefore a distancing from the centralizing complacencies of establishment patriotism. This book is therefore concerned with the emergence of what I thus call, in an opposing approach to Said's, 'realistic Orientalism'. It is my contention that orientalism need not necessarily be incompatible with a discovery of the Orient, but may indeed, however incompletely, encourage and foster it.

An important aspect of this issue has been commented upon by Marilyn Butler in her article, 'Revising the canon', in *The Times Literary Supplement*. In this she objects to the exclusiveness of the so-called 'literary canon' as defined by the critical establishment. The admission to the club of great poets who are considered in some sense to represent the national spirit of their age leads to the neglect and ultimately the oblivion of many 'minor' poets. But since these minor poets may not have seemed so in their time, and since they may therefore have exercised considerable influence on the major writers, it follows that exclusive canonization may distort literary history. Professor Butler discusses the case of Southey, who was, in his early career, as controversial a figure as Wordsworth, and was greeted by Francis Jeffrey as the leader of a 'sect of dissenters', a sect to which Wordsworth 'merely belonged'.[12] Why then did Southey come to be neglected? According to Professor Butler: 'Southey possessed non-canonical qualities — he was contentious rather than reassuring, common rather than genteel, provincial rather than metropolitan, international rather than national. And he was no solitary or recluse.'[13]

It is not easy to see how one can generalize from this admittedly just characterization of Southey. Keats was common rather than genteel, Shelley and Byron were both international and contentious, Crabbe and Clare were both provincial and reclusive — yet all of these are major canonical figures. On the other hand, Landor and Scott were, in their different ways, reassuring, genteel, metropolitan and national, yet they are excluded from the canon. Professor Butler's understanding of canonical criteria is not clear. Is Southey excluded because he possessed 'non-canonical' characteristics? (But, as I suggest, the characteristics she offers are implausible.) Or is he excluded because of his limited literary interest? (Yet, while she refers to his rhythmical feebleness, she does not wish to say that lack of literary quality is the reason for his failure to make it.) She seems to imply that a canon is 'constructed' on the basis of extra-literary criteria, i.e. the tastes and prejudices of the given political and social establishment, and that it owes nothing to the intrinsic merit of the texts selected. Thus Butler's perception of the canon seems in many ways complementary to Said's idea of orientalism. Both are merely perspectival, not objective. But it that case, the notion of a canon is open to the same objections as is Said's idea of orientalism. Much as a purely perspectival orientalism cannot establish contact with the real Orient, so a purely ideological canon is cut off from the literariness of texts. Nevertheless, any useful idea of a literary canon must surely establish some connection with literary and linguistic merit. Byron is canonical while Scott is not, not only because tastes have changed but also because he is a better poet.

In choosing works which (with the possible exception of *Gebir*) are today not considered to be masterpieces, I am challenging the existing canon. I do so, however, on grounds not independent of literary quality, but on those of suggesting that these writers are in fact better than they are thought to be, and that if we have failed to see this it is because we have failed to take their content — their orientalism — seriously enough. Within the term 'orientalism' I include the political and religious views relating to the Islamic orient, though this is not to say that they are interesting politically rather than aesthetically. My view is that their literary seriousness and their political seriousness are interdependent, and that the understanding of the one will lead to the understanding of the other.

The Orientalist Tradition

The achievement of my chosen poets as orientalists cannot be adequately evaluated outside the orientalist tradition they received. A brief outline of that tradition is therefore necessary.

The threat to Europe posed by the expansion of the Turkish Empire was checked in the 16th century, but clashes with Turkey only ceased in the middle of the 18th century. Turkey was associated with absolute despotism, and this image coloured the West's whole perception of Islam. Furthermore, unlike Christianity (in its spirit if not in its actions), Islam did not admit of an incompatibility between religion and politics — a point not lost on

Romantic poets inclined to associate literature and action. It could be said, therefore, that the central issue confronted by Romantic orientalism was despotism. Yet this would be too limited a view, for the Romantics had an ambiguous attitude to Islam: on the one hand, it offered a convenient symbol of the tyranny they all sought to overcome; but on the other, it offered an alternative to the compromised or corrupted political and social systems of Europe. It is therefore best to regard despotism not as the theme of Romantic orientalism, but as a major signpost.

The fact remains, however, that in the century that led up to the Romantics, the despotism of the Orient was an article of faith in the West. Even as liberal a figure as Montesquieu had regarded despotism as a basically oriental quality in *De l'Esprit des lois*, and endorsed the views of such orientalists as Chardin and Tavernier. Voltaire himself (1694–1778), in his play *Mahomet*, and in other writings, used the figure of the Islamic prophet to show up credulity and superstition as lying at the root of every religion. He was aware that there was some deliberate distortion in his picture of Muhammad, but, to him, the politics and religions of the Orient were equally suspect.

As the century advanced, there were some signs of a reaction against this prejudice. Antoine Boulanger, for example, argued in his *Recherches sur les origines du despotisme oriental* (1761) that oriental despotism was not a merely immoral phenomenon but the product of a religious and cultural matrix. More significant, though less well known, were the direct observations of oriental societies by Abraham-Hyacinthe Anquitel-Duperron (1731–1805), who was a long-term resident in India, and who greatly contributed to the dissemination of oriental history and culture. He translated and published the *Zend Avesta*, the sacred book of the Zoroastrians. But his major work was his *Législation orientale* (1778), which demonstrated, at a new level of scholarly accuracy, that Montesquieu and his followers had constructed their theory of oriental despotism on very insecure foundations. For instance, he showed that despotism was attributed to Turkey, Persia and India because they allegedly lacked a system of private property. He asserted 'that this distorted image of the Orient had provided the excuse for Europeans such as the English in India to confiscate native lands and wealth. If no private property existed under despotism, then the conqueror could take everything in the country because it had belonged to the defeated despot.'[14]

Anquitel-Duperron's attack on the generalized use of the phrase 'oriental despotism' (particularly relevant here, in that it concerns those areas of the orient whose culture is mostly Islamic) anticipates the stance of the Romantic poets I shall be examining. In various ways and degrees, the Romantics sought to demystify the image of the Orient, at least insofar as the mystification of the Orient was used to serve Anglo-centric interests and attitudes. Neither Landor, Southey, Moore or Byron, nor Coleridge, Shelley or Leigh Hunt (excluded from this book because it confines itself to the genre of the oriental narrative verse tale) were interested, in their earlier works, in fostering English self-complacency or in sharing the conventional denigration of Islam. At the very least, their attitude to their oriental material was ambiguous: it provided allegories of political despotism to be eschewed but also images of a foreign culture to be seduced by. Yet both these attitudes implied, under their apparent contradictions, a deeper unity in that both were critical of Europe — on the one hand for its despotic tendencies, on the other for its cultural imperialism or shortsightedness.

Two major thinkers may be identified as having had a major influence on Romantic openness to oriental reality: Jean-Jacques Rousseau and Edmund Burke. Their political assumptions were, of course, profoundly different, even antagonistic, but in their effects they were complementary. Rousseau's attack on tyranny was connected with his scepticism of the constructs of culture. His affirmation of the essential purity and innocence of nature (a repudiation of the doctrine of original sin) made English poets particularly responsive to the essential *pastoralism* of Islamic nomadic life in the early 19th century — a motif that occupies an important place in the narratives to be dealt with.

The case of Burke is more complex and less well known. The emphasis of his thought is on culture, not nature; but he has an *organic* conception of society, not a contractual one, and may therefore be said to have *naturalized* culture. This makes him specially imaginative about other cultures. Consider his contribution to the impeachment of Warren Hastings (1788), in the course of which he reviewed the history of Islam in India. Burke was not necessarily sympathetic to the speed with which Islam had spread across India.[15] Nevertheless he can say: 'The enthusiasm which animated [Muhammad's] first followers, the despotick power, which [his] religion obtained through that enthusiasm, and the advantages, derived from both, over the enervated great empires, and broken, disunited lesser governments of the world, extended the influence of that proud and domineering sect from the banks of the Ganges to the banks of the Loire.'[16] Yet Burke's examination of the Islamic domination of India and the different governments that came to power there enabled him to attack Hastings's claim that he adopted arbitrary power in India because the governments that had ruled there were themselves arbitrary and despotic. Burke thus asserts: 'But nothing is more false than that despotism is the constitution of any country in Asia . . . It is certainly not true of any Mahommedan constitution.'[17] Here is a clear echo of Anquitel-Duperron on the same issue, but

Burke goes even further: he implies that the Islamic constitution is an embodiment of the divine justice in that law is enhanced by religion:

> The greatest part of Asia is under Mahommedan governments. To name a Mahommedan government, is to name a government by law. It is a law enforced by stronger sanctions than any law, that can bind a Christian sovereign. Their law is believed to be given by God, and it has the double sanction of law and of religion which the prince is no more authorized to dispense with than any else. And, if any man will produce the Koran to me, and will but show me one text in it, that authorizes in any degree an arbitrary power in the government, I will confess, that I have read that book and been conversant in the affairs of Asia, in vain. There is not such a syllable in it; but, on the contrary, against oppressors by name every letter of that law is fulminated.[18]

Burke's original objective was to refute Hastings's imperialist claim that he had merely inherited an assumed Islamic arbitrary power over an enslaved population. But this leads him to crack open the carcass of ignorant prejudice to a quite remarkable degree.

It may be plausibly claimed that Burke anticipated and perhaps influenced an analogous openness in the relevant Romantic poets. The Byron who could write to Francis Hodgson on his return from the East (3 September 1811), 'I will bring you ten Mussulmans [who] shall shame you in all goodwill towards men, prayer to God, and duty to their neighbours,'[19] would certainly have approved of Burke's freedom from the prejudiced chauvinism of his insular compatriots.

Burke's independence from cliché was the fruit of direct experience — of Islamic writings rather than of Islamic life, as in the case of Byron. But readers and travellers can carry their prejudices with them; Burke and Byron were able to read or see with their own eyes because they were members of a culture in which such seeing was possible. They were the legatees of a tradition of increasing, if limited, honesty of testimony, mostly from travellers. One of the most remarkable of these travellers was Lady Mary Wortley Montagu (1689–1762), who as wife of the English ambassador lived in Constantinople between 1716 and 1718, and had virtually free access to Turkish women of the ruling class. Her so-called *Turkish Letters*, published in 1763, imparted a new direction to 18th-century orientalism in their freedom from the pieties of English culture and the acuteness and vivacity of their observation of Turkish life. As one would expect, she exercised a special influence on Byron, who was a member of her class and visited the same sites.

Another famous traveller of the period was James Bruce (1730–91), whose *Travels to Discover the Source of the Nile* (1790–91) awakened resonant chords in the Romantic imagination, particularly for his introduction of the Arab nomad as noble savage — a version of Rousseau's 'man of nature'. The following sample of his writing illustrates the extent to which perception of reality is related to the cultural stencils available to the perceiver:

> The dictates of nature in the heart of the honest Pagan [i.e. Arab nomad], constantly employed in long, lonely and dangerous voyages, awakened him often to reflect who that Providence was that invisibly governed him . . . Possessed of charity, steady in his duty to his parents, full of veneration for his superiors, attentive and merciful even to his beasts; in a word, containing in his heart the principles of the first religion, which God had inculcated in the heart of Noah, the Arab was already prepared to embrace a much more perfect

> one than what Christianity, at that time, disfigured by folly and superstition, appeared to him to be.[20]

This extract is all the more potent for its blend of Arab and Christian pastoralism, and the discovery in the sands of the Sahara of both the noble savage and the biblical original. This blend had special appeal to the pantisocratics Southey and Coleridge. Bruce's writings not only restored dignity to a patronized figure (the bedouin), but reality to a make-believe landscape. His portrayal of the landscapes and the weather (for example, the *simoom* wind) in the Orient made a powerful impact on the work of all the Romantic orientalists.

In fact two other travellers reinforced this effect: Constantin Volney (1757–1820) and Carsten Niebuhr (1733–1815). Volney's *Les Ruines* (1791) attracted the attention of many Romantic poets for its blend of antiquarian interest and Romantic themes of secularism and morality; whereas Niebuhr's *Travels through Arabia* (1774–8) vividly recorded the fierce climate and landscape of the Arabian deserts (including his observation of the famous 'mirage', known in Arabic as *sarab*, which had such an effect on the Romantic imagination), and applauded the Arab nomad for his freedom and purity.

But perhaps the most significant of these orientalist figures was Sir William Jones (1748–94), who uniquely joined the gifts of the scholar with those of the traveller, to impart a major impetus to an established tradition of oriental translation. In his 'Essay on the Poetry of the Eastern Nations', Jones urged the introduction of new imagery into English poetry, of which he recommended the Orient as a fecund source that could enrich western poetry as a whole. He thus asserts:

> I cannot but think that our *European* poetry has sustained too long on the perpetual repetition of

> the same images, and incessant allusions to the same fables: and it has been my endeavour for several years to inculcate this truth, if the principal writings of the *Asiaticks*, which are reposited in our publick libraries, were printed with the usual advantage of notes and illustrations, and if languages of the Eastern nations were studied in our great seminaries of learning, where every other branch of useful knowledge is taught to perfection, a new and ample field would be open for speculation; we should have a more extensive insight into the history of the human mind; we should be furnished with a new set of metaphors and similitudes; and a number of excellent compositions would be brought to light, which future scholars might explain and future poets might imitate.[21]

His magnificent translations of Islamic literatures and mythologies were informed by a remarkable scholarship and anchored in direct experience of the East, notably Bengal. He was particularly alert to the prejudice of ignorance, challenging the scholarship of such eminent historians as Richard Knolles and Paul Rycaut, who wrote on Turkish history and culture without possessing the Turkish language. He demonstrated the absurdity of the view that the Turks were ignorant because Islam taught ignorance (wrong both about the Turks and about Islam); he defended the subtlety and colour of ancient Indian mythology, the independence and simplicity of feeling of the Arab way of life, and the sophistication of Persian art and literature. The debt owed to Jones for his identification of the Arab nomad as the cousin, as it were, of the Ossianic outlaw and the republican mountaineer, and therefore as a political symbol of resistance to tyranny and monarchy, deserves to be noted. In his 'Discourse on the Arabs' (1787), Jones says:

> The *Arabs* never entirely subdued; nor has any impression been made on them, except on their borders . . . All the genuine *Arabs* of *Syria* whom I knew in *Europe*, those of *Yemen*, whom I saw in the isle of Hinzuàn . . . and those of *Hejaz*, whom I have met in *Bengal*, form a striking contrast to the *Hindu* inhabitants of these provinces: their eyes are full of vivacity, their speech valuable and articulate, their deportment manly and dignified, their apprehension quick, their minds always present and attentive; with a spirit of independence appearing in the countenances even of the lowest among them. Men will always differ in their ideas of civilization, each measuring it by the habits and prejudices of his own country; but if courtesy and urbanity, a love of poetry and eloquence, and the practice of exalted virtues be a juster measure of perfect society, we have certain proof, that the people of *Arabia*, both on plains and cities, in republican and monarchical states, were eminently civilized for many ages before their conquest of *Persia*.[22]

The tradition of translation available to Romantic orientalism has already been referred to. Two texts in particular need to be mentioned: the Koran and *The Arabian Nights*, both of which played a major part in defining the cultural and religious relations between West and East.

The Koran had long been known in Europe in Latin translations, made primarily by ecclesiastics who commented on issues concerning the divinity, and on Christo-Islamic controversies. One of the earliest translations of the Koran into English was by Alexander Ross (1590–1654), who used the French version of André du Ryer. But the great work of translation into English, well known to all the Romantic orientalists, was that of George Sale (*c.* 1697–1736) in 1734. Sale prefaced his translation with his famous 'Preliminary Discourse', which constitutes a major landmark in the evolution of orientalist scholarship. So striking was his knowledge of and identification with Islam, in an age of dogma and prejudice, that he was known in some conservative circles by the title 'half-Mussulman' for his positive view of the Koran. Sale's major innovation, the importance of which cannot be exaggerated, was his readiness to depend on the famous Muslim exegetists of the Koran — such as Beidawi and Zamakhshari; and on fundamental controversies he insisted on quoting Islamic rather than western authorities. Although Sale, conventionally enough, declared in his preface that the aim of his translation was to reveal the absurdity and imposture of the Koran, its effect was the exact opposite. The eloquence of his version led Byron himself to testify to the poetic sublimity of the original; the suggestiveness and depth of his commentary are everywhere visible in the works of all four poets figuring in the following chapters (in all cases reaching the point of emulation, with an entire apparatus of notes appended to the main texts); and all four remained deeply affected by the non-Christian moral power of the sacred Islamic text, and therefore of the profound viability of a civilization other than their own.

The practice of annotating one's own poem is not confined to the Romantic orientalists; but in their case it became so pervasive that it requires notice. It is not enough to suggest that they were simply showing off their erudition, or helping a reader with unfamiliar material, or yielding to a veritable infatuation with the Orient that made the accumulation of mere facts attractive in itself — though all these elements played their part. More important is the example of Sale. Sale's use of notes, which include many quotations elaborating on the Koranic text, reveals a clear division of purpose. On the one hand, it represents his official demonstration (with the striking exception of passages affirming the strong relationship between the Koran and the Bible, an element which left a profound mark on Southey in particular) of the inferiority of the Islamic text to the Christian one. On the other hand, they elaborate upon a translation which remains essentially intact, without editorial interpretations or even interference. In short, the *final* effect of the commentary is to impart dignity — to give weight and importance — to the original text. This is also the case with the Romantic narratives: the notes confer the substance of history, philosophy, learning to material that might otherwise seem no more substantial than the delightful but irresponsible stories of *The Arabian Nights*.

Not that the latter were regarded as merely frivolous, for they contained a very powerful charge of exoticism, as well as a narrative brilliance that had universal appeal. Antoine Galland's translation of 1704–17 into French had enormous success throughout Europe. Admittedly, Galland's work tailored the original to European taste; but the character of the original could not be suppressed — notably its emotional and erotic freedom, its oriental 'pagan' settings, its use of magic narratives. It certainly helps to explain the rapid growth of the 'oriental tale' genre in the 18th century: for example, Petis de la Croix's *Turkish Tales* (1707), and *The Persian Tales, or a Thousand and One Nights* (1710–12), Montesquieu's *Lettres persanes* (1721), Jean-Paul Bignon's *The Adventures of Abdalla, Son of Hanif* (1729), Voltaire's *Zadig* (1749), and across the Channel, Johnson's *Rasselas* (1759) and Goldsmith's *Citizen of the World* (1762). Most of these works had a satirical moral and allegorical tendency. This they owed to their ability to find a foothold, provided by the image of the Orient, in a society other than their own. To that extent at least they helped to relativize the European point of view, and thus to prepare the way for a more adequate perception of alternative cultural realities.

Beckford's Vathek

Vathek (English edition, translated with notes by Samuel Henley from Beckford's French prose, June 1786) marks the division between the 18th-century oriental tale and the Romantic verse romance. It is scarcely an exaggeration to suggest that it represents a quantum leap in the development of European literary orientalism, and the debt owed to it by the Romantic orientalists cannot be exaggerated. Though they are significantly reticent about acknowledging their indebtedness to Beckford's work, Landor, Southey and Moore undoubtedly grasped its imaginative and political implications. *Vathek*'s magnificent Halls of Eblis have their poignant echoes in both *Gebir* and *Thalaba*. The novel's exotic landscapes recur in the *Lalla Rookh* narratives. As for Byron, who devoted a powerful suppressed stanza to 'England's wealthiest son' in *Childe Harold's Pilgrimage*, he paid an extraordinary tribute to the 'sublime tale' of the 'Caliph Vathek' in his final note to *The Giaour*: 'For correctness of costume, beauty of description, and power of imagination, it far surpasses all European imitations, and bears such marks of originality, that those who have visited the East will find some difficulty in believing it to be more than a translation.'[23]

Vathek, with its brilliant notes taking up, in the first edition, almost as many pages as the text of the narrative itself, proved to be a rich cornucopia of oriental material for its Romantic successors. This debt has often been noticed, though it has not yet been fully explored. It consists in the supply of images (such as the wine of Shiraz, the nightingale and the rose, the butterfly of Cashmere, which recur in the verse romances) and in the imitation of phrases (Beckford's concluding summary, 'Thus the Caliph Vathek, who, for the sake of empty pomp and forbidden power, had sullied himself with a thousand crimes,' being echoed by Byron's concluding epigram on his Corsair: 'Linked with one virtue, and a thousand crimes . . .'). It consists in a wealth of local colour and local mythology (the Simorg, Houris, Peris, the Kaf mountains, etc) from which each of the Romantic poets took what suited his temperament and purposes: Landor the theme of arrogant construction and exemplary ruins, the figure of the sinister sorceress and the details of enchanting pastoral vegetation; Southey the Islamic piety, the encounter with sinister magicians, the sublime terror of the Halls of Eblis; Moore the jewelled seductive poise, the sinister despotism, the perversion and cruelty, the fire worship; and Byron the combination of aristocratic irony and sensual intensity, together with a sophisticated, and knowing, conduct of literary conventions. But more than those differentiated influences, *Vathek* opened wide the door to a world of new possibilities.

Vathek is a complex work, but the risk of over-simplification must not prevent the attempt at a brief characterization of it. Before Beckford, the 18th-century oriental tale had tended to treat Islamic material in an objective, that is a detached, manner.[24] Allegory, parable, satire had inhibited personal identification. Voltaire and Johnson (to cite the finest examples) never lost the air of producing a *demonstration*, tragic as it may have been in its implications. For Beckford, the orient became an opportunity for *experience* — certainly for intense personal fantasy and gratification. *Vathek* is part of his inner world. It is a projection of an amoral, secret life into the public domain; it gives the rein for the first time to what could well be called the outlawed self.

The structure of the narrative is, of course, orthodox. Its only eccentricity is to attribute to Islam a deep and central moral concern. Vathek is a self-indulgent tyrant, who renounces Allah and his Prophet, and is destroyed by his new master, Eblis. This ethical structure is given its fullest expression by the awe-inspiring shepherd ('a good

Genii') who makes a last attempt to divert Vathek from his 'atrocious purpose':

> abandon thy atrocious purpose: return: give back Nouronihar to her father, who still retains a few sparks of life: destroy thy tower, with all its abominations: drive Carathis from thy councils: be just to thy subjects: respect the ministers of the Prophet; compensate for thy impieties, by an exemplary life: and, instead of squandering thy days in voluptuous indulgence, lament thy crimes on the sepulchres of thy ancestors.[25]

This is undoubtedly impressive, even if the stylish succinctness and brio does not seem quite compatible with the deepest sincerity. But it is partly undone by the treatment of religion in everything that precedes this passage. The most religious figure encountered is Nouronihar's father, the Emir Fakreddin, an epitome of Muslim piety, faith and goodwill, but whose very earnestness gains Beckford's disrespect. This is how the emir receives the news that his daughter has given herself to Vathek:

> The news of so unlucky an event soon reached the ears of the emir, who abandoned himself to grief and despair, and began, as did his old grey-beards, to begrime his visage with ashes. A total supineness ensued; travellers were no longer entertained; no more plasters were spread; and, instead of the charitable activity that had distinguished this asylum, the whole of its inhabitants exhibited only faces of half a cubit long, and uttered groans that accorded with the forlorn situation.[26]

How seriously are we to take this piety, or, for that matter, the display of grief? The only element that brings the Fakreddin episode to life as far as the visitors are concerned is the erotic and voyeuristic; whenever it turns pious, the very worthiness produces only yawns and impatience. The reverse effect occurs in the eschatological conclusion. The Halls of Eblis inspire a terror and cruelty that is designed less to drive a moral point home than to provide a thrilling dimension to grandeur and sublimity. In other words, the ethical is put to the service of the aesthetic.

This deeply ambiguous work allows for no facile explanations. What its irony, its sardonic or grotesque humour, its systematic disrespect for every religious and social norm (even for its protagonist's appetites, which are treated like infantile gluttony) reveal is the author's sophisticated detachment from the literary and moral conventions that he inherited. This is precisely what one would expect from a work that is breaking and altering the existing mould. The conventions in place lose their stability, but without finding steadiness in a new set of expectations and norms. In the space opened out by detachment from inherited convention, new imaginative audacities become possible, and Beckford duly exploits them. But *Vathek* confronts us with something yet more interesting than acute literary transition. For what Beckford is really cutting loose from is his identity as a citizen of the 'tight little island' that is England. That *Vathek* was originally written in French is profoundly appropriate, for it is a radically unorthodox, and indeed cosmopolitan (as opposed to traditional and provincial) work. The first step in the direction of 'realistic orientalism' — the recognition by English culture of the reality and value of a *radically* foreign form of life — must be the loosening of one's literal-minded attachment to one's particular corner of the world. This *Vathek* exhibits to an extraordinary degree, and it is the secret of its appeal to those Romantic orientalists who began their career under the sign of the French Revolution, and who thereby declared their independence not only from political tyranny, but from national self-satisfaction. Whatever they became, Landor and Southey began as Jacobins; Moore never wholly lost his external perspective as an Irishman; and Byron remained, of course, the most relentless opponent of dogmatic Anglo-Saxon narrowness in the 19th century.

ISLAM AND ROMANTIC ORIENTALISM

Chapter 1

Landor's *Gebir* and the Establishment of Romantic Orientalism

LANDOR has been served in recent times by two outstanding biographies: R. H. Super's *Walter Savage Landor* (1953), a remarkable piece of front-line research, and Malcolm Elwin's more derivative, but more balanced and generous, *Landor: a Replevin* (1958). It is therefore possible to establish the dates and circumstances of the composition of the poem.

When he was only 22, Landor had been living in South Wales, where he met a young woman called Rose Aylmer (whom he was to immortalize after her premature death in a famous lyric), who got for him from the Swansea Circulating Library a copy of Clara Reeve's *The Progress of Romance* (1785). This was at the end of 1796. Mrs Reeve at that time rivalled Mrs Radcliffe as a popular novelist; the last story of her volume, entitled 'The History of Charoba Queen of Egypt', gave Landor the narrative substance of his poem, which was published anonymously before August 1798. To judge by the result, Landor was probably the most precocious of all the English Romantics — not only because of his youth, but also because he preceded even Wordsworth in his attempts to break away from the conventional diction of the late 18th Century.

To assess the place and function of the eastern elements in this ostensibly oriental — or at least Egyptian — tale, it is necessary to make a summary of the various traditional currents that flowed into it. The first significant element was the classical. Landor was perhaps the most remarkable Latinist of his age. It is possible that parts of *Gebir* were first written in Latin; certainly, when Landor published the second augmented and corrected edition of the poem in January or February 1803, he followed it in November of that year with a complete Latin version, *Gebirus*. The classical influences are therefore extremely powerful, not only on the style, which Landor claimed was, in its severity and compactness, affected by his reading of Pindar, but also in mode and substance.

The second of these elements, of even greater importance, was the oriental tradition. Mrs Reeve's narrative was taken from Pierre Vattier's 17th-century French translation of an Arabic book allegedly written by Murtadi, identified by Stephen Wheeler, the Oxford editor of Landor's *Poetical Works*, as Shaikh Murtada-'d Din, who died in Cairo in 1202.[1] The medieval Arab tale was apparently concerned with the invaders of Egypt. Jubair al-Mu'taffiki (the Jubair of the cities of the plain) was believed to be the first builder of Alexandria. Landor's Gebir (a name derived from the Arabic 'Jubair', but wrongly thought by Landor to be the etymological source of the name 'Gibraltar', whence his Gebir apparently originates) rebuilds a city called Gades (confounded by Landor with Gadis, the Phoenician name for the modern Cádiz). But Landor's wild fantasies and speculations cannot pull the root of the narrative out of its bed in medieval Egypt. In any case, his independent interest in oriental literature is testified to by his next publication, *Poems from the Arabic and Persian* (1800), a pastiche of two well-known collections: Sir William Jones's *Poems, Consisting Chiefly of Translations from the Arabick Languages* and John Nott's *Select Odes from the Persian Poet Hafez*, with the usual elaborate notes. Landor certainly had access in his father's well-stocked library to works by African and Asiatic travellers, and, of course, to Sale's famous translation of the Koran.

But apart from these two literary currents, the poem also received a determining impulse from Landor's own experiences. The first was a love affair in Wales with one Nancy Jones, to whom he wrote a moving elegy after her death in 1806. The second was the political events in France, to which Landor had responded with unusual sympathy and conviction. In 1796, when Landor was beginning to write *Gebir*, Napoleon was sweeping through northern Italy. Having quelled the last hiccups of the Terror in Paris, he seemed destined to carry the principles of the rights of man across the face of Europe, and inaugurate a golden age of liberty, equality and fraternity. The monarchies were against him, including England; but French troops against England had been mustered in Brest, and the future seemed open to the taking. Freedom in love and politics constitutes, as I shall emphasize, the governing idea of *Gebir*.

Exactly what weight one is therefore to give to the Islamic or oriental dimension of Landor's narrative is not easy to determine. The story is that two brothers, the military Gebir, who has been pledged as a child to avenge the wrongs suffered by his father by reconquering Egypt from which his people had been driven; and the pastoral Tamar, a shepherd whom Gebir (for a reason best known to his author) finds on the coastal plain of Egypt. Gebir falls in love with Charoba, Queen of Egypt, as she does with him; and Tamar falls in love with a sea-nymph, who challenges him to a wrestling match and defeats him. Gebir is persuaded by Charoba to rebuild the city of Cades, but the work is destroyed by mysterious powers. He discovers the cause of this destruction from his brother's nymph, whom he defeats in a contest, and with her help descends to the underworld. Here, meeting the spirit of his father, he discovers the vanity of ambition and tyranny. On his return to Gades he sponsors his brother's marriage to the nymph while deciding to marry Charoba himself and so end the Iberian-Egyptian conflict. Tamar's wedding is a happy one, but Gebir's ends in his death, the result of a devilish plot by Dalica, Charoba's nurse, who has mistakenly taken her mistress's agitation and silence as a symptom of her fear of, not her love for, Gebir.

Landor, in an unpublished 'Post-script to Gebir', written to defend his work against hostile reviewers, was quite clear about his independence from his source:

> . . . so far from a *translation,* there is not a single sentence, not a single sentiment, in common with the tale [as told by Clara Reeve]. Some characters are drawn more at large, some are brought out more prominent, and several are added. I have not changed the scene, which would have distorted the piece, but every line of appropriate description, and every shade of peculiar manners, is originally and entirely my own.[2]

This account is strictly accurate; and it makes it clear that Landor treated the material in his own way, and in terms of his own purpose. But what was this purpose?

In a note to *Gebirus* (the Latin version of the poem), Landor offers a possible answer: 'Our first book is almost wholly in the pastoral genre: nor could it be at all otherwise, having regard for propriety and the manner of the times in which it describes the events taking place:

but from that, step by step, rise greater things up to the end of the poem'.[3] This offers us a clue that may be readily tested. Book I, for example, is indeed *pastoral*, in that it is mostly concerned with Tamar's wrestling contest with the nymph, and his pangs of disappointed love, shared by Gebir. Book II is mostly devoted to Gebir's victory over the nymph, and his discovery of the secret cause of the destruction of the city he is trying to rebuild. The poem is thus in part *romance* — a more weighty genre than the pastoral. Book III is wholly taken up with Gebir's visit, with its prophetic lesson, to the underworld, and may therefore be thought of as *epic romance*. Book IV deals with the intensification of Charoba's love for Gebir, and her preparation to feast him: it has the excitement and display of *epic narrative*. Book V darkens the scene in that it describes Dalica's necromantic plot against Gebir, achieved by a sinister visit to her sister sorceress: the *demonic aspect* of epic narrative. Book VI celebrates the marriage of Tamar and the nymph, with its vision of a great historical future: a form of *epic prophecy*. And finally Book VII dramatizes the destruction of Gebir in what can only be thought of as the *tragic* genre. Thus, a movement, irregular in detail but plain in its general curve, develops from pastoral to romance, from romance to epic, from epic to tragedy.

This perspective is derived from the literature of classical antiquity. Impressive as it is, however, one cannot easily understand how, by itself, it clarifies Landor's intellectual and ideological purposes in the poem. But there lies another approach that may, without contradicting the first, prove more instructive — that the narrative form is based not on literary genre, but on what could be called the cultural context. Suppose that we ask, where are the oriental elements to be found in *Gebir*? The answer at once becomes obvious: in the main plot, involving Gebir with the Queen of Egypt. The subplot, involving the loves of

Tamar and the nymph, is entirely classical in feeling and colour, despite its initial setting in Egypt. This then has the effect of making a very sharp distinction between the two halves of the narrative. They are linked by two brothers (a relationship not in Reeve, but invented by Landor), one a soldier and architect, the other a shepherd and musician. Both of them are in love, one achieving disaster, the other happiness; the first descends into the infernal regions to discover the grim past of his ancestors, the other soars over the Mediterranean to discover a magnificent future for his progeny; the first is caught in the vice of nationalism and monarchy, the second carried by a vision of international justice and republican ideals. This systematic opposition is, as will be seen, given not only its focus but also its significance by the Islamic treatment of the main tragic plot as opposed to the secondary classical plot. We now turn, therefore, to an extended consideration of Landor's orientalism in *Gebir* — but with one word of caution. Even the main plot has profound classical elements, as Landor's own scheme of generic progression, outlined above, indicates. Theocritus, Virgil, Ovid and Milton are to be found behind much of the main action of the poem. To discuss the oriental elements is to pick only one imaginative layer from among several. Nevertheless my purpose is to demonstrate that it is a decisive one.

The Land of Egypt

The geographical and historical setting that Landor has created for his narrative is suffused with a wash of local colour. Primary to this must be the scene of Egyptian history — a period long after the decay and collapse of the great dynasties of kings and pharaohs, and vulnerable to foreign invasions: a sort of ancient 'third world', surrounded and dwarfed by the relics of a former gigantic civilization. We have seen that the historical source of Gebir himself was ultimately Jubair 'of the Cities of the Plain'. This Jubair was the leader of the Hyksos invaders, who could not have originated from Iberia, as Landor would have it. The young Queen of Egypt, Charoba (a name in Arabic meaning 'carob bean', emblem of constancy — a virtue which Landor's heroine certainly exhibits) is said to have been a friend of Abraham's wife, Sarah.[4] This is not a detail which Landor seems to have noticed, or perhaps rather chose to ignore. In any case, he sets the events rather later, in a fallow period that postdates the great Egyptian empires but antedates the appearance of Christianity and, of course, Islam. At one stroke, therefore, Landor eliminates the most potent source of cultural exoticism available to his orientalist successors: the Islamic tradition. What in that case remains?

First there are the geography and climate. We are in a country of empty plain and sterile mountains (though not without 'rich meadows where young Tamar fed/The royal flocks, entrusted to his care' (I, lines 88–9)),[5] with sands and dust and magnificent sunsets. We are, of course, conscious of the Nile and its alluvial delta. This is how Gebir greets his brother:

> Why, standing on the valley's utmost verge,
> Lookest thou on that dull and dreary shore
> Where many a league Nile blackens all the sand.
> [I, lines 95–7]

The Nile contains the creatures one would expect: when Gebir arrives in Egypt, his northern hunting dogs, 'shaggy, deep-chested', respond to unfamiliar sounds: 'the crocodile/ crying, oft made them raise their flaccid ears' (I, lines 65–6). The great river produces exotic fruit: '*Bring me a water-melon from the Nile*' (V, line 190), Charoba exclaims. Its arid plain swarms with strange and venomous snakes, like the 'grey cerastes' (or horned viper) used by Myrthyr,

Dalica's sister, for the 'viscuous poison' from its 'glowing gums' (V, lines 230–31), or, even more memorably, the cobra:

> . . . backward they start;
> And stop again, and see a serpent pant,
> See his throat thicken, and the crisped scales
> Rise ruffled; while upon the middle fold
> He keeps his wary head and blinking eye.
> Curling more close, and crouching ere he strike.
> [II, lines 27–32]

Plainly we are not in Tuscany, or even Athens, but in the Egyptian desert that fascinated Herodotus.

This austerity and sterile grandeur, however, offers a contrast, dear to the heart of the orientalists, with a profusion of material wealth and colourful luxury. The Egyptian festivity which Charoba, innocent of the dark plots of Dalica, orders for the reception of Gebir, has something of Cleopatra's style of conspicuous display. Tame crocodiles are crowned; women follow in barges; 'sweet airs' give rhythm to the rowers; distant spectators throng 'the sunny whiteness o'er the reeds' (IV, line 173). This movement is brought to a climax in the description of the procession from Charoba to Gebir:

> Meanwhile, with pomp august and solemn, borne
> On four white camels, tinkling plates of gold,
> Heralds before, and Ethiop slaves behind,
> Each with the signs of office in his hand,
> Each on his brow the sacred stamp of years,
> The four ambassadors of peace proceed.
> Rich carpets bear they, corn and generous wine;
> The Syrian olive's cheerful gifts they bear:
> With stubborn goats that eye the mountain-tops
> Askance, and riot with reluctant horn,

And steeds and stately camels in their train.
The king, who sat before his tent, descried
The dust rise redden'd from the setting sun . . .
[lines 182–94]

The formality and luxury of Egyptian life, as described here, is perfectly in keeping with a tribal society rather than an imperial or military one; and furthermore it is perfectly in accord with the concluding image which 'frames' the description in several ways: first by showing the scene in the perspective of distance, secondly by representing it as it appears to the eye of a foreigner alert to colourful detail, and thirdly by providing an appropriate setting of landscape and climate. In *Gebir*, the orientalism may be applied with a restrained brush, and it may be diluted by other styles and modes, but its effect remains extremely powerful.

Egyptian Ruins

A more specialized aspect of Landor's orientalism is his emphasis on the ruins of a once majestic but now decayed civilization. In this he was undoubtedly influenced by some of the 18th-century travel literature devoted to the Near East. In such works as Volney's *Les Ruines* (1791) one finds a sense of loss of and reverence for former grandeur. Landor alludes to James Bruce (a note to Book V, line 231, on the 'stunted shrub' under which the horned viper burrows) whose *Travels to Discover the Source of the Nile* (1790–91) was another influential book on ancient Egyptian relics. Here is a description of the ancient city of Masar, to which Dalica makes a pilgrimage in order to obtain means for destroying the invading Gebir:

ONCE a fair city, courted then by kings,
Mistress of nations, throng'd by palaces,
Raising her head o'er destiny, her face

Glowing with pleasure, and with palms refreshed,
Now, pointed at by Wisdom or by Wealth,
Bereft of Beauty, bare of ornaments,
Stood, in the wilderness of woe, Masar.
[V, lines 1–7]

Former splendour and pride have turned to decay and waste. Where once kings and warriors lived now lurk stealthy animals:

. . . at human step
The fierce hyæna, frighted from the walls,
Bristled his rising back, his teeth unsheathed,
Drew the long growl and with slow foot retired.
[lines 10–13]

This collapse is exemplary and has a meaning which both 'Wealth' and 'Wisdom' can recognize. It is nothing more or less than the vanity of earthly life. Human glory is at best a transitory thing. But the hidden meaning of this scene goes further than this commonplace. Masar (the Arabic word for 'Egypt' is 'Massr') is plainly the city known as 'Missr el Kahira', or 'Cairo' in English, and thus represents in a specially acute form the fall of Egyptian imperial power. This theme has already been sounded a number of times, and it features prominently in Landor's subtle treatment of the city of Gades. When he invades Egypt, Gebir discovers a ruined city on the northern coast:

. . . a city stood
Upon that coast, they say, by Sidad built,
Whose father Gad built Gades . . .
[I, lines 42–4)

The followers of Gebir are therefore called by Landor 'the Gadites' or 'the Gadite men'. According to Landor's garbled history, one Gad, ancestor of Gebir, built Gades (Cádiz in Spain near the eponymous 'Gibraltar' for Landor), and Gad's son, Sidad, having conquered Egypt, built 'a city' (I, line 42), now ruined, which Gebir, out of national and filial piety, decides to rebuild. What is the historical basis for this farrago? In his edition of the poem Wheeler draws attention to Sale's translation of the Koran, Chapter 89, and Sale's notes, which show that Landor failed to understand that Sidad (or rather Shaddat) built the city known as Iram, or Irem, in the desert near Aden, and not in the desert near the mouth of the Nile. In the Koran the people of Irem (Landor's Gadites) are called Adites. On these people the Koran is very instructive. The relevant Koranic verse runs thus: 'Hast thou not considered how thy LORD dealt with Ad, the people of Irem, adorned with lofty building [or "pillars"]?'[6] Sale's note runs thus: '[Irem was] the name of the territory or city of the Adites, and of the garden . . .; which were so called from Irem, or Aram, the grandfather of Ad, their progenitor.'[7]

According to the Koran, the Adites were tyrannical, corrupt and vainglorious; thus their punishment (the decline and destruction of their city and nation) was correspondingly severe. The Koran repeatedly drives the lesson home that great cities, turning tyrannical, inevitably earn God's vengeance and destruction. Let us consider as a further example the Koranic chapter entitled 'Houd', after the prophet of that name sent specifically to the Adites:

> But they who were unjust followed the delights which they enjoyed in this world, and were wicked doers: and thy LORD was not of such a disposition as to destroy the cities unjustly, while their inhabitants behaved themselves uprightly.[8]

Sale's comment here is equally relevant:

> Al Beidawi [the Muslim commentator on whose work Sale mainly depended] says that this passage gives the reason why the nations were destroyed of old; viz., for their violence and injustice, their following their own lawsuits, and for their idolatory and unbelief.[9]

Even more significantly, the Koran reserves a similar fate for the Egyptian pharaohs. The pharaoh to whom God sent Moses, overreaching himself, asked his people to recognize him as their deity, to the point of ordering his chief minister, Haman, to build a tower for him so that he could reach 'Moses's God'. Moses confronted the pharaoh:

> And Moses said, My Lord best knoweth who cometh with a direction from him; and who shall have success in this life, as well as the next: but the unjust shall not prosper. And Pharaoh said, O princes, I did not know that ye had any other god besides me. Wherefore do thou, O Haman, burn me clay into bricks; and build me a high tower, that I may ascend unto the God of Moses: for I verily believe him to be a liar. And both he and his forces, behaved themselves insolently and unjustly in the earth; and imagined that they should not be brought before us to be judged. Wherefore we took him and his forces, and cast them into the sea. Behold, therefore, what was the end of the unjust.[10]

In a note, Sale supplies a variant:

> It is said that Haman, having prepared bricks and other materials, employed no less than fifty thousand men, besides labourers, in the building; which they carried to so immense a height that the workmen could no longer stand on it; that Pharaoh, ascending

> this tower, threw a javelin towards heaven, which fell back again stained with blood, whereupon he impiously boasted that he had killed the God of Moses; but at sunset God sent the angel Gabriel, who, with one strike of his wing, demolished the tower, a part whereof, falling on the king's army, destroyed a million of men.[11]

In short, the Koran makes a causal connection between the ruins of great civilizations, of which Egypt was the leading example, and the moral and political corruption of its builders and rulers.

If we return to Gebir's city, what becomes specially significant is not only that he is facing the morally significant ruins of the city of his ancestors, *but that he proposes to rebuild it.* Gebir orders his men 'that from those ruins to their right/They forthwith raise a city' (I, lines 251–2). The transformation of rubble into architecture, as it were, incorporates the discoveries of the 18th-century travellers and amateur archaeologists, in that their rebuilding starts with the rediscovery of the original ruins:

> Some raise the painted pavement, some on wheels
> Draw slow its laminous length, some intersperse
> Salt waters thro' the sordid heaps, and seize
> The flowers and figures starting fresh to view.
> Others rub hard large masses, and essay
> To polish into white what they misdeem
> The growing green of many trackless years.
> [II, lines 8–14]

They are filled with archaeological excitement at the discoveries:

> Here, arches are discover'd, there, huge beams
> Resist the hatchet, but in fresher air

Soon drop away: there lies a marble, squar'd
And smoothen'd; some high pillar, for its base,
Chose it, which now lies ruin'd in the dust.
[lines 18–22]

This closely reflects the antiquarian interest in ruins that was beginning to assert itself at the end of the 18th century. As such it represents a fine example of straightforward orientalism. But the context provided by the Koranic suspicion, and even denunciation, of the pride of cities and civilizations, gives an altogether darker colouring to this act of rebuilding. There is something dangerous, if not impious, about it. To understand it more fully, we need to turn to Gebir himself.

Imperialism

Whether or not he is an imperialist by nature, Gebir is undoubtedly given an imperialist role. We may begin by observing that — whether or not Landor knew it — the very name 'Gebir' might derive its function from an Islamic etymological origin, for it is the type name in Koranic Arabic for those who have *behaved and ruled tyrannically*. In the Koran, Gebir's people (the Adites, or Gadites, as Landor calls them), are identified with *tajabor*, meaning 'being tyrannic'. Chapter V of the Koran has Moses conferring with his people just after the Exodus:

> Do you build a landmark on every high place, to divert yourselves [in delight]? And do you erect magnificent works, hoping that ye may continue in their possession for ever? And when you exercise your power, do you exercise it with cruelty and rigour?[12]

This last phrase represents Sale's attempt to identify the term *gebareen* with tyranny. (A modern translator of the

Koran, Marmaduke Pickthall, has rendered this final sentence: 'And if ye seize by force, seize ye as *tyrants*'.[13]) This sense of the word is maintained by Sale when explaining the cruelty of the Adites: 'Putting to death, and inflicting other corporal punishments without mercy, and rather for the satisfaction of your passion than the amendment of the sufferer'.[14] The Islamic connotation of Gebir and related names all confirm the general theme of tyranny which drew Landor's attention in the Koran.

Whether or not Landor was fully aware of this meaning inherent in the material he was using, there can be no doubt that the story of *Gebir* represents the nature and consequences of imperialism. In his preface to the 1803 edition, Landor added the following remark: 'In the moral are exhibited the folly, the injustice, and the punishment of Invasion, with the calamities which must ever attend the superfluous colonization of a peopled country'.[15] And this is indeed what the story of Gebir demonstrates. Gebir's fate tells:

> . . . how, incens'd
> By meditating on primeval wrongs,
> He blew his battle-horn, at which uprose
> Whole nations: how, ten thousand, mightiest men,
> He call'd aloud; and soon Charoba saw
> His dark helm hover o'er the land of Nile.
> [I, lines 16–21]

This is nothing less than a military occupation to reconquer lands won and lost ('ancient wrongs') by Gebir's forebears. The army of occupation inspires terror through its sheer size and power — 'Men of gigantic force, gigantic arms' (line 24); a trait, incidentally, also etymologically confirmed by the second meaning of *gebareen* as 'physical greatness' — and not merely 'outrageous pride'. Gebir and his Gadites represent imperialism, Charoba and the Egyptians the 'third world' nation vulnerable to conquest.

Insofar as Gebir can be considered a hero, his heroism is flawed. It is presented in his futile and abortive attempt to recover the glorious conquest of his forefathers. It is flawed on two grounds. First, conquests are intrinsically — or 'naturally', to follow Landor's argument — unacceptable as a foundation for heroism. He defines conquest as the 'superfluous colonization of a peopled country'. Secondly, the past he is trying to recover is itself already damaged in that it too was based on tyranny and oppression. Gebir does not discover this fact by himself. In a parody of God's creation of the world, the city he and his Gadites rebuild for six days is mysteriously destroyed on the seventh. He discovers that Egypt's undersea demons are responsible for this destruction, and he is vouchsafed entry into the underworld, like Odysseus, Aeneas, Dante, and even Milton's Satan, so as to be able to discover the reason for their action.

Despite powerful precedents in the classical and renaissance European epic, Landor's representation of hell is strongly affected by the Islamic hell as depicted in the Koran. Hell as a place of punishment for the wicked is, of course, so standard a feature of the negative underworld in all myths that nothing can be deduced from it. But there are two aspects of Landor's presentation that seem characteristically oriental: its appearance as a vast hall or architectural space, influenced too by Beckford's Halls of Eblis in *Vathek*; and its obsessive concentration on *tyranny* as the cause of infernal punishment.

Landor's portrayal of the infernal abyss into which Gebir descends has a dream-like terror and splendour that indicates that his imagination has been freed from the standard conventions of the classical or Christian hell:

. . . Now Gebir breath'd
Another air, another sky beheld.
Twilight broods here, lull'd by no nightingale,
Nor waken'd by the shrill lark dewy-winged,
But glowing with one sullen sunless heat.
Beneath his foot nor sprouted flower nor herb,
Nor chirp'd a grasshopper; above his head
Phlegethon form'd a fiery firmament:
Part were sulphurous clouds involving, part
Shining like solid ribs of moulten brass:
For the fierce element which else aspires
Higher and higher, and lessens to the sky,
Below, Earth's adamantine arch rebuffed.
[III, lines 83–95]

This combination of space and constriction, of immensity and confinement, is presented with a sensuous immediacy of a kind that seems without precedent in western literature. This agora-claustrophobia is achieved partly through an elimination of those contrasts on which an effect of life and vitality depends: 'But glowing with the one sullen sunless heat' — an impression immeasurably intensified by the effects of flames baffled by the 'adamantine arch' above his head, where swirling clouds of sulphur open to reveal the red-hot bars of the vast underworld prison. But the orient is present in more than these enormous subterranean halls. It is also present in the metaphysical idea, to be exploited by Moore in the third narrative of *Lalla Rookh*, that the fundamental reality of the world is made up of fire, and should therefore be worshipped as 'Phlegethon's eternal flame' (III, line 110). It is for this reason that the place of the punished and the place of the blessed are the opposite sides of one coin, so to speak. In the 'happy fields' on the other side of the 'adamantine arch', the breeze unites with heat to 'fill/With liquid light the marble bowl of Earth' (lines 104–5):

> Fire rules the realms of pleasure and of pain.
> Parent and element of elements,
> Changing, and yet unchanged, pervading heaven
> Purest . . .
>
> [lines 113–16]

The idea of fire as the fundamental reality of the cosmos (a fine Persian metaphor) is brilliantly amplified by a fusion of the sensory extremes of heat and cold (or *zamhareer*, a Koranic term), precisely as it features so prominently in the Islamic conception of hell in the after-life. The origins of this fire are 'the glowing oceans of the *Sun*', personified in a 'radiant robe . . . unseam'd and undefil'd'(lines 118–19) which diffuses to the stars and other lesser beings the element which is their life. Landor explicitly acknowledges the character of that image-cluster: 'This is a personification of an oriental cast, in which the stars are represented as crowding round their monarch, the sun, and as receiving from him those marks of favour, which inferior princes receive from their Sovereign'.[16] But this principle of life is either blended into a 'grateful symphony of guests' (line 121) or driven into conflict with its opposite. It dashes 'smaller streams' of fire

> on crystal cliffs of hail,
> And filters through black clouds and fleecy snows —
> But penetrates each cold and blue abyss
> Of trackless waves, and each white glimmering gem
> That crowns the victim's immolated brow.
>
> [lines 125–9]

This idea of common element, intolerably intensified on one side, tempered and diffused on the other, is given further development in the notion that every 100 years, the barrier dividing the two realms is removed to reveal and heighten the respective state of each. Such refinements are foreign to Landor's European and classical culture.

This account of the architecture of the next world seems to have involved specifically Koranic elements. The Koran tells us that the 'companions of the left hand [i.e. the wicked] shall dwell amidst burning winds, and scalding water, *under the shade of black smoke, neither cool nor agreeable*' (my italics).[17] On the other side, the companions of 'the right hand [i.e. the blessed] shall dwell in gardens of delight', [18] celebrated by Landor's gentle breezes 'that scatter freshness thro' the groves/And meadows of the fortunate' (lines 103–4). Furthermore, the arch separating the good from the wicked that parts open every century alludes to the Islamic notion of *Alsirat* or 'the straight bridge, leading directly to the other world'.[19] To be sure, this bridge is to be found outside Islam as well — as Sale notes, 'the Jews speak likewise of the bridge of hell, which they say is no broader than a thread';[20] but the *contrast* that Landor emphasizes is specially Koranic in that the Koran repeatedly declares that 'the realms of pleasure and of pain' are made aware of each other's state in order to increase respectively their delight and suffering. The Koran, for example, portrays the 'blessed' in their paradise viewing their polar opposites and questioning them about their conditions: ' . . . the companions of the right hand; who shall dwell in gardens, and shall ask one another questions concerning the wicked, and shall also ask the wicked themselves, saying What hath brought you into hell?'[21]

By adding an oriental layer to the classical and Christian tradition of hell, Landor feels free to introduce unexpected or unpredictable elements. The most important of these is his emphasis on *tyranny*. In his account, the division between the evil and the good resolves itself (to use his words in his 'Argument' featuring as headnote to Book

III) between '*the ambitious and . . . the peaceful*' (my italics). In this extraordinary emphasis on the sin of ambition, Landor is undoubtedly drawing on a major strand in Koranic ethics. The Koran reserves the punishment of hell for the impious who have committed sins against themselves and others. But this retributive justice is specially directed against those sinners who have 'behaved themselves unjustly'. The concept of 'injustice' in the Koran mainly includes *political* injustice, especially the oppression visited by despotic monarchs against their own subjects and those of other nations. For example, Chapter IX describes the fate of kings who have cheated their own people:

> On the day of judgement *their treasures* shall be intensely heated in the fire of hell, and their foreheads, and their sides, and their backs shall be stigmatized therewith; *and their tormentors shall say*, that is what ye have treasured up for your souls; taste therefore that which ye have treasured up.[22]

But what is emphasized in the Koran is not *avarice* or *greed*, as, for example, would be the case in Dante, but *illegality*. And this is something to which Landor is very responsive:

> Here are discover'd those who tortured Law
> To silence or to speech, as pleas'd themselves;
> Here also those who boasted of their zeal,
> And lov'd their country for the spoils it gave.
> [III, lines 283–6]

In contrast to tyrannical restlessness, the blessed are *peaceful*:

> . . . Here some observ'd
> Religious rites, some hospitality: . . .
> Some stopt revenge athirst for slaughter, some

Sow'd the slow olive for a race unborn.
[lines 299–300, 306–7]

They had no wishes, so that they are not the recipients of *ultimate* bliss — a state reserved for the 'supremely blest' (line 296) which Gebir is not allowed to witness ('We cannot see beyond' — line 297).

The reduction of hell and heaven, in line with the Koranic emphasis, to a system of tyranny and pacifism is naturally the appropriate context for the disclosure of an imperialist sin. Gebir descends into the underworld to discover why his ambitious city is mysteriously destroyed every seventh day. What he finds out is the true nature of his own past, and the values and obligations it has imposed on him. This information is partly supplied by his underworld interpreter, one Aroär, who had fought under his father:

'. . . Thou knowest not that here thy fathers lie,
The race of Sidad: their's was loud acclaim
When living; but their pleasure was in war:
Triumphs and hatred followed . . .
I still hear shrieking, through the moonless night,
Their discontented and deserted shades'.
[lines 35–8, 42–3]

And just in case Gebir is unreceptive, the message is made implicit:

'. . . It little now avails them to have rais'd
Beyond the Syrian regions, and beyond
Phœnicia, trophies, tributes, colonies . . .'
[lines 70–72]

Epic greatness is turned into its opposite — a life of misery and deprivation. Indeed, the inversion of values is such that it would not be an exaggeration to claim that heroism produces anti-heroism:

> . . . could they but revisit earth once more,
> How gladly would they Poverty embrace,
> How labour, even for their deadliest foe!
> [lines 67–9]

Eventually Gebir encounters his own father, who now bitterly regrets the imperative of honour that made him commit his young son to vengeance and retribution:

> O that I e'er extracted such a vow! . . .
> How against Egypt thou wouldst raise that hand
> And bruise the seed first risen from our line.
> Therefore, in death what pangs have I endured!
> [lines 241, 246–8]

In Landor's version, influenced in this respect too by the Koran, despots suffer less from physical torture than from psychological torment. Their agony lies in self-knowledge — in the 'tow'ring thoughts on their own breast o'erturned,/And piercing to the heart' (lines 63–4). (Compare this with the wicked in *Vathek*, whose inner pain makes them place their hands over their breasts.) Because the father's suffering is psychological, it conveys itself quickly and completely to the son. This produces an access of pain, for they are made to long all the more desperately for a personal contact forever denied them.

Gebir's discovery of the true nature of his past inevitably raises the question of his status as a tragic figure. Pierre Vitoux, in his essay 'Gebir as an Heroic Poem', has argued that, for example, as in conventional readings of *Hamlet*, the hero suffers from the tragic flaw of passivity in the face of an irremediable fate.[23] However, what Gebir actually learns is that his father, who had provided the cause and justification of his invasion of Egypt, is now repudiating precisely what he, the father, entrusted to the son. As an individual, Gebir is plainly guiltless; he may be objectively guilty; but he is subjectively innocent, and his fate may be less tragic than sacrificial and redemptive. Be that as it may, the powerful Koranic overtones of this magnificent episode greatly concentrates the theme of tyranny and imperialism.

The Conquered

Landor's orientalism is also justified by the fact that in his time Egypt was the archetypal victim of imperialist aggression, shortly to become, in 1798, the target of Napoleon's ambitions. The Egyptian reaction to Gebir's occupation is presented as a matter of considerable complexity, of which three aspects may be discriminated: the collective reaction, the response of Dalica, and the response of Charoba.

Gebir's invasion of northern Egypt provokes a reactive nationalism different in kind but scarcely less reprehensible in quality from the active action. It awakes the most prejudiced and self-serving form of patriotism.

> Determin'd to protect the country's gods,
> Still asking their protection, they adjure
> Each other to stand forward, and insist
> With zeal, and trample under foot the slow.
>
> [IV, lines 68–71]

Warning voices ('these men are not your enemies:/Enquire their errand; and resist when wrong'd' [lines 81–2]) are swept aside. Instead we hear the voice of paranoia ('seek they not hidden treasure in the tomb?'), of envy ('Build they not fairer cities than our own?' [line 88]), and of intolerance (they build temples not 'bearing gods like ours imbost./O profanation! O our ancestors!' [lines 94–5]). Landor's understanding of Egypt under threat is very acute, and may owe something to the fact that, while he was writing the poem in South Wales, he would have had an opportunity to observe for himself the reaction of the local population to the news that a French expeditionary force was mustering at Brest.

But this reactive nationalism, which demonstrates why imperialist invasion necessarily entails evil consequences, receives its keenest expression in Dalica, Charoba's old nurse and protectress. As Gebir himself learns early, 'This land of Egypt is a land/Of incantation' (II, lines 205–6); Dalica is a witch, and through her Landor is able to introduce another oriental theme — that of necromancy. Determined to destroy Gebir, Dalica visits her native city, Masar, now (as we have seen) a pile of ruins and rubble inhabited by hyenas and serpents. But this decay nourishes diminished and perverted talents and energies:

> Still were remaining some of ancient race,
> And ancient arts were now their sole delight.
> [V, lines 14–15]

And these arts are indeed mysterious and potent, mingling unnatural moonlight with the miraculous Red Sea wave that held itself back to allow the Children of Israel to cross out from Egypt:

> When at their incantation would the Moon
> Start back, and shuddering shed blue blasted light.
> The rifted rays they gather'd, and immersed
> In potent portion of that wonderous wave
> Which, hearing rescued Israel, stood erect,
> And led her armies through his crystal gates.
> [lines 17–22]

The mistress of these arts is the great enchantress Myrthyr, Dalica's sister, who, convinced that Charoba's life has been blighted by Gebir's occupation of the country, prepares a 'reeking garb', not unlike the shirt of Nessus that destroyed Hercules, which, as soon as he dons it, will instantly destroy the hated foreign despot.

These are the magical arts which, in a different form, are the cause of the destruction of the city that Gebir is trying to rebuild. Egyptian architecture and Egyptian necromancy seem antithetical. The latter is found among ruins; its function is to create *ruins*. If great cities are associated with imperialism, secret magic arts are associated with post-imperialism (the ruins of Masar) or anti-imperialism (the destruction of Sidad and Gebir). But the reaction of Egypt to the foreign conqueror is more subtle than that, for the conquered people not only loathe their conqueror: they often adore him. When, for example, Charoba, on the duplicitous advice of Dalica, decides to order a festival for Gebir, the xenophobic Egyptians suddenly applaud Gebir; and they participate with rapture in all the ceremonies of a day that 'Egypt with proud Iberia should unite' (VII, line 43). But the clearest case of this is Charoba's sudden and complete infatuation with Gebir.

The complex relationship between these reactions of hate and love is embodied in the plot of the poem. Dalica fails to notice that her young mistress's condition is symptomatic not of hate but of love, and it is under this misapprehension that she concocts her devilish retribution. Thus the relationship between them is one of systematic cross-purposes. For Dalica, Charoba's distress is a spur to action, for the Egyptian queen seems to Dalica too reticent to be in love with the Iberian despot;

> 'I have observ'd Charoba. I have asked
> If she loved Gebir: '*Love him*!' she exclaim'd,
> With such a start of terror, such a flush
> Of anger, '*I love Gebir? I in love?*'
> Then, looked so piteous, so impatient looked —

But burst, before I answer'd, into tears.
Then saw I, plainly saw I, 'twas not love.
For, such her natural temper, what she likes
She speaks it out, or rather, she commands.
And could Charoba say with greater ease
'*Bring me a water-melon from the Nile*'
Than, if she love'd him, '*Bring me him I love.*'
Therefor the death of Gebir is resolv'd.'
[V, lines 180–92]

For Charoba, on the other hand, Dalica's policy of honouring Gebir is a confirmation of her desires, for Dalica is playing too deep a game for her mistress to detect. This action undoubtedly serves to bind together apparently opposite responses to imperialism.

The response of Charoba is a sexual one, and thus permits Landor to exploit yet another major theme in orientalism: *exotic eroticism*. Charoba is the perfect oriental woman as imagined by the west, for she combines (in a feminine nature that will be fully exploited by later Romantics) radical innocence, even naivety, with an unconscious sensuality. Charoba's ablutions before her wedding make her the perfect odalisque:

Next to her chamber, closed by cedar doors,
A bath, of purest marble, purest wave,
On its fair surface bore its pavement high.
Arabian gold inclosed the crystal roof,
With fluttering boys adorn'd and girls unrobed,
These, when you touch the quiet water, start
From their aërial sunny arch, and pant
Entangled midst each other's flowery wreaths,
And each pursuing is in turn pursued.
Here came at last, as ever wont at morn,
Charoba: long she linger'd at the brink,
Often she sighed, and, naked as she was,

Sat down, and leaning on the couch's edge,
On the soft inward pillow of her arm
Rested her burning cheek: she moved her eyes;
She blush'd; and blushing plung'd into the wave.
[VII, lines 80–95]

It would be tempting here to associate Charoba, Queen of Egypt, with her historical successor Cleopatra, the arch-oriental seductress. And indeed there are signs in the poem — for example, the portrayal of Charoba's arrival at Gebir's camp for the ceremony (VII, lines 115–29) or the procession of barges on the Nile (IV, lines 159–81) — that Landor had remembered Shakespeare's great play. But Charoba is no Cleopatra: she is much too girlish and too passive. She has all the apparatus of oriental luxury — a luxury that is endorsed by no less an authority than the Koran itself, with its vision of a paradise filled with houris and 'fluttering boys': 'Verily we have created *the damsels of paradise* by a *peculiar* creation: and we have made them virgins, beloved by their husbands, of equal age *with them*; for *the delight of* the companions of the right hand'[24]; and with the furniture of a divine seraglio:

> . . . therein shall they repose themselves on couches; they shall see therein neither sun nor moon [i.e. *zamhareer*]: and the shades thereof *shall be* near *spreading* above them, and the fruits thereof shall hang low, so as to be easily gathered. And *their attendants* shall go round about unto them, with vessels of silver, and goblets: the bottles shall be bottles of silver *shining like glass*; they shall determine the measure thereof by *their wish*. And therein shall they be given to drink of a cup *of wine*, mixed with *the water* of Zenjebil, a fountain in *paradise* named Salsabil: and youths, which shall continue for ever in their bloom, shall go round to attend them; when thou seest them,

> thou shalt think them to be scattered pearls: and when thou lookest, there shalt thou behold delights, and a great kingdom.[25]

Perhaps the bathing Charoba has her antecedent in the Queen of Sheba. In the Koran, too, this queen's meeting with King Solomon is portrayed in political, luxurious and erotic terms (we should not overlook possible analogies between this encounter and Charoba's first meeting with Gebir in Book I):

> And when she saw it [the court], she imagined it to be a great water; and she discovered her legs, by lifting up her robe to pass through it. Whereupon Solomon said unto her, Verily this is a palace evenly floored with glass.[26]

What Landor has realized in his description of Charoba's bath is that there can be an innocent luxury and an innocent sexuality in the Islamic tradition. The bath is enclosed by a sensual space, and the ceiling, 'with fluttering boys adorn'd and girls unrobed' (VII, line 84), is brought into trembling life from the reflections of the water when its quiet surface is touched. In the midst of all this, Charoba's naked body is flushed with heightened feeling, as it sinks into the water. This scene is the distillation of oriental sensuality at once refined, guiltless and abandoned. What is its function?

If Dalica's necromancy represents perverted power, Charoba's sexual seductiveness stands for natural vitality. She is remarkably free from, because indifferent to, the imperialism symbolized by architecture and the pomp of monarchy. Dalica herself recognizes this. In her description of the young Queen of Egypt to Myrthyr, she recalls her childhood spontaneity:

> Shew her the graven sceptre; what its use? —

'Twas to beat dogs with, and to gather flies.
She thought the crown a plaything to amuse
Herself, and not the people . . .'
[V, lines 110–13]

This naturalism of feeling (which in its simplicity demystifies the constructs of pomp) is amplified, when the child turns into an adult, into the capacity for wonder ('That wond'rous soul Charoba once possessed . . . is gone'); but of course the reverse is true. And what is more, the feeling is reciprocated by Gebir, for he too is overwhelmed by the pangs of love, of which Dalica provides a circumstantial account. The oriental colour exploited by Landor permits him to present with intense vividness a natural good, free from the Hebraic sense of sin taken over by Christianity, fully experienced by his protagonists, but without their full understanding and consent (for theirs is the love of enemies), and exposed to the imperceptive manipulation of a destructive rationalist.

Thus the evil currents of imperialism and anti-imperialism are undercut by a deeper current of 'sympathy' expressing itself in the innocence of natural passion. Both Gebir and Charoba are essentially 'good', in the sense that they are naturally benign, responsive, generous, just and capable of delight. Both, however, are victims of their past — Gebir of the militarism of his ancestors, Charoba of the remnant of a much older tradition in Egyptian supernaturalism. Both start with the massive disadvantage of being monarchs, which divides them from their spontaneous feelings. But they are essentially free from the condition of 'original sin': they suffer from what could be called 'superficial sin' in that it is the roles they occupy, rather than their essential nature, that damage them. Landor could never have reached such a position on the basis of an orthodox Christianity. Whatever he may have become eventually, when he was writing *Gebir* he had explicitly taken his distance from Christianity, and, indeed, from the biblical overtones of the original story. (This may explain in part Landor's omission of the account of Abraham and his wife Sarah and their relationship with the Egyptian monarchy which is present in Mrs Reeve's story.) At the end of Gebir's sojourn in the underworld, he asks his guide to show him the wonders of the Christian heaven:

> Bring me among the wonders of a realm
> Admired by all, but like a tale admired.
> [III, lines 312–13]

He recognizes that believing is less than seeing, and that even when we convince our children of our life after death, we part from them as they do from us — with 'tears', and mutual 'agony':

> Wherefor should wretched mortals thus believe,
> Or wherefor should they hesitate to die?
> [lines 321–2]

But it is significant that this question is not answered. In fact, the absence of any answer forms the climax of the episode.

The Classical Element

The comprehensiveness and depth of what I have called the oriental layer in *Gebir* is confined to the main plot involving Gebir, Charoba and Dalica; and this only serves to underline its absence from the sub-plot involving Tamar and the nymph. Since this lack is felt as a positive presence, it is necessary to devote a little attention to Landor's conduct of this subordinate narrative.

With Gebir's abrupt arrival in Egypt, we discover that he has a brother who implausibly is a shepherd in a quasi-Arcadian landscape ('those rich meadows where Young Tamar fed/The royal flocks' [I, lines 88–9]) in an oriental setting (here the 'dull and dreary shore/Where many a league Nile blackens all the sand'[lines 96–7]). There is no attempt to integrate these landscapes; they are merely juxtaposed. The subplot introduces into the poem a powerful pastoral theme. But what is striking about it is that this pastoralism is *excluded* from the oriental main plot. There was no reason in orientalism for this to be so. As we shall see in Chapter 2, Southey exploits an oriental pastoralism, fully available to the West in the biblical narratives, and so in various other sources, including travellers' accounts of Bedouin simplicity of life with its nomadic flocks, its oases and its tents. Landor deliberately rejected this tradition in favour of the classical one.

The result is anachronism and inconsistency. The imagery has very little to do with Egypt, as even Landor is forced to acknowledge: 'I am afraid I have, in more than one instance, mentioned plants which are not natives of Egypt'.[27] When Gebir disguises himself as his brother in order to wrestle with the nymph, he wears a chaplet 'of the flowering raspberry and vine' (II, line 100). This he finds in 'brakes of roses; (line 107) and among 'chestnut . . . husk[s]' (line 111). When Gebir seeks to discover why his brother is languishing, he does not say that his sheep might have escaped from the field, but that the 'dew-drops were not shaken from the bar' (I, line 99). Even his reference to Tamar's occupation has been couched in classical images:

> Tamar! thy pastures large and rich, afford
> Flowers to thy bees, and herbage to thy sheep.
> [I, lines 245–6]

Tamar himself, being in love with the beautiful nymph, shows all the usual characteristics and symptoms of the typical pastoral lover. He attracts the nymph by playing on a pipe (an established symbol of the art of pastoral poetry); he falls in love with her, as in a story by, say, Ovid, first by seeing her feet (like 'long shells' [I, line 148]), then her eyes, then her garments ('not of wonted woof nor vulgar art'[line 154]); once in love, he can 'neither feed the flock, nor watch the fold' (line 117), but is overwhelmed by a debilitating and enfeebled longing.

This classical pastoralism, however, serves to bring out an underlying common element with the oriental narrative: a pagan eroticism. For all her supernatural origins, this nymph is no vapour. Hers is the most seductive fleshly existence, as is shown most clearly in her wrestling, which opposes her to her lover. She opposes to his sweet pipe the magical seductions of the seashell:

> . . . I have sinuous shells, of pearly hue
> Within, and they that lustre have imbibed
> In the sun's palace porch; where, when unyoked,
> His chariot wheel stands midway in the wave.
> Shake one, and it awakens; then apply
> Its polished lips to your attentive ear,
> And it remembers its august abodes,
> And murmurs as the ocean murmurs there.
> [I, lines 170–77]

This infinitely evocative appeal makes of her something of a Circe, or a Belle Dame sans Merci — a source of dangerous enchantment. The wrestling itself — significantly for the prize of a sheep, symbol of Tamar's occupation and self-control — is openly erotic:

> Above her knees she drew the robe succinct,
> Above her breast, and just below her arms . . .
> [lines 187–8]

And when she overcomes Tamar, himself overcome by an all-too-explicable physical paralysis, Tamar watches her leave with her spoils:

> But when I heard its bleating, as I did,
> And saw, she hastening on, its hinder feet
> Struggle, and from her snowy shoulder slip,
> (One shoulder its poor efforts had unveil'd;)
> Then, all my passions mingling fell in tears!
> [lines 220–24]

It is quite clear that Tamar is defeated by sexual love, and that he will not be able to extricate himself from his own predicament. He is saved by his brother's intervention. As this constitutes the moment of intersection of the two plots, it carries a great weight of significance, and full consideration is given to it in the following and final section of this chapter. For the moment I wish to show rather that there is a movement from pastoral lovesickness towards the harmony and security of marriage. In classical terms, this is a shift from the eclogue of Books I and II to the epithalamion of Book VI. It remains an unusual marriage in that the parties are mortal and supernatural. But the treatment of it accepts the convention of the epithalamion in all its details:

> Now to Aurora, borne by dappled steeds,
> The sacred gate of orient pearl and gold,
> Smitten with Lucifer's light silver wand,
> Expanded slow to strains of harmony;
> The waves beneath, in purpling rows, like doves
> Glancing with wanton coyness tow'rd their queen,
> Heav'd softly: thus the damsel's bosom heaves
> When, from her sleeping lover's downy cheek,
> To which so warily her own she brings
> Each moment nearer, she perceives the warmth

(Blithe warmth!) of kisses fann'd by playful Dreams.
Ocean, and earth, and heaven, was jubilee.
For 'twas the morning, pointed out by Fate,
When an immortal maid and mortal man
Should share each other's nature, knit in bliss.
[VI, lines 1–15]

All the classical conventions of the epithalamion are here present, from the dawning of the wedding day in standard Homeric images, to the sexually charged images of 'doves' and 'damsel's bosom', to the 'jubilee' of 'heaven' and 'earth' heralding the union of man and goddess, of the physical and the spiritual. The passage as a whole creates an impression of grand harmony, like a peal of bells.

And this is sustained throughout Book VI, which (not surprisingly, given the classical style) gives us a bird's-eye view of the Mediterranean, from the east to Italy and Corsica, and which anticipates, in the style of the marriage ode, the offspring of the pair who will together become the parents of history — the history of the west, rooted in classical and pagan optimism, not in Hebraic and Christian pessimism, to culminate in the achievements of Napoleon, the apostle and defender of liberty, equality and fraternity on an international scale. This grand vision of Tamar's future (which is — very briefly — the vision of the young Landor's present) is therefore sharply distinguished from the Islamic main plot, which ends in disaster and catastrophe, both personal and national. Yet, as I have suggested, the positive vision in some ways depends on the negative vision: Tamar's marriage, and all it represents, could not have taken place without Gebir's crucial intervention. To this we now turn.

Landor's Politics

It is essential to accept that *Gebir*, for all its orientalist and classical objectively, is in fact a deeply personal and expressive poem, and as such essentially a Romantic work. Furthermore, Landor makes no attempt to conceal this expressiveness, but confronts his reader with it at the very outset:

> WHEN old Silenus call'd the Satyrs home,
> Satyrs then tender-hooft and ruddy-horn'd,
> With Bacchus and the Nymphs, he sometimes rose
> Amidst the tale or pastoral, and shew'd
> The light of purest wisdom; and the God
> Scatter'd with wholesome fruit the pleasant plains.
> [I, lines 1–6]

These lines announce that the pastoral-erotic (satyrs, Bacchus and the nymphs) will have special importance in the poem to come, and that it will have a creative, procreative effect ('scatter'd with wholesome fruit . . .'). But this is how the verse proceeds:

> Ye woody vales of Cambria! and ye hills
> That hide in heaven your summits and your fame!
> Your ancient songs, and breezes pure, invite
> Me from my noon-tide rambles, and the force
> Of high example influences my lay.
> [I, lines 7–11]

As we have seen, the poem was largely inspired and written in Wales, a setting which Landor explicitly invites into the poem. He is writing for himself and his own time, and the pastoral-erotic is part of his own experience. We have seen that the writing of *Gebir* coincided with his first experience of love — his affair with Nancy Jones. And this, too, is explicitly introduced into the apparently objective narrative:

> Lo! mirror of delight in cloudless days!
> Lo! thy reflection: 'twas when I exclaim'd

— With kisses hurried as if each foresaw
Their end, and reckon'd on our broken bonds,
And could at such a price such loss endure —
'O what, to faithful lovers, met at morn,
What half so pleasant as imparted fears!'
How many a night serene, shall I behold
Those warm attractive orbits, close enshrined
In ether, over which Love's column rose
Marmoreal, trophied round with golden hair.
Within the valley of one lip, unseen,
Love slumber'd, one his unstrung bow impress'd.
Sweet wilderness of soul-entangling charms!
Led back by Memory, and each blissful maze
Retracing, me with magic power detain
Those dimpled cheeks, those temples, violet-tinged,
Those lips of nectar, and those eyes of heav'n!
[IV, lines 26–43]

This extraordinary effusion, in the voice of the narrator, serves to introduce the intensification of the loves of Charoba and Gebir, after the latter's return from the underworld. But it is impossible to miss hearing in it the note of impassioned confession, and I would argue that it forms the foundation of the poem as a whole.

We have seen how, from the very start, both brothers acknowledge that they are in love. The difference between them is simply that Gebir, as the combative imperialist figure, has the problem of acknowledging a love which contradicts his political and patriarchal mission, while Tamar (the name, incidentally, of a Cornish, hence Celtic, river, which helps to localize the allegory), as the defeated and sensitive shepherd, has to learn to conquer the love that has overwhelmed his life. Tamar, understanding his own situation, positively appeals for help to Gebir, as the elder and the stronger of the two; Gebir, after a short pause of misunderstanding, offers his help and defeats the nymph. He thus provides the necessary forcefulness to guarantee Tamar's happiness. But the effect is reciprocal. By letting his brother take his part, Tamar makes it possible for Gebir to discover the limitations of his imperialist city-building role. The nymph discloses to her conqueror the secret of the city's destruction and of the entrance to the underworld. And with the weakening of the grip of imperialism on him, Gebir is able more fully to admit his love for Charoba. From the point of view of the narrative action, love becomes fundamental.

But it is also fundamental for the political theme. Love is associated with pastoralism, and the pastoral is opposed to a whole cluster of associated ideas that include the building of cities, the institution of the monarchy and the court, the competing nationalisms behind imperialism and finally some of the defining tenets of Christianity. As we have seen, this is borne out by the structure of action and image that constitutes the poem. But it is also explicit. Landor was responsive to the criticism, particularly from his most favourable reader, Southey, that the first edition of the poem was unnecessarily obscure. Accordingly he provided explanatory summaries and notes, and certain amplifications to the text. Notable among the latter is an interpolation in Book VII, arguing that 'all nature dissuade from whatever is hostile to equality':

By every lake's and every river's side
The Nymphs and Naiads teach Equality:
In voices gently querulous they ask
'Who would with aching head and toiling arms
Bear the full pitcher to the stream far off?
Who would, of power intent on high emprize.
Deem less the praise to fill the vacant gulph
Than raise Charybdis upon Etna's brow?'
Amidst her darkest caverns most retired,
Nature calls forth her filial Elements

To close around and crush that monster *Void.* —
Fire, springing fierce from his resplendent throne,
And Water, dashing the devoted wretch
Woundless and whole, with iron-colour'd mace,
Or whirling headlong in his war-belt's fold.
Mark well the lesson, man! and spare thy kind.
Go, from their midnight darkness wake the woods,
Woo the lone forest in her last retreat —
Many still bend their beauteous heads unblest
And sigh aloud for elemental man.
Thro' palaces and porches, evil eyes
Light upon ev'n the wretched, who have fled
The house of bondage, or the house of birth:
Suspicions, murmurs, treacheries, taunts, retorts,
Attend the brighter banners that invade;
And the first horn of hunter, pale with want,
Sounds to the chase; the second to the war.
[lines 14–40]

This argument as it stands is not overwhelmingly convincing. The whole of nature takes the line of least resistance, and flows or drifts towards the lowest or emptiest point. Thus the pursuit of distinction and eminence is unnatural. Nature teaches us that such unnatural aspiration creates disorder and catastrophic conflict, as between volcano and torrent; so, too, in human society. It follows that imperialism, when involving the occupation of virgin woods and forests, is benign in that — like nature — man fills a void; but that if it involves the conquest of populated territories, it then implies ascent, the quest for superiority and war, with all the *unnatural* horrors that attend on *unnatural* action. The pastoral theme, with natural love at its centre, provides the foundation of the political theme.

Landor's politics in 1796–8, the period when he was writing and publishing the poem, were essentially those of a young idealist's interpretations of the programme of the French Revolution. He favoured a sort of republican internationalism. At its centre was a repudiation of monarchy as the keystone of the old despotic regime. Gebir's discoveries in the underworld are also Landor's except that Landor, in the reactionary Britain in which he was writing, had to conceal his meaning under narrative allegories. Gebir sees the shadowy shapes of his ancestors as his own past and present; but to Landor they are the figures of a later history.

'. . . what wretch
Is that with eyebrows white, and slanting brow?
Listen! him yonder, who, bound down supine,
Shrinks, yelling, from that sword there, engine-hung;
He too amongst my ancestors? I hate
The despot, but the dastard I despise.
Was he our countryman?'
'Alas, O King!
Iberia bore him, but the breed accurst
Inclement winds blew blighting from north-east.'
[III, lines 184–92]

As De Quincey noted, 'Aroär [Gebir's guide] is too *Tom-Painish*, and seems up to a little treason.'[28] The wretch or 'dastard' is recognizable as a caricature of George III, born in England ('Iberia') but originating from Hanover ('North-east'); the tyrant cowering under the guillotine ('engine-hung') is Louis XVI, whose fate threatens George. And the allegory continues. The 'giant next him', whose feet flounder in *yellow* flowers, writhing 'twixt the continent and isle', is William III, the '*Deliverer*', who brought the so-called 'Glorious Revolution'; the wretch 'who sold his people to a rival king' (line 215), is Charles II, who made secret deals with Louis XIV; the 'pale visage' with 'that space between the purple and the crown' (line 222), is the decapitated Charles I. This prophetic succession of kings represents an unrestrained attack on the institution of monarchy.

But what is the alternative? The answer is provided by the antithetical vision of the future, arising out of the wedding of Tamar and the nymph. At the climax of his Mediterranean honeymoon, Tamar is told of the fate of his descendants. This time the guide is the nymph herself:

> 'Look yonder!' Tamar look'd, and saw two isles
> Where the waves whiten'd on the desart shore.
> Then she continued. 'That which intervenes
> Scarcely the Nymphs themselves have known from Fame:
> But mark the furthest: *there* shall once arise,
> From Tamar shall arise, 'tis Fate's decree,
> A mortal man above all mortal praise . . .'
> [VI, lines 187–93]

The nearer island is Sardinia, the farther one Corsica, the birthplace of Napoleon — a figure who, for the Landor of the late 1790s, had arisen from the people, checked the excesses of the French Revolution (in particular, the attempted monarchist counter-coup of 1795), and was beginning to spread beyond the boundary of France the principles of republican democracy by taking Italy from the sway of the Austrian emperors.

In fact this adulation of Napoleon was to prove short-lived. By the time Landor was revising his poem for its 1803 edition, Napoleon had conquered Egypt in 1798 (but not, as the 1798 version foretold, in the name of justice: 'equal Egypt bid her shepherds reign' [line 227]), had returned to seize power in 1799 and in 1802 to nominate himself life consul. Thus Landor was moved, in his second edition, to include a cancellation of his Napoleonic hopes. His comment upon his famous line, 'A mortal man above all mortal praise', runs thus:

> Bonaparte might have been so, and in the beginning of his career it was argued that he would be. But unhappily he thinks, that to produce great changes, is to perform great actions: to annihilate antient freedom and to substitute new . . .; in short, to overthrow by violence all the institutions, and to tear from the heart all the social habits of men, has been the tenor of his politics to the present hour.[29]

But he still clung to a vision of liberty, equality and fraternity. This vision, born in Italy — Roman and Florentine republican Italy, 'clime of unbounded liberty and love' (VI, line 251) — awaited its fulfilment in Europe, where 'Time himself throws off his motly garb' in line 301 (viz. the traditional names of the months and days, 'figur'd with monstrous men and monstrous gods', that the French Convention suppressed). And as for the 'pure' festivals of reason:

> Captivity led captive. War o'erthrown,
> They shall o'er Europe, shall o'er Earth extend
> Empire that seas alone and skies confine,
> And glory that shall strike the crystal stars.
> [VI, lines 305–8]

How completely this vision presupposes an optimistic view of human nature is finally demonstrated, however, by the main 'oriental' plot, not by the sub-'classical' one. Landor makes a number of important alterations to his source, including the making of Gebir and Tamar *brothers*, which symbolizes the profound affinities between the two stories. But no change is more significant than the transformation of the characters of Gebir and Charoba. In Reeve, Gebir was a fierce, gigantic king, barbaric and overwhelming; Charoba was a devious, wily queen who deliberately deluded and destroyed Gebir in order to save her country. Both figures are committed to national interest, and are therefore wholly in opposition to each other, sexually as well as politically. In Landor, all this has gone, or rather it has shrunk to the circumstance of their predestined roles. What they are in themselves is quite different. Gebir is essentially humane: responsive, generous, trusting, brave; Charoba is essentially loving: innocent, timid, passionate. She is not affected by the coldness and superiority of her court, and she does not find in Gebir the arrogance of a conqueror; hence her inescapable infatuation with him. But they are both destroyed by a mistake: from modesty and inexperience they misinterpret each other's love; while the destructive Dalica misinterprets her adored queen's feelings from literal-mindedness and lack of imagination. In short, Landor does all he can to make them victims. In this he is powerfully aided by his oriental setting. On the one hand, it enables him to represent those imperialist and monarchic conflicts in a more highly coloured, and more fatalistic, guise; while on the other it permits him to deal with sexual passion much more directly as *natural*, without the constraints of Christian taboos and guilts. The oriental perspective therefore serves his revolutionary politics well, for it makes it possible for him to suggest that human beings are cruel and unjust, not because of what they are, but because of what their own past and traditions have obliged them to be, and that all one has to do to achieve collective happiness is to throw off, in the name of nature, the superficial and unnecessary burden of inherited institutions.

Chapter 2

Southey's *Thalaba* and Christo-Islamic Ethics

WE have Southey's word for it that his *Thalaba* was intimately influenced by *Gebir*. The earliest reference to *Thalaba* we possess antedates the publication of *Gebir* by two years. In a letter of 1796 to his lifelong friend Grosvenor Bedford, he referred to 'my Oriental poem of the Destruction of the Dom Daniel'.[1] By the middle of 1798, however, *Gebir* had come into his hands, and its effect was instantaneous. In August of that year he wrote to Joseph Cottle, a rising Bristol bookseller who had published his first narrative romance, *Joan of Arc*:

> You know my tale of the 'Adite', in the garden of Irem. I have tacked it on to an old plan of mine upon the destruction of the Domdanyel, and made the beginning, middle and end. There is a tolerable skeleton formed. It will extend to ten or twelve books, and they appear to me to possess much strong conception in the Arabian manner. It will

> at least prove that I did not reject machinery in my Epics, because I could not wield it. This only forms part of a magnificent project, which I do not despair of one day completing, in the destruction of the Domdanyel. *My intention is to show off all the splendour of the Mohammedan belief. I intend to do the same to the Runic, and Oriental systems; to preserve the costume of place as well as of religion* [my italics].[2]

Southey was overwhelmed with admiration for Landor's poem. He had been a contemporary of Landor's at Oxford, but did not meet him until 1808 in Bristol. Nevertheless, as soon as he had read his anonymous review copy of *Gebir*, he was converted; he wrote to his friends about it; he produced an enthusiastic review — 'the miraculous work of a madman' — for the *Critical Review* in September 1799. How much he owed to the poem is indicated by his later references to it. 'It was certainly from *Gebir*,' he once wrote, 'that I learnt ever to have my eye awake — to bring images to sight, and to convey a picture in a word. I know no poem from which I have ever derived so much improvement.'[3] And finally, in the 1837 preface to the 1846 edition of *Thalaba*, he wrote: '. . . I walked on the beach, caught soldier-crabs, admired the sea-anemonies in their ever-varying shapes of beauty, read Gebir, and wrote half a book of Thalaba . . . I am sensible of having derived great improvement from the frequent perusal of Gebir at that time.'[4] The beach in question was at Falmouth, where Southey and his wife, in April 1800, were waiting for the passage to Portugal. The book in question was Book IX of the poem he had started writing in July 1799 in Bristol, and was to complete in Lisbon exactly a year afterwards, just before his 26th birthday. The completed manuscript was sold to Longman for £115, published in July 1801, shortly after Southey's return from Portugal, and sold so slowly (despite a respectful if unfavourable notice by Lord Jeffrey in the *Edinburgh Review* of October 1801), that by the spring of 1804 the publisher had disposed of only 500 copies.

The importance of *Gebir* for *Thalaba* prompts the question of affinities and differences. In the references already quoted, Southey highlights the visual brilliance of *Gebir*. The importance of the poetic — i.e. verbal — example set by Landor is undeniable, but Southey's tone makes it clear that there was a deeper affinity. It was not only Landor's new orientalism (new in relation not only to such 18th-century oriental-tale imitations as Goldsmith's *Citizen of the World* and Dr Johnson's *Rasselas* but also to the brilliant excitement provided by Beckford's *Vathek*) that inspired Southey, but also his *politicization* of the oriental material (or rather, the *orientalizing* of western politics). In fact it was this connection with politics that largely constituted Landor's novelty. It may seem that Southey's own political enthusiasms followed, or ran parallel to, those of Landor — the 'mad Jacobin' sent down from Oxford for irregular conduct. Southey had entered Westminster School the year before the outbreak of the French Revolution. Looking back in 1824 on that phase of his youth, he wrote: 'Few persons but those who have lived in it can conceive or comprehend what the memory of the French Revolution was, nor *what a visionary world seemed to open upon those who were first entering it. Old things seemed passing away, and nothing was dreamt of it but the regeneration of the human race*' (my italics).[5] At the time, Southey's radicalism was such that neither the imprisonment of the French royal family in 1792 nor the slaughter of the Swiss guards, nor even the September massacres, provoked any overt protest from him. In 1793, as he was settling in at Balliol College, the guillotining of Louis XVI, following the declaration of a French republic and provoking war between England and France, found him sympathizing with France. By 1796, however, when he returned from his first visit to Portugal, he had begun to warm to the social culture, if not to the politics, of England, and to cool to a revolution that had executed the Girondins and permitted a reign of terror. By the time he was beginning to write *Thalaba*, he had started to become interested in the practical alleviation of poverty, though without yet losing his interest in theories of progress. During his second sojourn in Portugal, as he was finishing *Thalaba*, he was slow to understand the full menace of Napoleon, perhaps in part because of his almost obsessive hatred of Pitt's politics. 'England is now the bedarkening power,' he wrote at the time; 'she is in politics what Spain was to religion at the Reformation.'[6] These views would have been closely congruent with Landor's: France was the great example of the overthrow of hated monarchic tyrannies, like Austria and Russia, the allies of England. What was to accelerate Southey's shift to the right — the resignation of Pitt in February 1801, and the Peace of Amiens in March 1802 — was yet to come, and could not be said to have marked the meaning of *Thalaba*.

Yet, in some central respects, Southey's politics were distinct from Landor's, and this certainly influenced his particular orientalism. Landor's republicanism was deeply rooted in a European seedbed, nourished by the politics of classical and republican Rome; and his interest in the East was rhetorical and allegorical — part of an elaborate literary strategy. Southey's republicanism was much more diffuse, and, in a different sense, more scholarly. The French Revolution, as we have seen, provided 'a visionary world' in which one could dream of 'the regeneration of mankind'. In fact his politics were never practical; his political vision was essentially moral and humanitarian. As a student, he had serious religious doubts: but his attack on the established church, as Simmons notes, was on it as an *institution* rather than for its doctrines. His opposition was to any exclusive social formation claiming privileged truth: hence his almost pathological loathing of the Catholic church. But there can, of course, be no serious political action outside institutions. Like some other Romantics of the period — particularly Wordsworth — Southey's politics were not easily distinguishable from his ethics and his religion. He sought, above all, for human unity and harmony. He was profoundly responsive to Utopian projects, and for several months thought of emigration. In June 1794, Coleridge, then at Cambridge, visited Oxford, where he met Southey (like him known as a 'Jacobin', but of the 'soft' rather than the 'hard' variety), and together they dreamt up the creation of a private communal society in America. The project, strongly influenced by Godwin's *Political Justice* (1793), was called by Coleridge 'Pantisocracy', and glossed by Southey as 'equal government for all'.[7] Although this plan came to nothing, it demonstrates not only the nature of Southey's moral idealism, but also how serious he was about it.

This too served to distinguish Southey's orientalism from Landor's. Landor was, in the neutral sense of the term, profoundly egoistical: his own sense of the self was so strong that it naturally diminished his power to imagine others as independent of himself. His classicism, for example, was made a part of himself, and not studied for its distinctive character. Southey, on the other hand, was not only a universalist, but deeply interested in forms of life other than his own. Of the four writers this account is concerned with, he alone had the instincts of a scholar, as his editions of other men's work, his translations and his biographies indicate. As we have already seen, he planned a series of epics dealing with the principal religious-cultural 'systems' of the world — the 'Mohammedan' (Islamic), the 'Runic' (Celtic) and the 'Oriental' (Hindu). As it happens he produced five full-scale romances, which made his reputation in the 19th century: *Joan of Arc* (written at the age of 21, and published in 1796), based on the Christian legend, but preaching pacifism and democracy, and branding Henry V as a wicked tyrant; *Madoc* (written just before *Thalaba*, but published in 1805), inspired by the establishment of a Welsh ('Runic') community in South America; *Thalaba* itself; *The Curse of Kehama* (written over a long period and published in 1810), making powerful use of Hindu mythology in opposing the despotic 'raja' Kehama by the brave peasant, Ludurlad; and finally *Roderick, the Last of the Goths* (1814), a tale of vengeance in the context of the Moorish-Spanish conflict, written in response to Landor's treatment of the same material in *Count Julian* (1812). *Roderick* was considered the best of the five by contemporaries like Coleridge and Lamb;[8] *Kehama* has more recently been regarded as the best orientalist verse narrative of the period. It 'stands', as Simmons puts it, 'with *Gebir* at the head of English Oriental poems of the Romantic period, a very much more distinguished work than *Lalla Rookh* or *The Giaour*'.[9] Whatever *Kehama*'s merits, the present purpose is to concentrate on Islamic, not Hindu, material (which thus excludes *Kehama*) and in due course to suggest in Chapter 3 that Moore's *Lalla Rookh* is a much better poem than it is often reckoned to be, and in Chapter 4 that Byron's *The Giaour* is a special masterpiece.

What Southey's huge project shows is the extent to which he was interested in common factors binding together a variety of mythological and religious 'systems', and at the same time (for otherwise the affirmation of shared values would have no force) how much he was interested in the distinctive and specific character of each. If we recall a phrase already quoted, 'to preserve the costume of place as well as of religion', his use of the term 'costume' — also a favourite word with Byron, who prided himself on the accuracy of his oriental material — Southey's standards of fidelity to a whole complex unity, made up of physical as well as of spiritual elements, become apparent. Nor is this just a connoisseur's interest. He is caught up and excited by the prospect opening out before him: 'My intention is to show off *all the splendours* of the Mohammedan belief.' In this he was more responsive to the work of Beckford than to that of Landor; but what distinguishes his orientalism from Landor's is his commitment to the life of Islam for its own sake, and thus for the sake of the human values it may contain. As I will seek to show, Southey's purpose is to discover the common ethical denominator between Islam and Christianity so as to liberate the West from a self-regarding, therefore tyrannical, perspective. In his perception of the reality and independence of Islam, he took an important step in an evolution which found its fullest expression in Byron, and which I have called *realistic orientalism*.

Byron lived in the Orient; Southey did not. However, this deficiency was made up in part at least by Southey's truly impressive orientalist learning, to which the extensive notes to each of the 12 books of the poem bear ample testimony. He was certainly much better read in oriental literature than Landor. Originally a passionate reader of the 18th-century pseudo-oriental tales, and of *The Arabian Nights*, he became a scholar of the Koran. 'Of the books with me,' he wrote to John May in 1799, 'I'm most engaged by the Koran.'[10] In fact, no other Romantic writer had absorbed George Sale's excellent translation of the Koran to the same degree. He cites from the Koran and from Sale's 'Preliminary Discourse' with great frequency in *Thalaba*. Moreover, his enthusiasm for orientalism puts him in contact with travel books, histories and romances, in French and Latin as well as in English, produced during the previous two centuries. Having started writing *Thalaba*, he visited Exeter, where he read the travels of John Fryer and Sir John Chardin in the Municipal Library.[11] His notes to *Thalaba* include quotations from Sir William Jones's translation of the Arabic 'Seven Odes' known as *Mualakat*, Bruce's *Travels to Discover the Source of the Nile*, Niebuhr's *Travels through Arabia* and Gibbon's *The Decline and Fall of the Roman Empire*, to mention only the most significant. Of course, some of these were known to Southey's predecessors, including Landor; but it seems they influenced Southey to a degree not recognized by his critics or even acknowledged by himself. My claim is that they drove him towards a deeper understanding of the Islamic form of life considered as part of a universal humanitarianism based on the idea of 'intuitive morality' — the idea that man is provided with an inborn moral sense, as opposed to values acquired socially or by revelation, and that he is surrounded by an external divinity omnipresent in nature.

The Structure of Thalaba

The immediate source of *Thalaba* was Henry Weber's translation from the French, entitled *New Arabian Tales*, and in particular his identification of magic as the symbolic source of evil. In the 1837 preface to *Thalaba* Southey writes: 'In the continuation of the Arabian Tales, the Dom Daniel is mentioned; a seminary for evil magicians, under the roots of the sea. From this seed the present romance has grown.'[12] The French original of the *New Oriental Tales* was itself a translation from the Arabic, or so it was claimed, made by Dom Chavis and M. Gazette in 1792; and it contained 'The History of Maugraby the Magician', which suggested not only the plot of *Thalaba* but also its theme: the trans-political struggle between good and evil, in terms of two symbolic opponents, Thalaba and Maugraby.

The hero of 'The History of Maugraby' is an Arab youth named Habed, who is engaged in a mortal struggle with the evil enchanter Maugraby; the latter abducts children to his domain under Mount Atlas, where he alternately tortures and caresses them in order to enslave them to his master, Zatani (or Satan). Once subjugated, these children are taken to caverns under the sea, adjoining the dreaded Domdaniel, located near Tunis, from where the magicians of the dark world wield their power. In the narrative, Habed manages to destroy Maugraby and his followers, and to set free his beloved, the Princess of Egypt.

Southey's elaboration of this story is extensive, but his obligations to it are unmistakable. The 12 books of *Thalaba, the Destroyer* dramatize the destruction of the Domdaniel by Thalaba, a 'dedicated youth' chosen by destiny and divinity for the task, which he accomplishes in the final book. The evil magicians have got wind of their fate, and do their utmost to annihilate Thalaba's family — his father, Hodeirah, and his seven brothers and sisters. But Thalaba and his mother, Zeinab, escape into the desert, the boy being determined to avenge his father and regain the paternal sword ringed by fire in the very depths of the Domdaniel.

Like Habed, Thalaba is essentially a figure of vengeance. But like his model, he is a *pious* avenger, requiring the utmost purity and courage of dedication to his task. Moreover, as in the original tale, the protagonist's opponents are magicians, magic being opposed to rational ethics, as a symbol of human evil. 'Cannot the Dom Daniel,' Southey writes in his *Common-place Book*, 'be made to allegorize those systems that make the misery of mankind?'[13] Southey thus seeks to represent not only the power but also the irrationality of evil. He retains some of the revolutionary horror of 'superstitions', though he does not remain there.

But Southey's treatment of the narrative structure of vengeance is distinctive. After completing *Thalaba*, he was quoted as saying, 'My next mythological poem, should I ever write another, would be founded upon the system of Zoroaster. I should represent the chief personage as persecuted by the evil powers, and *make every calamity they brought upon him the means of evolving some virtue*, which would never else have been called into action' (my italics).[14] But this is precisely a definition of the procedure of *Thalaba*. The narrative represents, through the variety of vicissitudes its protagonist endures, the elaboration of an opposition to 'magic' which becomes a transcendence of it. As the magicians themselves openly declare (notably Lobaba in Book IV — a 'temptation in the desert' — and the arch-magician Mohareb in Book IX), they live in a world of power, in which the only value is the means to power (necromancy). To this Thalaba presents an alternative and ultimately irresistible force, which is that of the divine will, manifested to human beings as *Destiny*. He is a 'delegated youth', and his task is not to gain possession of the instruments of destiny, but to become himself an instrument of power. And how is this done? In the two major discoveries he makes in his restless wanderings, first through *Faith* (the 'talisman' disclosed to him in the ruins of Babylon by the two penitent angels, Haruth and Maruth, in Book V), then through *Forgiveness* (the lesson taught to him by Laila, the daughter of his father's magician-murderer, Okba, in Books X–XI).

Thalaba's travels, then, represent a quest that is also a trial, an appointed task that is also a purification. Brought up in pastoral simplicity in the Arabian desert, he journeys on foot to the ruins of Babylon, then on horseback to an enchanted paradise, then through mountainous cold on foot to 'Kaf', via a diversion in an aerial car to Mohareb's magic island. The 'Simorg' (a mythological all-knowing bird) then gives him directions to the Domdaniel, reached by dog-sledge and boat to the island-cavern which is the entrance to his final destination. In the course of these bizarre voyages, he is subjected to repeated assaults from the magicians and their associates, introduced in Book II in the Domdaniel in the process of discovering with consternation the survival of the one who is to destroy them: from Abdaldar (Book II) who, as a wayfarer, finds the boy Thalaba, but is destroyed by a *simoom*; from a demon (Book III), who tries to recover the potent ring Thalaba has taken from Abdaldar; from Lobaba (Book IV), who, disguised as an old man, tries to tempt the adult Thalaba to his destruction in the desert; from Mohareb (Book V), who, as a martial youth, tries to dominate Thalaba in the Babylonian ruins; from Aloadin (Books VI–VII), who exposes Thalaba to earthly delights; from the witch sisters, Maimuna and Khawla (Books VIII–IX), who fetter Thalaba to deliver him to Mohareb; and finally from the murderer Okba (Book X), who tempts him to violence. The dedicated youth is tested and tempered by these successive attacks, but they all break like waves against the rock of his faith in God's omnipotence and omniscience.

At its most general, the value system of *Thalaba* has the closest associations with that of *Gebir*, for it involves an antithesis between pastoral humility and urban pride. In this respect, the opening book of Southey's poem sets the scene. The narrative involves an encounter with one Aswad, the sole survivor of the destruction of the palace of Irem, founded by the familiar people of Ad (which, with a greater historical scrupulousness than Landor, Southey correctly locates in Arabia). It involves an implacable struggle between the worldly and vainglorious tyrant Shedad and the pastoral prophet Houd, which the latter wins. The great city, of which Babylon is the archetype (along with the tower of Babel and the Pyramids), is associated with the infernal palace, whether as earthly paradise of pleasure (Aloadin's domains in Book VI) or as sumptuous demonic cavern (the Domdaniel in Book XII); and all three are ranged against the vision of true happiness offered by the pastoral childhood of Thalaba in Book III, with its kindly foster-father Moath, and his sweetly dutiful daughter, Oneiza, who becomes the object of Thalaba's love. But here the differences between

Southey and Landor assert themselves more clearly. For the latter, the good life is achieved through sexual passion, for the former, against it. For Southey, paradise is not intensity of feeling but domesticity. 'Domestic Peace and Comfort are within': this is Southey's summary of his ideal of happiness (Book III, stanza 18), and it is to *this* paradise that Thalaba goes after bringing down — like Samson — the Domdaniel on the heads of his enemies as well as his own head to rejoin his demure 'houri' and her father, whose physical deaths have anticipated his. It follows therefore that the worst temptation he can suffer is to seek woman's love instead of God's service. This he undergoes in Book VII after the destruction of Aloadin, when, having been lavished with imperial honours by a sultan, grateful for the defeat of his enemy, he decides to marry Oneiza. The fact that he has committed himself to a *superior* glory and pleasure only makes his case more serious, and the sumptuous wedding he rashly insists on having has to end in Oneiza's sudden death. Landor was nourished on pagan writers; Southey is more high-minded and altogether more Protestant.

Before going on to discuss how Islam is represented in and influences this narrative, a final distinction between the two writers should be noticed. Although, perhaps inspired by *Gebir*'s example, Southey proposes, as we have seen, to make the 'Domdaniel allegorize those systems that make misery of mankind', his poem has no practical political dimension. The fact remains that *Thalaba* is ultimately a story of apocalyptic destruction. It is in this sense that it is a product of the French Revolution, that great event which, to its sympathizers, sought to extirpate the tyranny of the *ancien régime* in order to make possible the regeneration of mankind.

Thalaba as a Moral and Political Poem

Perhaps the most striking characteristic of *Thalaba* is its association of political tyranny with evil and the worship of Satan, or the Islamic Eblis. This is quite as important a theme in the poem as its hypothesis, ultimately derived from Locke, of intuitive morality and man's innate good. That Southey received in this the strongest confirmation from Islam cannot be doubted. Islam is full of traditions enforcing such an association, and Southey exploited everything he came across in his reading about oriental religions that endorsed it. What he would have found above all in this material is the view that oriental despotism had its root in the fall of Adam.

The Morality of the Koran

The Koran, in line with other traditional Islamic writings, naturally has much to say in this regard. As already noted in the discussion of *Gebir*, it contains several passages alluding to the decay of ancient cities and civilizations, shown to have forfeited their glory as a punishment from God. What Southey and Landor found in the Koran was a new emphasis on the commonplace that pride and tyranny are at best transitory. In *Thalaba*, this theme achieves its most sustained treatment in the description of the ruins of Babylon:

Once from her lofty walls the Charioteer
Look'd down on swarming myriads; once she flung
Her arches o'er Euphrates' conquer'd tide,
And through her brazen portals when she pour'd
Her armies forth, the distant nations look'd
As men who watch the thunder-cloud in fear,
Lest it should burst above them. She was fallen,
The Queen of cities, Babylon, was fallen!
Low lay her bulwarks; the black Scorpion bask'd
In the palace courts; within the sanctuary
The She-Wolf hid her whelps.
Is yonder huge and shapeless heap, what once
Hath been aërial Gardens, height on height

Rising like Media's mountains crown'd with wood,
Work of imperial dotage? Where the fane
Of Belus? Where the Golden Image now,
Which at the sound of dulcimer and lute,
Cornet and sacbut, harp and psaltery,
The Assyrian slaves adored?
A labyrinth of ruins, Babylon
Spreads o'er the blasted plain:
The wandering Arab never sets his tent
Within her walls; the Shepherd eyes afar
Her evil towers, and devious drives his flock.
Alone unchanged, a free and bridgeless tide,
Euphrates rolls along,
Eternal Nature's work.

[V, stanza 10]

The irony of Babylon's former greatness is that it seemed to constitute a new nature, greater and more magnificent than that of God. Her original power is represented in quasi-religious terms: it 'looked down' on *swarms*, it flung bridges over the 'conquered tide', it *pour'd* armies out; it was feared like the *thunder-cloud*, its aerial gardens were like *Media's mountains*. But God's creation cannot be rivalled or conquered; its symbol, the great river, now 'free and bridgeless' rolls along, *Eternal Nature's work*, and the pastoral realities — the scorpion, the she-wolf, the wandering Arab, the shepherd — reassume the landscape.

This huge collapse is felt to be a sort of divine curse, and is thus shunned by natural beings. The curse was provoked by the idolatry of worldly power — Belus, 'the Golden Image', and the instruments 'adored' by 'Assyrian slaves'. This impiety captures the essence of the Koranic attitude to the fall of civilizations. The Koran frequently urges man to consider, and take warning from, the fate of preceding generations:

> Do they not pass through the earth, and see what hath been the end of those who were before them? They excelled in strength, and broke up the earth, and inhabited it with greater affluence and prosperity than they inhabit the same: and their apostles came unto them with evident miracles: and God was not disposed to treat them unjustly, but they injured their own souls by their obstinate infidelity: and the end of those who had done evil, was evil, because they charged the signs of God with falsehood, and laughed the same to scorn.[15]

These 'apostles' represent God's disposition of righteousness towards great nations; these arrogant nations earn divine punishment because they reject that quality of God, and not because of any intrinsic wickedness of wealth and power. The danger inherent in power is, for Southey as for the Koran, very considerable. In the poem this is represented by the extreme caution with which Thalaba handles Abdaldar's magic ring, and which — though it saves him repeatedly — he has to discard before each of his supreme tests: the defeat of Mohareb in the Babylonian cavern (Book V), and his destruction of the same in the Domdaniel (Book XII).

One of the Koranic stories that appealed most to Southey was one which Landor had already used in *Gebir* — the chastisement of the Adites. As it forms the foundation of the entire narrative, it deserves detailed analysis. Both Landor and Southey found its most complete treatment in Sale's 'Preliminary Discourse':

> The tribe of Ad were descended from Ad, the son of Aws, the son of Aram, the son of Sem, the son of Noah, who, after the confusion of the tongues, settled in al Ahkaf, or the winding sands in the province of

Hadramaut, where his posterity greatly multiplied. Their first king was Shedad the son of Ad, of whom the eastern writers deliver many fabulous things, particularly that he finished the magnificent city his father had begun, wherein he built a fine palace, adorned with delicious gardens, to embellish which he spared neither cost nor labour, proposing thereby to create in his subjects superstitious veneration of himself as a god. This garden or paradise was called the garden of Irem, and is mentioned in the Koran, and often alluded to by the oriental writers. The city, they tell us, is still standing in the deserts of Aden, being preserved by providence as a monument of divine justice, though it be invisible, unless very rarely, when God permits it to be seen . . .

The descendants of Ad in process of time falling from the worship of the true GOD into idolatry, sent the prophet Hud (who is generally agreed to be Heber) to preach to and reclaim them. But they refusing to acknowledge his mission, or to obey him, GOD sent a hot and suffocating wind, which blew seven nights and eight days together, and entering at their nostrils passed through their bodies, and destroyed them all, a very few only excepted, who had believed in Hud and retired with him to another place. That prophet afterwards retired into Hadramaut, and was buried near Hasec, where there is a small town now standing called Kabr Hud, or the sepulchre of Hud. Before the Adites were thus severely punished, GOD, to humble them and incline them to hearken to the preaching of his prophet, afflicted them with drought for four years, so that all their cattle perished, and themselves were very near it; upon which they sent Lokman (different from one of the same name who lived in David's time) with sixty others to Mecca to beg rain . . .[16]

Southey was so impressed by this story that he thought of writing a separate poem on it. He copied the bulk of this quotation into his *Common-place Book*, and retained it in full in his notes to *Thalaba*.[17] The Koran does not provide all the details which Sale collected from reliable and unreliable Islamic sources, but limits itself to the destruction of the tribe's city, Irem, after its arrogant and unjust rejection of God:

> Hast thou not considered how thy LORD dealt with Ad, the people of Irem, adorned with lofty buildings, the like whereof hath not been erected in the land; and with Thamud, who hewed the rocks in the valley into houses; and with Pharaoh, the contriver of the stakes: who had behaved insolently in the earth, and multiplied corruption therein? Wherefore thy LORD poured on them various chastisements: for thy LORD *is surely in a watch-tower*, whence he observeth the actions of men.[18]

The insolence of the tribe of Ad — which, in this part of the Koran, appears as one of a number of nations sharing the same fate — is elaborated in another passage:

> As to the tribe of Ad, they behaved insolently in the earth, without reason, and said, who is more mighty than we in strength? Did they not see that God, who had created them, was more mighty than them in strength? And they knowingly rejected our signs. Wherefore we sent against them a piercing wind . . .[19]

The destruction of the Adites was accomplished, as the Koran puts it, 'by a roaring and furious wind; which God caused to assail them for seven nights and eight days successively'.[20]

Southey reproduces this story point by point in *Thalaba* (Book I). The invisible city of Irem suddenly appears to the innocent eyes of Zeinab (Thalaba's just-widowed mother) and her little son. The arrogant magnificence of the construction, both palace and gardens, is emphasized; so are the warnings of the prophet (here spelt 'Houd' rather than 'Hud') being ignored; the four-year drought is described, as is the final destruction by the 'piercing wind', called in Arabic the 'Sarsar': 'The Sarsar can pierce through,/The Icy Wind of Death' (I, stanza 36) — which performs its fatal work in stanza 44.

The significance of this punishment, repeatedly foretold by the Prophet Houd ('Woe, Woe to Irem! woe to Ad!' and so forth), is summed up by the survivor Aswad, who confesses the cause of his city's destruction and his own punishment to young Thalaba:

> 'Boy, who hast reach'd my solitude,
> Fear the Lord in the days of thy youth!
> My knee was never taught
> To bend before my God;
> My voice was never taught
> To shape one holy prayer.
> We worshipp'd Idols, wood and stone,
> The work of our own foolish hands,
> We worshipp'd in our foolishness,
> Vainly the Prophet's voice
> Its frequent warning raised,
> "REPENT AND BE FORGIVEN!". . .
> We mock'd the messenger of God,
> We mock'd the Lord, long-suffering, slow to wrath.'
>
> [I, stanza 21]

Aswad expresses exactly the Koranic condemnation of impiety from arrogance and of idolatry from power.

He would, however, be equally plausible in a Christian context. In fact, Southey's one significant addition to his sources is the reason for Aswad's escape from the common fate. Sale refers to 'very few excepted who had believed in Hud' and, like Lot, 'retired to another place'. Southey's Aswad is saved from death by an act of kindness to an animal *in defiance of religious formalities*, and although his impiety condemns him to centuries of isolation (like Ahasuerus or Coleridge's wedding guest), this act of merely human feeling against institutionalized dogma recommends him to the Prophet, and so generalizes the Islamic point without cancelling it.

However, there then enters another element in Southey's treatment of constructed splendour. Consider his description of the palace and gardens of Irem, also mentioned in the Koran:

A mighty work the pride of Shedad plann'd,
Here in the wilderness to form
A Garden more surpassing fair
Than that before whose gate
The lightning of the Cherub's fiery sword
Waves wide to bar access,
Since Adam, the transgressor, thence was driven.
Here, too, would Shedad build
A kingly pile sublime,
The Palace of his pride.
For this exhausted mines
Supplied their golden store;
For this the central caverns gave their gems;
For this the woodman's axe
Open'd the cedar forest to the sun;
The silkworm of the East
Spun her sepulchral egg;
The hunter Afri
Provok'd the danger of the Elephant's rage;

The Ethiop, keen of scent,
Detects the ebony,
That deep-inearth'd, and hating light,
A leafless tree and barren of all fruit,
With darkness feeds its boughs of raven grain.
Such were the treasures lavish'd in yon pile;
Ages have past away,
And never mortal eye
Gazed on their vanity.
[I, stanza 22]

The explicit evocation of the banishment of Adam from the Garden of Eden (itself part of Islamic traditions) serves to remind us of the impiety of Shedad's project. But the actual description of the building presents this impiety in terms of *unnaturalness*. It requires an unhealthy and reckless exploitation and concentration of the earth's resources, from gold, gems, cedarwood, to silk, ivory, ebony. In each case, we are reminded of the violence with which they are torn out of their natural habitat or environment. Of course there is a recognition here of oriental splendour; but unlike that of his cynical predecessor Beckford, the morality is not merely a device to legitimate the thrill: it is the central emotion informing the description. In its 'ecological' protest — its concern for nature — it not only reproduces but also develops the Koranic warnings.

When Southey deals with ruins, as he frequently does in *Thalaba*, he never strikes the note of archaeological curiosity seen in *Gebir*, or of secular nostalgia for lost grandeur struck by orientalists like Volney, Bruce, Niebuhr or Pococke. He is much more in tune with a deistic traveller like John Chardin, who moralizes the ruins he finds. Like his contemporaries a disciple of Rousseau, Southey condemns palaces and cities, not only because they challenge the authority of God (the Islamic view) but also because they violate the modesty of nature (the Romantic view). For example, the marble statues left in the garden of Shedad allegorize in their vacuity the essential soullessness of the great 'unjust men' they represent:

> Here, frequent in the walks
> The marble statues stood
> Of heroes and of chiefs.
> The trees and flowers remain,
> By Nature's care perpetuate and self-sown.
> The marble statues long have lost all trace
> Of heroes and of chiefs;
> Huge shapeless stones they lie,
> O'ergrown with many a flower.
>
> [I, stanza 23]

By a typical Romantic paradox, this passage demonstrates that permanence is not found in carved stones, but in trees and flowers. For Southey, as with many other Romantics, nature, not architecture, is the true source of value. His fundamental attitude is the pastoral one.

Nevertheless it remains true to say that Southey is in genuine sympathy with the Islamic point of view. How far he goes can be seen from his treatment of Baghdad, the capital of Muslim civilization. Once Thalaba has been directed to Babylon via Baghdad, to consult the two penitent angels, his journey is interrupted by Lobaba in the shape of an old man who pretends to join him in his quest:

> It is a noble city that we seek.
> Thou wilt behold magnificent palaces,
> And lofty minarets, and high-domed Mosques,
> And rich Bazars, whither from all the world
> Industrious merchants meet . . .
>
> [IV, stanza 9]

But this is exactly the language that an orientalist traveller would use. To Southey, the attitude of the average western traveller is exactly suited to the characterization of a demonic magician in disguise. Not only is it detached from and external to the civilization it appreciates, it is also secularist and empirical, and therefore out of sympathy with the moral and religious perspectives of Islam. To this Thalaba replies:

> 'Stands not Bagdad
> Near the site of ancient Babylon
> And Nimrod's impious temple?'

The 'old man' retorts:

> 'A mighty mass remains; enough to tell us
> How great our fathers were, how little we.
> Men are not what they were; their crimes and follies
> Have dwarfed them down from the old hero race
> To such poor things as we!. . .'
>
> [IV, stanza 9]

Lobaba has now turned into the Muslim Arab as pictured in the travel literature of the period, for he thinks of himself as one degenerated from further glory. This too seemed to Southey a perversion both of the spirit of Islam and of moral and political commitment. Romantic nostalgia, in whatever form it assumed, was a recipe for defeatism and passivity.

Southey's more complete attitude is disclosed in Book V, when he provides his own account of Baghdad. Having extricated himself from the snares of Lobaba, Southey's hero, 'with strength renewed' and confident in faith, seeks the consolidation of his beliefs.

At length Bagdad appear'd,
The City of his search.
He hastening to the gate,
Roams o'er the city with insatiate eyes;
Its thousand dwellings, o'er whose level roofs
Fair cupolas appear'd, and high-domed mosques,
And pointed minarets, and cypress groves,
Every where scatter'd in unwithering green.
[V, stanza 5]

Thalaba sees the city in the splendour of its apogee. But in a sudden and striking shift in perspective, the next stanza gives us Baghdad as it is 'today':

Thou too art fallen, Bagdad! City of Peace,
Thou too hast had thy day;
And loathsome Ignorance and brute Servitude,
Pollute thy dwellings now,
Erst for thy Mighty and the Wise renown'd.
O yet illustrious for remember'd fame, —
Thy founder the Victorious, — and the pomp
Of Haroun, for whose name by blood defiled,
Yahia's and the blameless Barmecides',
Genius hath wrought salvation, — and the years
When Science with the good Al-Maimon dwelt . . .
[V, stanza 6]

The unusual note of grief for lost greatness here is owed to the fact that Southey, in addressing Baghdad, is actually addressing Islam. We deduce from Southey's description ('loathsome Ignorance', 'brute Servitude') that the capital of Islam's golden age was destroyed by the effects of tyranny. To those, like Southey, who knew Islamic history, the Califs — the 'Victorious' (or, Almansoor) and 'Al-Maimon' (correctly Al-Ma'amoon) — refer us to periods in which despotic rule was commonly practised. The genius of the Islamic mind and its scientific achievements could not survive political disorder — which led eventually to the withering of the Islamic empire and its culture. Thus, although the stanzas would seem to conclude with the classic rationalization of the self-satisfied imperialist —

> So one day may the Crescent from thy Mosques
> Be pluck'd by Wisdom, when the enlighten'd arm
> Of Europe conquers to redeem the East!
> [V, stanza 6]

— it is the redemption of the East *as the East*, and not in the imposition of western ideology, that is Southey's fundamental concern.

In any case, Islam itself is more self-critical than Southey at this point, for it recognizes its responsibility — in political tyranny and injustice — for the collapse of its greatness. If *Thalaba* cites the pyramids of Egypt as the exemplary case of retribution for arrogance, it is only following the precepts of Islam.

> . . . ye have seen
> The mighty Pyramids,. . .
> For sure those awful piles have overlived
> The feeble generations of mankind.
> What though unmoved they bore the deluge weight,
> Survivors of the ruined world?
> What though their founder fill'd with miracles
> And wealth miraculous their spacious vaults?
> [I, stanza 29]

In a note to this passage Southey quotes an Arab account (apparently taken from folk tradition) cited in Greaves's *Pyramidographia*, which offers an explanation for the building of the pyramids.[21] Sourid Ibn Salhouk, the King of Egypt, had a dream one day in which he saw the apocalyptic end of the world. The dream was interpreted by his chief priest as a flood that would destroy Egypt. The king decided to build the pyramids by the river Nile, to escape this deluge, and to fill them with all kinds of treasures, engraving on them all the sciences of the world. When the flood came, however, the king and his people were destroyed; but their now useless wealth survived. The moral of this fable matches exactly the message proclaimed by the pyramids remaining today: that neither God nor death can be defeated.

Oriental Despotism

Even though Southey did not attempt allegorical allusions to European politics, political despotism was so strongly associated with the orient that it could scarcely fail to feature prominently in his poem. A fact less well known, but of equal importance to him, is that the Islamic scripture itself accounts for the decay that overtakes ancient civilization in terms of political tyranny. Thus Southey's denunciation of such oriental despots as the pharaoh, Shedad or Nimrod is exactly in line with the Koranic doctrines. As the Koran puts it: 'and these their habitations remain empty, because of the injustice which they committed'.[22]

Islam seemed to Southey to be dominated by tyranny and submission. From the sources available to him on the Near Orient, he could hardly have perceived Islamic society as being otherwise. Almost all orientalists' sources, from d'Herbelot's *Bibliothèque orientale* to Henley's notes in Beckford's *Vathek*, repeat stories that centre on oriental tyranny of one kind or another. Sale's account of the ancient Arab King of Tasm, the Yemeni Jewish king, Dhu Nowas, and the Nooman of Hirah are only three among innumerable examples. The King of Tasm was a tyrant who ruled over the tribe of Jadis. He 'made a law that no maid of the tribe of Jadis should marry unless first deflowered by him'.[23] Dhu Nowas was a Jewish king who ruled in Yemen and persecuted those who embraced the newly introduced religion of Christianity: the 'bigoted tyrant commanded all those who would not renounce their faith to be cast into a pit, or trench, filled with fire, and there burnt to ashes'. Al Nooman of Hirah was another tyrant, who, in Sale's own words,

> in a drunken fit, ordered two of his intimate companions, who overcome with liquor had fallen asleep, to be buried alive. When he came to himself, he was extremely concerned at what he had done, and to expiate his crime, not only raised a monument to the memory of his friends, but set apart two days, one of which he called the unfortunate, and the other the fortunate day, making it a perpetual rule to himself that whoever met him on the former day should be slain, and his blood sprinkled on the monument, but he that met him on the other day should be dismissed in safety, with magnificent gifts.'[24]

On one of those unfortunate days, an Arab of the tribe of Tay, who had once entertained the king when he was fatigued with hunting, visited him. Being grateful to this man, the king could neither kill him nor discharge him, so instead offered him a year's remission. The Arab returned on the exact day appointed for his death. Admiring his courage, the king asked the Arab what made him fulfil his promise on such conditions. The answer was because the religion he professed taught him to. The man's religion was Christianity, which the king then embraced because of this incident.

The Nooman of Hirah's tale was an example of conversion, but most of the tyrants Southey refers to are megalomaniacs, who demand of their people submission, and even worship — a sin fully recognized as such by the Koran. This is what the Islamic scriptures say about the pharaoh who claimed divinity, and who required his minister Haman to build him a tower high enough to see Moses' God:

> And Pharaoh said, O princes, I did not know that ye had any other god besides me. Wherefore do thou, O Haman, burn me clay into bricks; and build me a high tower, that I may ascend unto the GOD of Moses; for I verily believe him to be a liar.[25]

Elsewhere the Koran refers to the pharaoh's pride and stubbornness: 'thus doth God seal up every proud and stubborn heart. And Pharaoh said, O Haman, build me a tower, that I may reach the tracts, the tracts of heaven, and may view the God of Moses.'[26] According to an Islamic account (which was reported by Sale), as soon as the tower was built, the pharaoh and his army started to climb to its top, but God sent Gabriel to destroy it over them. This pharaoh was only one of a line of despots whose tyranny was such that they required their subjects to worship them. And although the Koran condemns tyranny, it at the same time blames the people who submit to it: 'And Pharaoh *made fools of his people*; and they obeyed him: for they were a wicked people.'[27]

Here, too, Southey is in accord with Koranic precept. *Thalaba* blames the Adites for their resignation to the tyranny imposed on them, a subject on which Aswad is eloquent:

> 'O Ad! my country! evil
> . . . evil was the day
> That thy unhappy sons
> Crouch'd at this Nimrod's throne,
> And placed him on the pedestal of power,

And laid their liberties beneath his feet . . .'
[I, stanza 32]

And this is reinforced in the following stanza:

They saw their King's magnificence, beheld
His palace sparkling like the Angel domes
Of Paradise, his Garden like the bowers
Of early Eden, and they shouted out,
'Great is the King! a God upon the earth!'
[I, stanza 33]

But perhaps the place where Southey comes closest to identifying *royalty* (and by implication European kings) as the object of his attack occurs in a passage in the first edition, but significantly suppressed in later editions. It depicts an oriental despot sitting in a luxurious tent, receiving 'homage and worship' from his people. He enters his tent with the pompous and blatant accompaniment of 'swelling horn', 'the trumpet's spreading blair', and 'the heary Gong . . . that falls like thunder on the dizzy ear'.[28] Worshippers crowd on his path:

On either hand the thick-wedged crowd
Fall from the royal path.
Recumbent in the palanguin he casts
On the wide tumult of the waving throng
A proud and idle eye.
Now in his tent alighted, he receives
Homage and worship. The slave multitude
With shouts of blasphemy adore
Him, father of his people! him their Lord!
Great king, all-wise, all-mighty, and all good.
Whose smile was happiness, whose frown was death,
Their present Deity!
[II, stanza 10; 1st edn, p 190]

Very little adjustment would be required to make this passage fit a European court of the *ancien régime*. The passage as a whole (which is taken from Tavernier's account of Persia) highlights the reckless exoticism and extravagance of the oriental despot. But Southey's prudent, and doubtless sincere, excision of it makes its original target unmistakable. In fact, the first edition was generally less compromising in its representation of despotism than the latter ones. To take another example: the sultan who honours Thalaba in Book VII for having destroyed his arch-enemy Aloadin is, in the first edition, a vicious sadist who relishes the agony of his victims. (Beckford's *Vathek* had exhibited similar perversions.) One of the Sultan's victims is a Christian boy, brought to Turkey to enable magicians to extract poison from his dying body. He has been chosen for his red hair, a feature allegedly regarded by the Turks as specially suited to their experiment. Southey found this story in Tristan's *Plaidoyers Historiques*, and gave as his reason for withdrawing it from later editions its irrelevance to the general purpose of *Thalaba*. Whatever the truth of the matter, there can be no doubt that such anecdotes nourished his interest in demonology, and increased his sense of the profound connection between witchcraft and tyranny — a subject to which we shall return.

Southey's poem discovers in oriental ruins the fate of tyranny. But it also affirms the meaning of this fate — divine retribution. His narrative presents the collapse of despotic regimes in accelerated form, as it were, for it is Thalaba, and not time, that is the 'destroyer'. The poem exhibits a succession of such retributions, the leading ones being Shedad (Book I), destroyed by the Sarsar, and Aloadin (Books VI–VII), extinguished by Thalaba and Oneiza. But it is the evil magicians of the Domdaniel, and in particular the chief magician Mohareb, who represent despotism at its most absolute, and whose fate represents the destruction of despotism at its most complete. The Domdaniel is presented twice — in Book II, where we are introduced to the assembled magicians plotting how to deflect, and eliminate, their appointed destroyer; and in Book XII, where it becomes the site on which the destroyer accomplishes his task, sacrificing his earthly life to gain a heavenly one.

The pattern of these narrative incidents is revealing. In each case, the tyrants possess an extraordinary earthly power that is at the same time extremely frail and insecure. The might of Shedad is demolished by a wind. The power of Aloadin seems invulnerable: Thalaba crushes his head with a club improvised from an uprooted poplar tree, but — 'Aloadin fell not', and the gigantic bird of prey hovering over his head is about to attack Thalaba when it is shot by Oneiza with Thalaba's bow; then — 'darkness covered all . . . /Earth shook, Heaven thunder'd, and amid the yells/Of evil Spirits perished/The Paradise of Sin' (VII, stanza 18).[29] Although much amplified, exactly the same pattern returns in the apocalyptic final book (XII). The power of the Domdaniel, but also its vulnerability, is embodied in a giant 'Living Image' of Eblis, the cause of storms, earthquakes and eruptions on earth, but also the pillar that holds up the floor of the sea forming the roof of the cavern (stanza 27). So, in the poem's ultimate stanza:

> Thalaba knew that his death-hour was come;
> And on he leapt, and springing up,
> Into the Idol's heart
> Hilt-deep he plunged the Sword.
> The Ocean-vault fell in, and all were crush'd.
> [stanza 36]

The pattern is clearly symbolic of the essential hollowness of terrestrial might. For this reason, the destroyer's task is at once extremely arduous and extremely easy. When he is finally in a position to challenge tyranny, it seems to collapse of its own accord. The omnipotence of God is co-extensive with the weakness of His opponents. Thus Southey drives home the real significance of divine retribution: that it is accomplished by a single, unprotected, faithful individual, shorn of all artificial aids (such as magic rings), armed only in his own honesty and with his father's sword — the emblem of inherited honour. Only a small effort is required to dislodge an avalanche.

What happens to tyrants after apocalypse? On this question, unlike Landor, Southey is strangely reticent. The great set piece of *Gebir*, the descent to the underworld, has incidental influences on Southey's description of Thalaba's descent into the Domdaniel. But it is not the place in which tyrants suffer: it is their headquarters and fortress. The only moment strictly comparable to *Gebir*, Book III, is Thalaba's descent into the chasm adjoining Babylon, guarded by the screaming giant Zohak:

. . . o'er the vaulted cave,
Trembles the accursed taper's feeble light.
There where the narrowing chasm
Rose loftier in the hill,
Stood Zohak, wretched man, condemn'd to keep
His Cave of punishment.
His was the frequent scream
Which when far off the prowling Jackal heard,
He howl'd in terror back:
For from his shoulders grew
Two snakes of monster size,
Which ever at his head
Aim'd their rapacious teeth
To satiate raving hunger with his brain.
He, in the eternal conflict, oft would seize
Their swelling necks, and in his giant grasp
Bruise them, and rend their flesh with bloody nails,

And howl for agony,
Feeling the pangs he gave, for of himself
Co-sentient and inseparable parts,
The snaky torturers grew.
[V, stanza 28]

The notion of being at once the cause and effect of one's own torment is a horrifying one, made the more vivid by the image of a huge body contorted and bulging with pain. The extravagance of the tortures reveals gothic elements. In a general way, moreover, this Romantic tradition is blended with Islamic tradition, which pictures the eternal torture of tyrants from their very sepulchres, so that gothic horror flows into the Islamic hell. Yet it remains quite unclear as to why Zohak is suffering. The feeling that the 'wretched man' arouses is, if anything, compassionate. Perhaps, as 'that Giant of primeval days' (stanza 27), he recalls the classical Titans condemned to suffer eternally for their revolt against heaven. Yet that very vagueness serves Southey's distinctive purpose, which is less to punish the abuse of power than to disclose the nature of power.

Thalaba as a Christo-Islamic Hero

Vengeance and Redemption

Southey's Thalaba is a hero of both Islamic and Christian ideals. He has two of the widely accepted qualifications for the role of hero. On the one hand, he has a destiny and an appointed task — the destruction of evil. On the other, he pursues this task with unwavering fidelity and courage. And his heroism is recognizable as such by both East and West. His role as a 'delegated' destroyer of evil is perfectly compatible with Islamic values. The support of God or Allah in the accomplishment of the task is equally characteristic of both religions. Whenever he is tempted to turn away from his divinely appointed mission, he is forced to return to it by what appears to be a providential act working through human beings and the ghosts of human beings. Three times he seeks the consolation of the private life — first in the company of his mother, Zeinab (Book I), who dies yet encourages him from the grave; then with Oneiza (Books II and VII), who, as we have seen, is taken from him by the angel of death Azrael the moment he marries her, but who also continues to exhort him from the other world; and finally with Laila (Book X), who is killed by her father, Okba, when she receives the arrow meant for Thalaba, and who in the shape of a green bird then leads him to the all-knowing Simorg.

Despite all this oriental machinery and the fulfilment of Thalaba's destructive role, Southey's development of his hero's career acquires distinctly Christian overtones. It takes the form of an evolution from vengeance to forgiveness, traceable in Thalaba's relationship with all three women, based, in all three cases, on *love* — filial, passionate and protective, respectively — and therefore leading towards the discovery of compassion. As a young boy whose family has been killed, he cannot accept his mother's profound fatalism — i.e. the conviction that whatever happens is the will of God ('Allah, thy will be done!' [I, stanza 7]). To this, Thalaba replies ('his brow in manly frowns was knit'):

> 'Tell me who slew my father?'. . .
>
> 'But I will hunt him through the world!. . .'
>
> 'Already I can bend my father's bow;
> Soon will my arm have strength
> To drive the arrow-feathers to his heart.'
>
> [stanzas 8, 9]

But this is clearly an immature and primitive motive, devoid of the universal morality that Southey seeks to proclaim.

His relationship with Oneiza is central to his career. Although he loses her at the end of Book VII, his death at the end of Book XII is presented as his recovery of her. The entire poem concludes with this orthodox Islamic idea:

> In the same moment, at the gate
> Of Paradise, Oneiza's Houri form
> Welcomed her Husband to eternal bliss.
>
> [stanza 36]

If vengeance involves too strong a personal attachment, what he has to learn is a measure of detachment or impersonality. As we have seen, Thalaba has married Oneiza in a flush of worldly triumph. Moreover, he does so despite her personal distaste for the life of the court in comparison with the pastoral life of the desert (VII, stanza 29), and despite her most serious forebodings: 'Remember, Destiny/Hath mark'd thee from Mankind!' she tells him. Her death therefore throws him into an uncontrollable excess of guilt and grief. Eventually he is found by Moath next to Oneiza's tomb in a state of demented deprivation, and, like Zeinab before him, Moath counsels resignation: 'God is good! His will be done!' He discovers that Thalaba has been haunted nightly by the 'vampire corpse' of Oneiza, who urges him to despair; he kills the creature, and, to Thalaba's infinite relief, it is instantly replaced by the spirit of the true Oneiza, who urges Thalaba: 'O my husband,/Go and fulfil thy quest . . .' (VIII, stanza 11). This is clearly an allegory of liberation from the excessive love of the creation, as opposed to the dutiful love of the Creator.

But detachment is not enough: it is only a stage to the final attitude, an emptying of the self of false attitudes as a preliminary to the acquisition of true ones. And this is accomplished in Thalaba's meeting with Laila, the only daughter of Okba, the murderer of his father, brothers and sisters. Having escaped the clutches of the witch sisters, Maimuna and Khawla, he continues his frozen journey until he comes to a refuge. This offers the image of domestic felicity in a garden ('whose delightful air/Was mild and fragrant as the evening wind/Passing in summer o'er the coffee-groves/Of Yemen . . .') and a warm cottage — and inside it a sleeping damsel. She awakes and produces a magic meal, which he refuses. He learns that she is called Laila, and that she has been hidden in this solitude by Okba so as to escape a prediction of her death. He is sympathetic, and she responds to his kindness. Thereupon Okba, whom Thalaba has recognized as the killer of his family, urges him to take part of his vengeance against his own daughter. This would represent a perfect reply to the original crime — a relative for relatives.

Thalaba refuses, however, despite assurances from no less than Azrael himself that Laila must indeed be killed. The straight satisfaction of the impulse of revenge is no longer possible. The exasperated Okba then makes another strike at him; and this time Laila offers her breast to receive the blow. The contradiction is thus resolved: she loses her life as a predestined retributor for a crime, and also performs an act of self-sacrificing gratitude. Furthermore, this episode determines the final phase of the plot. By refusing to kill Laila, even though prompted by the will of heaven, Thalaba has replaced vengeance with compassion as the driving theme of the narrative, for he has secured the further means to reach the Domdaniel, and the fulfilment of his destiny. This attempt to reconcile retribution and compassion is really quite remarkable. Laila, transformed by her death into the green bird of Paradise, prepares the way to the final, catastrophic annihilation of the Domdaniel, by leading Thalaba to the brink of his destination, where she takes her leave of him. 'Son of Hodeirah!' she says, with a deliberate allusion to his motive for revenge,

> 'When thou shalt see an Old Man bent beneath
> The burthen of his earthly punishment,
> Forgive him; Thalaba!
> Yea, send a prayer to God on his behalf!'
>
> [XI, stanza 26]

And his response shows how far he has transcended the avenging impulse:

> A flush o'erspread the young Destroyer's cheek;
> He turn'd his eye towards the Bird
> As if in half repentance; for he thought
> Of Okba; and his father's dying groan
> Came on his memory.
>
> [stanza 27]

So Thalaba sacrifices his own grievance to the redemption of Okba. His final act, before the Armageddon, is to spare a despairing Okba from his avenging sword:

> 'The evil thou hast done to me and mine
> Brought its own bitter punishment.
> For thy dear daughter's sake I pardon thee . . .
> Repent while time is yet!. . .
> . . . hath not Allah made
> Al-Araf, in his wisdom?. . .'
>
> [XII, stanza 30]

And only at this supreme moment does a voice announce that the final hour has struck at last; and his fate is to be accomplished. Al-Araf is the purgatory of the Muslims which, according to Southey's note, quoting the Persian poet Sadi, 'appears a Hell to the happy, and a Paradise to the damned'.[30]

Thus it is that Southey reconciles the idea of a just or holy war, associated with Islam, to the idea of non-violence and forgiveness associated with Christianity. How close the two great traditions are in Southey's conception may be judged by recalling the Koran's commendation of those who die for the sake of God:

> Now in the creation of heaven and earth, and the vicissitude of night and day, are signs unto those who are endued with understanding; who remember God . . . and meditate on the creation of heaven and earth, saying, O LORD, thou has not created this in vain . . . O LORD, forgive us therefore our sins, and expiate our evil deeds from us, and make us to die with the righteous . . . Their LORD therefore answereth them, saying, I will not suffer the work of him among you who worketh to be lost, whether he be male or female. They therefore who have . . . suffered for my sake, and have been slain in battle; verily I will expiate their evil deeds from them, and it will surely bring them into gardens watered by rivers; a reward from God.[31]

The spirit of this passage is exactly echoed in Thalaba's repudiation of Mohareb's values, when the latter challenges him to 'abandon him who has abandon'd thee':

> 'And this then is thy faith! this monstrous creed!
> This lie against the Sun, and Moon, and Stars,
> And Earth, and Heaven!. . .
> . . . Shall danger daunt,

Shall death dismay his soul, whose life is given
For God, and for his brethren of mankind?
Alike, rewarded in that holy cause,
The Conqueror's and the Martyr's palm above
Beam with one glory. Hope ye that my blood
Can quench the dreaded flame? and know ye not,
That leagued against ye are the Just and Wise,
And all Good Actions of all ages past,
Yea, your own crimes, and Truth, and God in Heaven?'
[IX, stanza 15]

The Magic Ring

The degree to which Thalaba's submission to the will of God constitutes an achievement — the result of fidelity, effort and intelligence — is demonstrated by means of one of the main threads of the narrative: the talismanic ring which at once assists and impedes his quest. The paradox is easily stated. The ring which helps Thalaba represents magic, the force that stands in opposition to the power of God. The problem is that since God and the magicians (and behind them their master Eblis) are in implacable opposition, the servant of God must attain a faith that is entirely purified of all dependence on the magicians' art. But such a faith cannot be achieved without exposure to what is contrary to it.

When the magicians realize that Thalaba has escaped the extermination of his family by Okba, they forge a potent ring that will identify Thalaba when he is found and protect its wearer from harm or even death (Book II). Abdaldar is sent out to find the surviving boy, and with the help of the ring does so, but is destroyed by a *simoom* as he is about to kill him. Thalaba notices the ring on the dead man's finger, but Moath warns him against it, saying that its mysterious power cannot be good, being the property of wizards. Thalaba, however, decides to take it:

In God's name, and the Prophet's! be its power
 Good, let it serve the righteous; if for evil,
 God, and my trust in Him, shall hallow it.
[III, stanza 1]

Whatever its power, then, it is subordinate to God's power, and cannot harm those who acknowledge the fact. But once they have lost the ring, the magicians become desperate to recover it. That evening a demon appears in Thalaba's tent, but is foiled by the power of the ring, and obliged to reply to Thalaba's questions about the identity and location of his father's killers, and to bring his father's bow and arrows.

The next attempt to regain the ring is made by Lobaba, who is more subtle than his predecessor. Having led Thalaba into the most inhospitable part of the desert and exposed him to the destructive force of a sandstorm, he tries to tempt him into substituting the ring's magical power for dependence on God. His argument is that what makes magic powers (such as those possessed by gems) good or bad is the use they are put to ('All things have a double power,/Alike for good or evil'), and that there is no *intrinsic* good or evil determined by God's will. It is clear that Thalaba will not be swayed by such an argument, for it was precisely the view he rejected when he took the ring from Abdaldar.

The third attempt to check Thalaba is made by no less a figure than the chief magician Mohareb himself as Thalaba descends into the chasm in Babylon. This seeming warrior is wholly contemptuous of Thalaba's piety: 'Idiot! that I have led/Some camel-kneed prayer-monger through the cave!' (V, 36). His contempt is increased when his physical assault on Thalaba is checked by power of the ring rather than Thalaba's own power. Thalaba therefore throws it into a nearby bitumen spring, where it is collected by 'A skinny hand' to the sound of 'devilish laughter' — a reaction which warns us that he has at last been tricked into parting with the ring; but he succeeds in ridding himself temporarily of Mohareb by hurling him into the chasm.

But Mohareb is to return for yet another temptation attempt. This time he is the ruler of the magic island to which the witch sisters have borne Thalaba in Book VIII, and where they discover by divination from Eblis, their master, that Mohareb's life is tied to Thalaba's (as the destruction of the Domdaniel indeed eventually demonstrates). Mohareb therefore, out of self-preservation, returns the protecting ring to Thalaba. 'Locked in his magic chain,' as he is, Thalaba cannot resist receiving it, but repeats the same faith in God's superior power which he originally declared when he first took the ring (IX, stanza 13). This draws from Mohareb the most sustained statement of the enchanters' — that is, the secular — point of view in the poem (stanza 14): that since life and death coexist, so there are in nature 'two hostile Gods,/Makers and Masters of existing things,/Equal in power . . .'; so that 'Evil and Good' are 'but words', and thus 'power must decide'. This doctrine Thalaba rejects with abhorrence. The more wicked of the two sisters tries, by means of a spell, to turn the harmful powers of nature against Thalaba, but he is saved by the ring. The kinder of the witches is melted into self-realization by the beauty of natural life; she frees Thalaba, and escapes with him from the island.

The ring will protect Thalaba one last time, against the attack of Okba in Laila's cottage. But when, at last, he reaches the mouth of the Domdaniel, he finally casts it into the sea, exclaiming:

'Thou art my shield, my trust, my hope, O God!
Behold and guard me now,
Thou who alone canst save . . .

If of all selfish passions purified
I go to work thy will, and from the world
Root up the ill-doing race,
Lord, let not thou the weakness of my arm
Make vain the enterprize!'
[XII, stanza 1]

This ultimate gesture, then, is a declaration of Thalaba's complete faith in and full submission to God. The temptations preceding it have been deliberately designed by the magicians to make him doubt the power of God. In this, Southey expresses a typically Islamic attitude, which regards temptation as vital in the making of a strong faith. 'Magic' represents one important aspect of the test Thalaba has to undergo to reach the full status of a faithful martyr, the other, as we have seen, being 'nature' and the temptation of the paradisal refuge it offers. The equation of magic with Eblis is not clearly established in the major Islamic sources, though it is clear from the translations of *The Arabian Nights* that for any westerner necromancy and the demonic world might seem an integral part of Islamic culture. The issue of evil in general, however, is canonically associated with Eblis, the arch-devil, whose temptation caused the fall of Adam and Eve, and who therefore will continue to exert influence in the world, under divine respite, until the day of judgement, as the Koran puts it. To worship Eblis is to worship the self. This means turning away from God, and towards an idea of the energies of nature from which the idea of Good and Evil is absent.[32]

But to Southey the question of the magic ring has a deeper philosophical significance. When Thalaba decides to wear the ring, seeing no contradiction in using it for righteous ends, the next relevant episode complicates matters. He dismisses the demon who seeks to recover the ring in the following terms:

'Go thy way, and never more,
Evil spirit, haunt our tent!
By the virtue of the Ring,
By Mohammed's holier might,
By the holiest name of God,
Thee, and all the Powers of Hell,
I adjure and I command
Never more to trouble us!'
[III, stanza 12]

The passage reveals Thalaba's inadequate and vacillating attitude towards magic, for he places the ring on an ascending scale of 'virtue' that rises through Mohammed to God. Yet he has already recognized that the point of departure of this ladder is not magic but pastoral nature — God's creation. And that he has doubts is shown by the fact that though he keeps on wearing the ring, he is very reluctant to use its power to save him from the perils he encounters. When Lobaba urges him to use the ring to escape the whirlwind, he replies: 'Nay!. . ./Shall I distrust the providence of God?/Is it not He must save?' (IV, stanza 29). And he immediately goes on to demonstrate that he has fully grasped what is at issue: '. . . If Allah wills it not,/Vain were the Genii's aid' (stanza 29). But even now, Thalaba is still not free of temptation. When Mohareb, to his own secret joy, gets him to take the ring back, Thalaba retains his sense of having to depend on a compromised and dangerous power:

'In God's name and the Prophet's! be its power
Good, let it serve the righteous! if for evil,
God and my trust in Him shall hallow it.
Blindly the wicked work
The righteous will of Heaven!'
[IX, stanza 13]

What the ring episode demonstrates is that as long as one is still part of the world, and entangled in its snares (in the poem: the activity of magicians), one cannot be entirely free of dependence on its power. Only at the supreme moment of self-sacrifice and martyrdom, when one is on the point of relinquishing one's place in nature, can one finally renounce one's necessary compromises with the impurities of 'magic'.

This amounts to saying that submission to the will of God is the supreme achievement of the individual human being. This idea, common to the major religions of the world, has a place of special importance in Islam, from which the word 'submission' (*istislam*) is a derivation. Thalaba — and perhaps Roderick (unlike Southey's other epic heroes, who never experience a tragic conflict, and are virtuous to the point of infallibility) — is exposed to a process of testing and purification. In Christian terms, this is usually justified on the basis of the doctrine of original sin, which holds that man, left to his own devices, is helpless to achieve salvation. The episodes of the ring are skilfully devised to hold a position half-way between Christian original sin and Islamic providentiality — which regards error as a necessary stage in the achievement of purity, and indeed (as the action of the ring demonstrates) productive of future good. Southey's reconciliation of the two religions, or rather his discovery of a common ground between them, shows a subtlety rarely encountered in world literature.

A final example should enhance this view. As Thalaba's pilgrimage develops, it becomes more and more difficult, and physically more and more harsh and painful. Yet, the greater his suffering, the more completely he is sustained by God: 'He who has led me here, will sustain me/Through cold and hunger' (X, stanza 11). God's final support comes in the form of the Simorg, the ancient 'all-knowing bird' (XI, stanza 11) — a creature of nature, or super-nature, and not a magic amulet or spell, like the ring — to guide him to his goal. It is therefore not surprising if the concluding part of the journey acquires spiritual connotations. Echoing an Islamic parallel, Southey's hero undergoes a final ritual of purification. Thalaba may, as a redeemer who forgives, act as an imitator of Christ; but at this stage in his adventure, he recalls the Prophet Muhammad's 'Nocturnal Journey to the Heavens'. The Simorg requires Thalaba to 'Wash away [his] worldly stains' in the 'Fountain of the Rock'. This he does:

> There, in the cold clear well,
> Thalaba wash'd away his earthly stains,
> And bow'd his face before the Lord,
> And fortified his soul with prayer.
>
> [XI, stanza 15]

In a similar way, Muhammad is invited by his guide, Gabriel, to a ritual of purification and prayers before he commences his journey. The Archangel Gabriel provides Muhammad with a horse-like creature (the 'Borag') as a mount;[33] Thalaba's Simorg equips him with a sledge and a wingless car. At the end of Muhammad's journey to the heavens, during which he is exposed to scenes of an apocalyptic nature, he receives confirmation of his prophethood. So Thalaba, at the end of *his* journey, achieves his full status as God's 'purified servant': 'Thou hast done well, my Servant!' (XII, stanza 31). In fact the very word 'servant' is the term employed by the Koran to define the status Muhammad achieves through this journey.[34] Thus, even at the climax of the action, when Thalaba triumphs over evil by renouncing vengeance in favour of forgiveness — that is to say, when the poem seems most Christian and least Islamic — Southey continues to reveal the depth of his response to Islam.

Islamic Beliefs and Customs in *Thalaba*

Islamic Post-Lapsarianism

It will be clear by now how important a source of inspiration Islam was to the writing of *Thalaba*. Southey's work was much more than a contribution to the development of the literary form known as the oriental tale. It became a vehicle for the communication of the nature of the Islamic faith in the West, and in England in particular; it treated Islam with scholarly seriousness that left its undoubted impact on many Romantic poets.

Thalaba and the notes annexed to it include many references to Islamic beliefs and customs. These do not present Islam as an alternative to Christianity, but serve to confirm and consolidate a number of Christian beliefs. One of these references deals with the creation of Adam and his fall as recounted in Islamic writings, especially the Koran. However, this reference is less concerned with the causes of the fall than with its consequences, alluding to the great store of post-lapsarian details and episodes to be found in Islamic literature.

The Islamic perspective of the fall seems to enhance Southey's conviction of an implicit accord between Islam and Christianity. In *Thalaba*, Arabia is presented as the land into which Adam and Eve were exiled from Eden. Thus Mecca is described as 'the Place of Concourse' (I, stanza 25). In the notes, Southey emphasizes that the inhabitants of Mecca had, in pre-Islamic times, preserved ancient rituals going back at least to Abraham, who had dwelt in that city and built its holy house, Câba, with the help of his son, Ishmael. The Koran mentions this episode in several places; and Sale devoted many pages of his 'Preliminary Discourse' to describing the house and its history. One passage from Sale is noteworthy for its relevance to Southey's view of the relationship between Islam and Christianity:

> The temple of Mecca was a place of worship, and in singular veneration with the Arabs from great antiquity, and many centuries before Mohammed . . . . The Mohammedans are generally persuaded that the Caaba is almost coeval with the world: for they say that Adam, after his expulsion from paradise, begged of GOD that he might erect a building like that he had seen there, called Beit al Mamur, or the frequented house, and al Dorah, towards which he might direct his prayers, and which he might compass, as the angels do the celestial one. Whereupon GOD let down a representation of that house in curtains of light, and set it in Mecca, perpendicularly under its original, ordering the patriarch to turn towards it when he prayed, and to compass it by way of devotion. After Adam's death, his son Seth built a house in the same form of stones and clay, which being destroyed by the Deluge, was built up by Abraham and Ismael, at God's command, in the place where the former had stood, and after the same model, they being directed therein by revelation.[35]

Two footnotes to this passage reinforce this relationship further. The first reads: 'Some say that the Beit al Mamur itself was the Caaba of Adam, which, having been let down from Heaven, was at the Flood, taken up again into heaven, and is there kept.'[36] The second footnote is even stronger:

> It has been observed that the primitive Christian church held a parallel opinion as to the situation of the celestial Jerusalem with respect to the terrestrial: for in the apocryphal book of the revelations of St Peter (chap. 27), after Jesus has mentioned unto Peter the creation of the seven heavens — whence, by the way, it appears that this number of heavens

> was not devised by Mohammed — and of the angels, begins the description of the heavenly Jerusalem above the waters, which are above the third heaven, hanging directly over the lower, Jerusalem . . .[37]

Southey undoubtedly absorbed this view into *Thalaba*. After quoting in the notes a passage describing Mecca from Joseph Pitts's *A Faithful Account of the Religion and Manners of the Mahommedans*, he repeats another passage from the French traveller D'Ohsson, who cited Islamic accounts of Adam's post-lapsarian life. This passage is again important, for it gives us an idea of the elements which influenced Southey's opinion of Arabia as a locus for biblical associations:

> Adam after his fall was placed upon the mountain of *Vassem*, in the eastern region of the globe. Eve was banished to a place, since called Djidda, which signifies the first of mothers, (the celebrated port of Gedda on the coast of Arabia). The Serpent was cast into the most horrid desart of the East . . . The fall of our first parent was followed by the infidelity and sedition of all the spirits, *Djinn*, who were spread over the surface of the earth . . . Some time after, Adam, conducted by the spirit of God, travelled into Arabia, and advanced as far as Mecca. His footsteps diffused on all sides abundance and fertility. His figure was enchanting, his stature lofty, his complexion brown, his hair thick, long and curled; and he then wore a beard and mustachios. After a separation of a hundred years, he rejoined Eve on Mount *Arafaith*, near Mecca; an event which gave that mount the name of *Arafaith*, or *Arefe*, that is, the Place of Remembrance. This favour of the Eternal Deity, was accomplished by another not less striking. By his orders the angels took a tent, *Khayme*,

> from Paradise, and pitched it on the very spot where afterwards the *Keabe* was erected. This is the most sacred of the tabernacles, and the first Temple which was consecrated to the worship of the Eternal Deity by the first of men, and by all his posterity. Seth was the founder of the sacred Keabe: in the same place where the angels had pitched the celestial tent, he erected a stone edifice, which he consecrated to the worship of the Eternal Deity.[38]

D'Ohsson drew mostly on the Koran and other associated traditions dealing with the creation of Mecca. He must have given Southey a strong sense of the importance of Mecca for the Islamic religion, for Southey asserts in one of his notes that the Prophet Muhammad owed his veneration of this spot to his awareness of its ancient holiness. 'Mohammed,' he states with conviction, 'destroyed the other superstitions of the Arabs, but he was obliged to adopt their old and rooted veneration for the Well and the Black Stone, and transfer to Mecca the respect which he had designed for Jerusalem.'[39] It remains here uncertain whether Southey is emphasizing his claim of an existing connection between Islam and Christianity by showing the veneration Muhammad held for the biblical capital; but his statement underlines an important view which seems to regard Muhammad as an originally biblical prophet, who, because of certain local necessities, made his religion depart from its precursor, Christianity, without actually meaning to.

Southey's dependence on the Islamic view of Adam is demonstrated in another aspect of the story — the Koranic account of the conflict between Adam and Satan, to which he refers in *Thalaba*:

> But Eblis would not stoop to Man,
> When Man, fair-statured as the stately palm

From his Creator's hand
Was undefiled and pure . . .
But who is he of woman born
That shall vie with the might of Eblis?
[II, stanza 13]

This passage is only one of several in the poem which present the struggle between man and devil, or good and evil. It is, in fact, a distillation of several Koranic accounts of the original confrontation with Eblis, one of which summarizes it thus:

> And remember when thy LORD said before the angels, Verily I am about to create man of dried clay, of black mud, wrought into shape; when therefore I shall have completely formed him, and shall have breathed of my spirit into him; do you fall down and worship him. And all the angels worshipped Adam together, except Eblis, who refused to be with those who worshipped him. And God said unto him, O Eblis, what hindered thee from being with those who worshipped Adam? He answered, it is not fit that I should worship man, whom thou hast created of dried clay, of black mud, wrought into shape. God said, Get thee therefore hence; for thou shalt be driven away with stones: and a curse shall be on thee, until the day of judgement. The devil said, O LORD, give me respite until the day of resurrection. God answered, Verily thou shalt be one of those who are respited until the day of the appointed time. The devil replied, O LORD, because thou hast seduced me, I will surely tempt them to disobedience in the earth, and I will seduce them all, except such of them as shall be thy chosen servants.[40]

The care with which Southey studied such passages can be shown from a single detail: his substitution of the word 'worship' used by Sale by the word 'stoop' (see first line of above quotation, II, stanza 13). In fact it is incorrect to translate the original Arabic *sajada* as 'worship', though Sale refers the reader to a footnote to explain why he has done so:

> The original word ['worship'] signifies properly to prostrate one's self till the forehead touches the ground, which is the humblest posture of adoration, and strictly due to GOD only; but it is sometimes, as in this place that civil worship or homage, which may be paid to creatures.[41]

But this, as it reads, cannot be supported, for the Koran reiterates that there can be no worship of any creature or object other than God.

There is a further point of interest relating to the stanza quoted above (II, stanza 13). Sale dismissed as inaccurate the notion, advanced in some primitive accounts, that Adam was of a gigantic stature. He quotes these accounts as saying that 'their prophet . . . affirmed Adam to have been as tall as a high palm tree'.[42] But Southey adopts this myth in his allusion to 'man, fair-statured as the stately palm'. It is remarkable that Southey, whose stern Christian attitudes might have led him to manipulate such opportunities as these, chooses a word more faithful to the Islamic original; it shows that the poet Southey was more *imaginatively* open to Islam than was the scholar Sale.

It is not too much to say that Southey was convinced that Islam, despite its 'superstitions', has originated from the same source as the Bible. Southey, as is clear from his preface, could not be more explicit. But it is plausible to conclude from his extraordinary deployment of information about the Islamic religion in *Thalaba* and its notes, and in his letters and diaries, that he held the faith of Islam and its monotheism and morality in high esteem.

Islamic Fatalism

We have seen something of Southey's admiration for the spirit of resignation which dominates the good personalities in *Thalaba*, and which he regards as a mark of an authentic faith.[43] This, too, of course, has its roots in Islamic as well as western traditions. *Thalaba* has several passages which breathe Islamic fatalism. 'Fate favour'd thee,/Young Arab! when she wrote upon thy brow/The meeting of tonight,' cries one of the Arabians to Thalaba. The belief that what God had decreed cannot be changed becomes a leitmotiv in a poem whose protagonist is a man appointed and subjected to a divine mission. And here, too, Southey's project of synthesis is evident: Thalaba's heroic fate brilliantly combines Islamic fatalism with (Christian) epic heroism.

In its Islamic context, fatalism is often seen as a strong conviction that all that God has decreed to his prophets will inevitably come to pass. This is called dependence on God (*tawakul*), and Thalaba's confidence in the positive outcome of his quest is an expression of it:

> He raised his hands to Heaven,
> 'Is there not God, Oneiza?
> I have a Talisman, that, whoso bears,
> Him, nor the Earthly, nor the Infernal Powers
> Of Evil, can cast down.
> Remember, Destiny
> Hath mark'd me from mankind!'
> [VII, stanza 12]

One of Southey's notes reinforces the Islamic inspiration of this:

> The Mohammedans believe, that the decreed events of every man's life are impressed in divine characters on his forehead, though not to be seen by mortal eye.

> Hence they use the word Nusseeb, *anglicé* stamped, for destiny. Most probably the idea was taken up by Mohummed from the sealing of the Elect, mentioned in the Revelations.[44]

The general sense of this quotation rests on well-attested sources, but Southey, along with his orientalist predecessors, did not seem to have had access to more reliable sources to explain the context of this doctrine. For the proverb to which he alludes, and which in modern Arabic runs: 'That which hath been written on the forehead will have to be seen by the eye,' cannot be taken literally. And although one may suspect that Southey was aware of this, he is sufficiently intrigued by traditional orientalist literalism to cite a story taken from a translation of an Indian popular narrative, *Ayeen Akbery*. This story tells how a faithful vizier was dismissed from office and later crucified by his prince, the Rajah Chunder of Cashmeer, because of false rumours accusing him of conspiracy. A short time after his execution, so the story continues,

> the Vizier's peer (his spiritual guide) passed the corpse, and read it decreed in his forehead as follows: 'That he should be dismissed from his office, be sent to prison, and then crucified, but that after all, he should be restored to life, and obtain the kingdom.' . . . one night the aërial spirits assembled together, and restored the body to life by repeating incantations. He shortly after mounted the throne, but, despising worldly pomp, soon abdicated it.[45]

While such a story cannot but carry powerful political overtones, the point here is that Southey, by insisting on a more primitive or superstitious version, was attempting to underline what he took to be characteristic Islamic colouring.

Southey's poem gives an outstanding expression to the spirit of the age in viewing Muslims as fatalists who accept every dilemma that befalls them as the work of God. In the beginning of the poem, Zeinab, Thalaba's mother, makes no protest against the murder of her husband and seven children:

She raised her swimming eyes to Heaven,
'Allah, thy will be done!
Beneath the dispensations of that will
I groan, but murmur not.
A day will come, when all things that are dark
Will be made clear;. . . then shall I know, O Lord!
Why in thy mercy thou hast stricken me.'
[I, stanza 7]

Zeinab's resignation is plainly based on her faith in the providentiality of existence. This, too, is a Christian tradition; but the completeness — or even the fanaticism — of her resignation bears the signs, for Southey, of an Islamic perspective. And, indeed, destiny is fundamental to Islam, for it is determined by God, and inscribed in the Book of Fate. For man to protest against his fate is considered an act of impiety, a challenge to God himself. Thus we find a new contest for the role of the magicians in Southey. In *Thalaba* it is the magicians who, concerned as they are to achieve power for themselves, seek to change what has been written in the Book of Fate. But their impiety involves them in a contradiction, for, like their master, Eblis, they remain aware of God's power. Khawla, the sorceress, addresses her fellow-magicians thus:

Ye can shatter the dwelling of man;
Ye can open the womb of the rock;
Ye can shake the foundations of earth,
But not the Word of God:

But not one letter can ye change
Of what his Will hath written!
[II, stanza 23]

In fact these magicians remain convinced that God can protect his agent, Thalaba, through stronger and more effective means than theirs. One of these magicians, Okba, recounts how he successfully slew Hodeirah and seven of his children: 'Eight blows I struck, eight home-driven blows,/Needed no second stroke.' But as he is about to direct his blow against Thalaba:

A cloud unpierceable had risen,
A cloud that mock'd my searching eyes.
I would have probed it with the dagger-point,
The dagger was repell'd;
A Voice came forth and said,
Son of Perdition, cease! Thou canst not change
What in the Book of Destiny is written.
[II, stanza 8]

Thalaba is frequently saved from destruction by natural forces under God's agency. All nature is marshalled to serve God's protective purposes: clouds, simoom winds, devastating whirlwinds and so on, are continually called to his rescue. But even here the western traditions are not forgotten, for these Islamic elements, viewed from a different perspective, are also the expression of a Romantic theme in which the hero acts directly under the inspiration or protection of nature. Thalaba's faith, for example, is constantly strengthened by his observation of how natural elements 'obey' the will of God:

. . . a cloud
Of locusts, from the desolated fields
Of Syria, wing'd their way.

'Lo! how created things
Obey the written doom!'
[III, stanza 29]

This law of reinforcement encompasses all that God has created, as Moath's interpretation of the locust cloud indicates:

'Behold the mighty army!' Moath cried,
'Blindly they move, impell'd
By the blind Element.
And yonder birds, our welcome visitants,
See! where they soar above the embodied host,
Pursue their way, and hang upon the rear,
And thin the spreading flanks,
Rejoicing o'er their banquet! Deemest thou
The scent of water on some Syrian mosque
Placed with priest-mummery and fantastic rites
Which fool the multitude, hath led them here
From far Khorassan? Allah who appoints
Yon swarms to be a punishment of man,
These also hath he doom'd to meet their way:
Both passive instruments
Of his all-acting will,
Sole mover He, and only spring of all.'
[stanza 31]

Here Romantic animism (in the sense that nature has a moral purpose) meets Islamic fatalism. This passage, which seems to have a tone of piety, alludes to several Koranic verses which describe God's creation of all that is in heaven and earth as 'the armies that execute his will'.[46]

A final illustration of the pervasiveness of faith-inspired fatalism in this poem may be found in Thalaba's response to his mother's death. As Azrael, the angel of death, arrives to take the soul of his dying mother, the young man asks him to take his soul too. But Azrael replies:

> 'It is not yet the hour.
> Son of Hodeirah, thou art chosen forth
> To do the will of Heaven;. . .
> Live! and REMEMBER DESTINY
> HATH MARKED THEE FROM MANKIND!'
> [I, stanza 54]

The last lines serve as a refrain in Thalaba's journey. The poem's reiteration of fatalism reveals the importance this theme acquired for Southey. As his later correspondence explicitly suggests, it plays a crucial part in bringing the individual to terms with the mysterious issues raised by evil and good under God's providentiality.

Arabic Mentality

Southey's admiration of the Arab wilderness, about which he learnt from travel books, also led him to admire the Arab nomads and the mentality that was the product of their environment. Before showing how Arab mentality is portrayed in *Thalaba*, it is essential to note that Southey, following the practice of 18th-century orientalists, does not attempt to distinguish between Islamic faith and pre-Islamic mythology. The lack of such a distinction could lead — as, indeed, it did — to the assumption that Islam itself included a wide range of primitive beliefs, or even a strong dose of paganism. The extent to which Southey was influenced by such a mistaken assumption is not hard to trace.

For example, in his note on the deity of the Adites he writes: 'The Adites worshipped four idols, Sakiah the dispenser of rain, Hafedah the protector of travellers, Razekah the giver of food, and Salemah the preserver in sickness.'[47] He took this quotation from d'Herbelot in order to show the dependence of superstitious Arabs on these domestic deities. Southey also relied on several other orientalists, particularly Volney, D'Ohsson and Niebuhr, who were attempting to explain 'Arab mentality' as an essentially practical tendency that deified what it could find of use in the environment. This type of 'paganism' was promulgated in the writings of the age, and became a standard attribute of ancient Arabs and modern Muslims alike.

Southey's notes also frequently cite travel works dealing with animals and birds which are venerated for their usefulness. The camel, for example, is so important in the Arabian desert that, according to an anonymous quotation, 'Some of the pagan Arabs had their Camel tied by their Sepulchres, and so left without meat or drink to perish, and accompany them to the other world, lest they should be obliged at the Resurrection to go on foot, which was accounted very scandalous.'[48] Southey finds confirmation of this rather absurd idea in Sale: 'All affirmed that the pious, when they come forth from their sepulchres, shall find ready prepared for them white-winged Camels with saddles of gold. Here are some footsteps of the doctrine of ancient Arabians.'[49]

Actually there is no basis for this belief in the main traditions of Arabic and Islamic thought. On the other hand, what is of special interest here is that, although Southey's notes seem to endorse it, his poetry does not. The reason why Aswad is spared the fate of the citizens of Irem is that he could not bear to have his father's and his own favourite camel ritualistically sacrificed at his father's funeral:

'The funeral rites were duly paid,
We bound a Camel to his grave,
And left it there to die,
So if the resurrection came
Together they might rise.

I past my father's grave,
I heard the Camel moan.
She was his favourite beast,
One who had carried me in infancy.
The first that by myself I learn'd to mount.
Her limbs were lean with famine, and her eyes
Ghastly and sunk and dim.
She knew me as I past,
She stared me in the face;
My heart was touch'd,. . . had it been human else?
I thought that none was near, and cut her bonds,
And drove her forth to liberty and life.'
[I, stanza 27]

Human and sympathetic impulses, powerfully conveyed in the choice of detail (the camel 'moaning', and especially the bond between man and animal marked by the exchange of glances) completely overwhelm the dogma of resurrection. The poet repudiates his own bad scholarship by other means. To live with animals is to make them part of your life. This is true even of the vulture.

Southey also finds confirmation in Niebuhr, this time in reference to the vulture of the usefulness of which he had learnt during his journey in Arabia: 'The Vulture is very serviceable in Arabia, clearing the earth of all carcasses [and] destroys the field mice.' And Niebuhr concludes: 'Their [the vultures'] performance of these important services induced the ancient Egyptians to pay those birds divine honours, and even at present it is held unlawful to kill them in all the countries which they frequent.'[50] A related story is reported by travellers such as Sonnini, which Southey quotes in a note to the passage describing Thalaba's characteristic Bedouin stance 'with his dog beside him': 'Bedouins take care of these useful servants, and have such an affection for them, that to kill the dog of a Bedouin would be to endanger your own life.'[51] Orientalist books abound with analogous examples.

Arab convictions and beliefs were shown by 18th-century orientalists like Volney and Niebuhr to be the reaction of men to the natural environment in which they lived and on which they depended. One popular example is the scene of a desert mirage, which is frequently encountered in many travel works on the Near Orient. It represents one of several natural phenomena, freeing the imagination to indulge in fanciful escape from the hardships of the wilderness. Southey is impressed by this idea, which he used successfully in *Thalaba* and other works to reflect on the subtle contradistinction between reality and dream. The notes to *Thalaba* abound with references to this phenomenon, drawn from detailed first-hand reports. For example, from the early explorer Shaw:

> Where any part of these Deserts is sandy and level is as fit for astronomical observations as the sea, and appears, at a small distance, to be no less a collection of water. It was likewise surprising to observe, in what an extraordinary manner every object appeared to be magnified within it; insomuch, that a shrub seemed as big as a tree, and a flock of Achbobbas might be mistaken for a caravan of Camels. This seeming collection of water always advances about a quarter of a mile before us, whilst the intermediate space appears to be in one continued glow, occasional by the quivering undulating motion of that quick succession of vapours and exhalations, which are extracted by the powerful influence of the sun.[52]

This account is ingeniously transformed by Southey into a complex image of a literal thirst which becomes itself, in the context, expressive of a spiritual thirst:

. . . Long their craving thirst
Struggled with fear, by fear itself inflamed;. . .
Still the same burning sun! no cloud in heaven!
The hot air quivers, and the sultry mist
Floats o'er the desert, with a show
Of distant waters, mocking their distress.
[IV, stanza 27]

But this passage bears strong affinities to the Koran, which also uses the image of the mirage in spiritual terms. The works of unbelievers are described as being 'like the vapour in a plain, which the thirsty traveller thinketh to be water, until when he cometh thereto, he findeth to be nothing'.[53] Surely Southey would not have missed Sale's note to the above Koranic verse: 'The Arabic word *Serab* signifies that false appearance which, in the eastern countries, is often seen in sandy plains about noon, resembling a large lake of water in motion, and is occasioned by the reverberation of the sunbeams.'[54]

Niebuhr's experience of this phenomenon, also quoted by Southey, adds an interesting dimension:

> One of the Arabs, whom we saw from afar, and who was mounted upon a camel, seemed higher than a tower, and to be moving in the air; at first this was to me a strange appearance, however it was only the effect of refraction; the Camel which the Arab was upon touching the ground like others. There was nothing then extraordinary in this phenomenon, and I afterwards saw many appearances exactly similar in the dry countries.[55]

The notes then proceed to cite with remarkable appropriateness a verse on mirages taken from Alhareth Ibn Hilzah, the author of one of the celebrated pre-Islamic *Seven Odes*: 'They surprised you, not indeed by a sudden assault; but they advanced, and the sultry vapour of noon, through which you saw them, increased their magnitude.'[56] The juxtaposition of these different passages is a mark of Southey's range and sympathy of erudition. But even more impressive is the way in which he turns them into poetry. The magician Lobaba, disguised as an old man, attempts to make Thalaba doubt the reality of God's punishment of the angels Haruth and Maruth:

> Son, thou hast seen the Traveller in the sands
> Move through the dizzy light of hot noon-day,
> Huge as the giant race of elder times;
> And his Camel, than the monstrous Elephant,
> Seem of a vaster bulk . . .
> And hast thou never, in the twilight, fancied
> Familiar object into some strange shape
> And form uncouth?. . .
> Things view'd at distance through the mist of fear;
> By their distortion terrify and shock
> The abused sight . . .
> Wisely from legendary fables, Heaven
> Inculcates wisdom.
>
> [IV, stanza 9]

This passage offers a remarkable example of the way in which Southey's imagination works. Obviously it elaborates the mirage and related phenomena for rhetorical purposes: through it the old man tries to persuade Thalaba of the unreality of God's judgement. But the way Southey manipulates the speech is less obvious. The old man moves from a familiar experience ('a frequent sight') to a more threatening one ('strange shape/And form uncouth') to the 'distortion' of fear itself. The very subtlety of his slide from one image to another, however, itself creates an effect of insubstantiality, and seems to enact precisely what is condemned. In other words, the argument that

God's judgement is a mirage itself turns into a mirage, and so undoes itself.

But the mirage is not only an image of deceptive uncertainty or illusion. Southey can develop it into strikingly positive effects. Earlier in the same book, old Moath and his daughter, Oneiza, watch the 'delegated' youth's departure into the sunrise:

Day dawns, the twilight gleam dilates,
The Sun comes forth, and like a god
Rides through rejoicing heaven.
Old Moath and his daughter, from their tent,
Beheld the adventurous youth,
Dark-moving o'er the sands,
A lessening image, trembling through their tears.
Visions of high emprize
Beguiled his lonely road;
And if sometimes to Moath's tent
The involuntary mind recurr'd,
Fancy, impatient of all painful thoughts,
Pictured the bliss should welcome his return.
In dreams like these he went,
And still of every dream
Oneiza form'd a part,
And hope and memory made a mingled joy.
[IV, stanza 4]

If the figure of Thalaba, mirage-like, begins to 'tremble', this is not only an effect of sunlight and distance, it also becomes an effect of emotion: he is refracted through their tears. He leaves on his quest with all their hopes and fears for him. The mirage's effect here is a spiritual one, and serves to intensify the young man's value in the eyes of Oneiza and Moath (as well as in the minds of the readers). But paradoxically, Thalaba too has his own visions, both of his goal ('emprize') and of her love for him ('fancy').

His dream, both forward looking and backward looking, facing the future courageously but without diminishing the loss of the past, is a sign of his greatness and seriousness as one undertaking a special destiny. The mirage here is an indirect means of expressing heroic dream.

The Arab's interaction with his natural environment served to define for the western travellers of the period a limited and patronizing conception of the 'Arab mentality'. Starting with the same material, however, Southey achieves an opposite effect. This is because his imaginary Arabs are not merely primitive superstitious people, but cultured beings capable of spiritual experience. For this reason, their environment is not merely limiting, but becomes a source of rich images that reflect their complexity and aspiration. The amalgamation of these elements in the character of the Arab nomad (his piety, spirituality and simplicity) is what makes this poem unique in comparison to other Romantic poems that treated similar issues. In this we have, in fact, another example of Southey's special contribution to Romanticism.

Thalaba and European Regeneration

Islam and the European Regeneration

In *Thalaba* Islam is used as a model for the regeneration of European civilization. Southey's insight, which only a few other orientalists attained, that Islam possessed moral principles of considerable appeal and depth, led him to use it to explore new religious and political forces at work in the society of his time. Southey's aim was broadly 'political'. Like many other European contemporaries, he saw in the East a medium for the spiritual restoration of Europe and European civilization.

Southey's poem exhibits an important tendency in the Romantic Movement which M. H. Abrams describes as 'a reversion to the stark drama and suprarational mysteries of the Christian story and doctrine and to the violent conflicts and abrupt reversal of the Christian inner life, turning on the extremes of destruction and creation, hell and heaven, exile and reunion, birth and rebirth, dejection and joy, paradise lost and paradise regained'.[57] In the case of Southey, this reversion was less towards the original drama of Christianity than towards its fundamental ethics; and it was Islam that served as a means for the revival of Christian morality which he sought to reconstitute and, to borrow Abrams's phrase, to 'make . . . intellectually acceptable, as well as emotionally pertinent . . .'.[58]

While Southey at first regarded Islam as supporting the existence of a connection with Christianity, as he became more engaged with Islamic materials, particularly with the Koran, he grew more convinced that Islam in itself could play an effective part in the understanding of man and human consciousness. This view develops the tendency of late 18th-century orientalists like Sir William Jones and John Richardson to regard the East as a whole constituting a culture that could revive Europe. The last decade of the 18th century, as the most revolutionary in modern times, was ripe for such a revival because, as Southey himself puts it, 'Old things seemed passing away, and nothing was dreamt of but the regeneration of the human race.'[59]

During the period of the Enlightenment, religious values had begun to lose relevance under the double effect of science and absolutism. The latter most obviously manifested itself in France under Napoleon, whose expansionist policies, following the devastations of the French Revolution, shook the basis of belief throughout Europe. In writing *Thalaba*, Southey was conscious of both these dangers, and his poem reflected the age's need for reassuring alternatives. His attempt to reassert a broader moral base for Christianity was conducted on many fronts, the one with which we are concerned being that of his most original invocation of the moral traditions of Islam.

The Arabian Desert as a Romantic Landscape

In the poem, nature is presented in terms of the struggle between good and evil. Southey's view of nature confirms his Romantic moralism, for in the wilderness of the Arabian desert, which he considers to be the origin of biblical life, he seeks not the exotic thrill but the disclosure of the right relationship between man and nature. Like various anticipatory works written in the second half of the 18th century, *Thalaba* discovers the existence of a hidden connection between nature and morality. Nature is not only pure in itself, but it can help man gain virtue and purity. The Arabian desert thus forms an appropriate setting for a moral epic.

In his description of the Arabian desert, Southey depends, as we have seen, on works written by travellers to the Near East. He was particularly impressed by accounts of the fierceness of oriental nature. His decision to emphasize this side of nature is in line with his rejection of the 'soft' strain of pastoral idealism in Romantic writing.

Following the Islamic example, Southey treats nature as a place for experience and suffering and not merely for joy and happiness. Thus the desert in which the hero is brought up and 'disciplined' provides an ideal setting for, and representation of, spiritual hardship and supernatural perception. Here, for example, is a general evocation of the environment in which Zeinab and her son undertake their arduous journey:

She cast her eyes around,
Alas, no tents were there
Beside the bending sands,
No palm-tree rose to spot the wilderness;
The dark blue sky closed round

And rested like a dome
Upon the circling waste.
She cast her eyes around,
Famine and Thirst were there . . .
[I, stanza 11]

This inhospitability and austerity will stand in contrast with representations of the worldly paradises of the wicked magicians.

The setting of *Thalaba* is not confined to desert landscapes. In the poem, rugged mountains, deep and dark vales, wild forests, cold icy plains and endless oceans all feature as part of its spiritual and physical wastelands. The absence of the consolations of social life is felt throughout:

All waste! no sign of life
But the track of the wolf and the bear!
No sound but the wild, wild wind . . .
[VIII, stanza 22]

This almost gothic picturing of fierce and empty landscapes insists on the absence of human achievement. Elemental nature is all-pervasive and omnipotent. Man is shown to be overpowered by it — indeed unfitted for it, not so much because of his weakness but because of his pride and vanity. In fact it reflects, in a quite unpastoral fashion, the apparent futility of man's existence and, more crucially, his incapacity to withstand moral degeneration and collapse.

Paradoxically, however, what Southey sees as inevitable and pervasive in nature is precisely what becomes the basis for moral regeneration and salvation. For that which threatens man's existence is also a challenge and a discipline. The ardour of his hero's devotion and piety is tested and strengthened by his experience of the wildness and inhospitability of remote mountains:

This was a wild and wonderous scene,
Strange and beautiful, as where
By Oton-tala, like a sea of stars,
The hundred sources of Hoangho burst.
High mountains closed the vale,
Bare rocky mountains, to all living things
Inhospitable; on whose sides no herb
Rooted, no insect fed, no bird awoke
Their echoes, save the Eagle, strong of wing,
A lonely plunderer, that afar
Sought in the vales his prey.

Thither toward those mountains Thalaba
Following, as he believed, the path prescribed
By Destiny, advanced.
Up a wide vale that led into their depths,
A stony vale between receding heights
Of stone, he wound his way.
A cheerless place! the solitary Bee,
Whose buzzing was the only sound of life,
Flew there on restless wing,
Seeking in vain one flower, whereon to fix.
[VI, stanzas 12–13]

What is immediately striking about these two magnificent stanzas is that the desolation they describe does not represent the realms of death. The mountains possess an unearthly beauty, for they are seen almost as the original source of life, the place where the rivers spring — cosmically, so to speak, like a 'sea of stars'. Furthermore, they also contain life, from the majestic eagle to the humble bee. The fact that these can barely survive does not merely reinforce the sense of desolation from a socially human point of view; it also reinforces the essential indestructibility of life. There are in fact three purposive elements in this landscape: the eagle, the bee and the man, and the qualities of the first two are, by association, shared with the third.

Thus it is in passages like these that the wilderness seems to strengthen the hero's determination to follow 'the path prescribed/By Destiny'. Thalaba's whole pilgrimage turns into a succession of reinforcements of moral purpose. As the Koran teaches, contemplation of the hardships of nature gradually reveals the meaning both of the soul and of original nature: namely, that God's purposes exist. Southey's apparent ambivalence towards nature, which seems to him both inspiring and destructive, in fact anchors his moral stand in nature as a whole. Like the other Romantics, he is passionately moved and comforted by the beauty of natural landscape; however, he seems to glorify the arduous solitude of elemental nature not because of human happiness but because of human wickedness. The great quality of elemental nature is its purity, as the two stanzas just quoted make clear. Nature then becomes a pacific means of purification. For Southey, as for the Koran, all men require purgation. The Islamic fascination with the emptiness and cleanliness of the desert, found by Southey in his sources, confirmed for him the importance of solitude as a means to spiritual experience.

In *Thalaba*, Southey's protagonist seems, on account of his constant awareness of his divine mission, to be the only one who can survive exposure to the Arabian desert. Even Aswad, the Adite survivor, cannot come to terms with the 'unspeakable misery' of his solitude (though, to be sure, his solitude is fixed by a spell):

'No sound hath ever reach'd my ear
Save of the passing wind,
The fountain's everlasting flow,
The forest in the gale,
The pattering of the shower,

Sounds dead and mournful all.
No bird hath ever closed her wing
Upon these solitary bowers,
No insect sweetly buzz'd amid these groves,
From all things that have life,
Save only me, conceal'd.
This Tree alone, that o'er my head
Hangs down its hospitable boughs,
And bends its whispering leaves
As though to welcome me,
Seems to partake of life;
I love it as my friend, my only friend!'
[I, stanza 48]

In contrast to the mountain scene described above, there is no grandeur, energy and purpose here — only survival and stasis — a dull, hopeless waiting. For Aswad, this solitude is a torturing immobility, a divine punishment for his sins. In a Sybil-like manner, Aswad recalls the contrast between his arrested misery and a nature that constantly changes and renews itself:

'I know not for what ages I have dragg'd
This miserable life;
How often I have seen
These ancient trees renew'd;
What countless generations of mankind
Have risen and fallen asleep,
And I remain the same!
My garment hath not waxen old,
And the sole of my shoe is not worn.'
[stanza 49]

Aswad's sole desire is that his portion of suffering be accomplished so that he can find atonement, for his 'iniquities'

'And sufferings have made pure
My soul with sin defiled,
Release me in thine own good time;. . .
I will not cease to praise thee, O my God!'
[stanza 50]

So what we may call the passive way of Aswad, as opposed to the active way of Thalaba, is not meaningless either. Sustained by Islamic fatalism, Thalaba's resignation to his fate in the belief of the irresistible omnipotence of God adds a solemnity to the scene of his suffering. From such encounters Thalaba learns that natural solitude itself is an instrument of God, and he becomes better fitted to deal with the hardships ahead. In short, the Arabian desert becomes Southey's ideal location for the forging of moral integrity.

False Paradises

The inhospitable environment described has to be embraced and accepted, for it has been ordained by God for man's purification and salvation. But it can provoke an alternative response. Faced by the deprivation and austerity of nature, man may seek to alter this God-given condition by his own creativity and energy, and create an artificial world in which he can live in the illusion of pleasure, comfort and power. According to the Koran, which admittedly parallels the Bible in this regard, life on earth is designed for the overcoming of the hardships which test and forge faith. Because good and evil exist, it is necessary for man to run through the ordeals of earthly purgation before reaching his final goal: God's paradise. Thus turning life on earth into a paradise of sensual saturation is to undo the whole purpose of the divine creation.

Accordingly, Thalaba's quest does not merely expose him to the hardships of the wilderness; it also unveils to him the temptations of man-made gardens and cities. The most striking of these is Aloadin's earthly paradise, to which Thalaba is conveyed after his encounter with Mohareb, and his rejection of the false talisman of the ring for the alternative 'talisman': faith. He is dazzled by what he sees: 'The glittering tents,/The odorous groves,/The Gorgeous palaces' (VI, stanza 18). This seems to him like Eden, but: 'earthly Eden boasts/No terraced palaces.' He is met by an old man who invites him in terms that define quite clearly the impiety of this splendour: '"Favour'd of Fortune," thus he said, "go taste/The joys of Paradise!"' (stanza 19). He enters and finds a cornucopia of earthly delights: 'streams of liquid light', flowers, water, trees, nightingales, jasmines; and, in the banquet hall, all the refinements of sensuality: feasting, lascivious dancing girls and 'the delicious juice/Of Shiraz' golden grape' (stanza 24). But this last the dutiful follower of the Prophet cannot take, and finally he flees these luxurious splendours, resolved that what he sees is nothing but a 'Paradise of Sin'.

Thalaba's rejection of Aloadin's paradise has implications which cannot be accounted for simply in terms of Islamic puritanism, for he is repudiating nothing less than a human project in direct rivalry with the divine purpose. Tyrants who build huge palaces and gardens do so on the assumption that their life will be eternal. 'Shall ye,' the Koran addresses such tyrants, 'be left for ever secure in the possessions of things which are here; among gardens, and fountains, and corn, and palm trees, whose branches sheathe their flowers?'[60] What is at issue is made explicit in Samuel Purchas's story of Aloadin's paradise, which was one of Southey's main sources.

> In the N.E. parts of Persia there was an old man named Aloadin, a Mahumetan, which had inclosed a goodly valley, situate between two hilles, and furnished

> it with all variety which nature and art could yield; as fruits, pictures, rills of milk, wine, honey, water pallaces and beautiful domoselles, richly attired, and called it Paradise. To this was no passage but by an impregnable castle; and daily preaching the pleasures of this Paradise to the youth which he kept in his court, sometimes he would minister a sleepy drinke to some of them, and then conveigh them thither, where, being entertained with these pleasures four or five days, they supposed themselves rapt into Paradise, and then being again cast into a trance by the said drink, he caused them to be carried forth, and then would examine them of what they had seene, and by this delusion would make them resolute for any enterprise which he should appoint them; as to murther any prince his enemy, for they feared not death in hope of their Mahumetical Paradise. But Haslor or Ulan, after three years' siege, destroyed him, and this is fool's Paradise.[61]

God's authoritative and benevolent mastery of the created world has been replaced by a ruthless and systematic tyranny, which treats human beings not as responsible agents, but as helpless slaves.

But the divine purpose is violated in ways that run still deeper, as Thalaba's encounter with Lobaba makes clear. The power that seeks to rival God's undoes the very basis of good and evil. In trying to persuade Thalaba to feel free to seek out magic powers — ultimately the powers behind the creation of earthly paradises — Lobaba reaffirms that good and evil are but abstracts, like the desert mirages, created, or imagined, by man himself:

> . . . nothing in itself is good or evil,
> But only in its use. Think you the man
> Praiseworthy, who by painful study learns

> The knowledge of all simples, and their power,
> Healing or harmful?
> [IV, stanza 15]

In this Lobaba acts as an Islamic Mephistopheles. He could be alluding to the question of the origin of good and evil, long debated in early Islamic times, when some argued that the essence of things was neither good nor evil, while others claimed the opposite. The debate that ensues between Thalaba and Lobaba turns on the definition of the legitimate power of man, which, according to Thalaba, should be governed by God's determination of what constitutes good and evil, but to which, according to Lobaba, no limits should be set. Ultimately, Lobaba applies a satanic logic, the nature of which is revealed more explicitly in the Koranic than the biblical account of the temptation of Adam and Eve in Eden: 'And Satan suggested to them both . . . Your LORD hath not forbidden you this tree, for any other reason but lest ye should become angels, or lest ye become immortal.'[62]

A more extended and more powerful argument is provided by Mohareb when, later in the narrative, he seeks an alliance with Thalaba and returns the ring to him, as yet another trial of temptation. For him good and evil are intrinsic in nature, and not subject to God's decrees:

> 'Hear me! in Nature are two hostile Gods,
> Makers and Masters of existing things,
> Equal in power . . .
> . . . From the first,
> Eternal as themselves their warfare is.'
> [IX, stanza 14]

In this impersonal contest of opposing forces, good and evil lose their meaning: 'What are they, Thalaba, but words?' And the conclusion is plain: 'Power must decide.' As the greatest magician himself, Mohareb has the greatest power:

> 'Thou seest what I am, the Sultan here,
> The Lord of Life and Death.
> Abandon him who has abandon'd thee,
> And be, as I am, great among mankind!'
> [IX, stanza 14]

The assault on a God-ordained universe could not be more complete.

Magic and necromancy finally demonstrate the degree to which the man-made paradises are perversions of God's creation. Ultimately what wizards like Shedad and Aloadin are doing is to mystify God's nature. The paradises they create to seduce credulous humanity are a form of 'anti-nature':

> 'Impious! the Trees of vegetable gold
> Such as in Eden's groves
> Yet innocent it grew;
> Impious! he made his boast, though Heaven had hid
> So deep the baneful ore,
> That they should branch and bud for him,
> That art should force their blossoms and their fruit,
> And re-create for him whate'er
> Was lost in Paradise.
> Therefore at Shedad's voice
> Here tower'd the palm, a silver trunk,
> The fine gold net-work growing out
> Loose from its rugged boughs.
> Tall as the cedar of the mountain, here
> Rose the gold branches, hung with emerald leaves,
> Blossom'd with pearls, and rich with ruby fruit.
> [I, stanza 31]

Shedad's immense palace, next to which the pyramids are no more than 'the baby wonders of a woman's work' (stanza 29), attempts to recreate artificially, and for the sake of the artificer, God's paradise, created for, and lost by, mankind. But this creation is a perversion of a living nature. It is no longer 'innocent', but is the product of a nature 'ordered' and 'forced', constructed out of minerals and metals, silver and gold, ruby and pearl. Its beauty is wholly oppressive, a product of the perverted energies of magic, and therefore blasphemous.

The Moral Transformation of Islamic Material

The travellers' tales on which Southey partly depended for his representation of the Near Orient were designed to appeal to contemporary European tastes, which discovered in the Arab world an abundance of picturesque, sublime and gothic elements. But obviously this could not have formed a basis for a programme of moral regeneration in the way Southey had undertaken, where these elements are shown to be subservient to the divine will of God. Although he is responsive to Romantic beauty, what dominate his use of the oriental material are his moral and religious concerns.

We should recognize, however, that Southey's attitude to his source was quasi-historical. He wished to base his structure on foundations of truth and fact. His claim that valuable moral inspiration could be found in the Arab environment depended on his poem making real contact with a real world. Here his notes play a distinctive part in realizing his aim, and should, despite their obscurity, be regarded as an integral part of the poem itself.

For the moment, however, our main purpose is to see how the poet's imagination transforms the facts provided by the travellers into poetry in which the Romantic tonalities of the picturesque, the sublime and the gothic, are subordinated to the moral impulse of the poem. As a demonstration of this kind of transformation, take two of the most impressive oriental images in *Thalaba*: the 'Sarsar' and the 'Simoom'. To start with, there are the moral connotations which these two images offer Southey, for they refer to natural forces which, as Islamic sources would have it, were let loose to punish the wicked.

As the Koran mentions, the Sarsar is a piercing cold wind sent by God to chastise the Adites for their injustices. Southey's description of the Sarsar incident draws upon d'Herbelot's Islamic account of how the Adites, having rejected God's message through the words of Prophet Houd, were hit by a drought and sent a messenger to Mecca to pray for rain. As Kail, the messenger, returned, a dark cloud appeared in the sky which suddenly produced the Sarsar, 'a wind, most cold and most violent'. D'Herbelot's account draws mostly from the Koran, which describes how this wind 'continued to blow for seven days and seven nights, and exterminated all the unbelievers in the country, leaving only the Prophet Houd alive, and those who had heard him and turned to the faith'.[63]

Southey's version of this incident reflects his knowledge of the Koran's description of the suffering and abuse endured by God's messengers. He casts it in the form of a first-person narrative by one survivor, Aswad, who, as he tells Thalaba his story, remains appalled by the memory of how God destroyed those who had offended His Prophet Houd:

'. . . Fly the wrath,
Ye who would live and save your souls alive!
For strong is his right hand that bends the Bow,
The Arrows that he shoots are sharp,
And err not from their aim!'

'With that a faithful few
Prest through the throng to join him. Then arose

Mockery and mirth; "Go, bald head!" and they mix'd
Curses with laughter . . .'

'He went, and darker grew
The deepening cloud above.
At length it open'd, and . . . O God! O God!
There were no waters there!
There fell no kindly rain!
The Sarsar from its womb went forth,
The Icey Wind of Death.'
[I, stanzas 42–4]

Southey's achievement is to fuse the moral point with the poetic life of the passage. The language gains in power and seriousness even as it acquires the imaginative reality which only local colour can provide. First, the moral is dramatized in the terrified recollection of the survivor, as he relives in the interrupted rhythms and exclamations of speech the dreadful experience. Secondly, the complete reversal of God's providence is brought to life in the reversal of the expectations of the tribe: the cloud that gathers in the heavens and promises life-giving rain to the desert suddenly discharges the wind of death, and the promise of fertility is fulfilled in destruction and waste. Thirdly, and perhaps most strikingly, the words of the Prophet Houd are literally become the unnatural phenomenon: the 'Arrows' of God that 'err not in their aim' are translated exactly into the icy blast from above. Prophetic speech is transformed into a natural event, and human rhetoric is turned into a message from the sky.

There is a final poetic effect. As so often in Southey, the power of a destructive event is not described directly, but suggested through its effects on the narrator — here, on the impious tribe. One moment they are alive, either jeering at the Prophet Houd or cowering in terror; the next moment:

'They fell around me; thousands fell around,
The King and all his people fell.
All! all! they perish'd all!
I . . . only I . . . was left . . .'
[I, stanza 45]

Southey's method allows him to convey the blinding speed of the calamity, and thus the irresistible power of God.

A similar fusion of morality and oriental landscape, or divine and natural destruction, may be seen in Southey's use of the image of the *simoom*, the hot and suffocating wind common in the Arabian deserts. Detailed descriptions of it were provided by such celebrated travellers as Volney, Bruce and Niebuhr, whom Southey consulted extensively. Volney, for example, writes:

> The Arabs of the desert call these winds *Semoum*, or poison, and the Turks *Shamyla*, or wind of Syria, from which is formed the *Samiel*.
>
> Their heat is sometimes so excessive, that it is difficult to form any idea of its violence without having experienced it; but it may be compared to the heat of a large oven at the moment of drawing out the bread.[64]

Or again, Niebuhr's somewhat overstated account reads: 'The effects of the Simoom are instant suffocation to every living creature that happens to be within the sphere of its activity, and immediate putrefaction of the carcasses of the dead'.[65] Thus Southey had at his disposal, so to speak, a potentially destructive force that could easily be turned into an agent of divine retribution.

The earliest example in *Thalaba* places the emphasis slightly differently, for there the *simoom* is used by God to protect his appropriate agent. The magician Abdaldar is about to assassinate Thalaba while praying when God intervenes:

> . . . over Thalaba
> He stands, and lifts the dagger to destroy.
> Before his lifted arm received
> Its impulse to descend,
> The Blast of the Desert came.
> Prostrate in prayer, the pious family
> Felt not the Simoom pass.
> They rose, and lo! the Sorcerer lying dead,
> Holding the dagger in his blasted hand.
> [II, stanza 40]

The effect of this stanza, which sounds trivial, cannot be felt until one remembers that it is the concluding stanza of a 'book'. The matter-of-fact brevity then becomes impressive, for in its placing it achieves a climax of understatement. Nothing can be said about a divine intervention, particularly a miraculous one, except that it has happened. Only a statement of the bare fact will do. Of course, the linguistic imagination is still functioning. For example, the word 'blast' in the phrase 'Blast of the Desert' simply means a violent gust of wind. But by the time it has had its effect on Abdaldar, whose hand has been 'blasted', the word has acquired the force of a lightning flash, and one discovers that the first 'Blast' contained all the destructive heat implied in the second 'blasted'. But essentially here the sense of miraculous intervention — God's protective agency — is conveyed by what is *not* said.

A more elaborate example of the transformation of travellers' material into moral poetry may be found in the passage in which Lobaba and Thalaba witness an approaching whirlwind. In his notes, Southey quotes the following passage from Bruce's *Travels to Discover the Source of the Nile*.

> In that vast expanse of desert . . . we saw a number of prodigious pillars of sand at different distances, at times moving with great celerity, at others stalking with a majestic slowness . . . . They retired from us with a wind from S.E. leaving an impression upon my mind to which I can give no name; though surely one ingredient in it was fear, with a considerable deal of wonder and astonishment. It was in vain to think of flying, the swiftest horse, or the fastest sailing ship, could be of no use to carry us out of this danger . . . . On the 15th, the same appearance of moving pillars of sand presented themselves to us, only they seemed to be more in numbers, and less in size. They came several times in a direction close upon us . . . They began immediately after sun-rise, like a thick wood, and almost darkened the sun. His rays shining through them for near an hour, gave them an appearance of pillars of fire.[66]

Southey skilfully absorbs Bruce's description without losing his grip on the characteristically oriental elements. His poetry retains the essentials of Bruce's report: the size and violent movement of the whirlwind, as well as the fear and hopelessness it inspires in the travellers.

> Whilst he spake, Lobaba's eye,
> Upon the distance fix'd,
> Attended not his speech.
> Its fearful meaning drew
> The looks of Thalaba;
> Columns of sand came moving on,
> Red in the burning ray,
> Like obelisks of fire,

They rush'd before the driving wind.
Vain were all thoughts of flight!

High . . . high in Heaven upcurl'd
The dreadful sand-spouts moved;
Swift as the whirlwind that impell'd their way,
They came toward the travellers!
[IV, stanzas 30–31]

This incident occurs at the end of the elaborate debate between Thalaba and Lobaba concerning the status of good and evil. What is in question is whether 'the providence of God' can be trusted. The whirlwind therefore does not come to destroy or protect, but to manifest and display the power of God. It is a test rather than an admonishment. Should one wait on God's providence, or should one, as Lobaba urges, 'call on the [occult] powers' that will save (stanza 32)? Will Thalaba make use of the magic properties of the ring — 'thy charmed signet' (stanza 34)? Southey's description of the whirlwind shows that God is present in it. The terms that he uses to make it vivid also convey the divine presence. For example, the neutral term 'columns' becomes, in the burning sun, an 'obelisk of fire' which unmistakably recalls the biblical column of fire that guided the Children of Israel in their journey across Sinai from Egypt to Palestine. Or again, the great height of the whirlwind associates it quite explicitly with 'Heaven'. The whirlwind finally sorts out the just and the unjust: Lobaba's terrified dependence on magic powers contrasts dramatically with Thalaba's calm independence of them. All that remains, therefore, is for Thalaba to turn magic against the magician — which he does.

Southey's distinctive achievement as a poet in *Thalaba* has been, as it were, to moralize the Arabian landscape. He does not use Arabia as a moral antidote valuable for European doubt or scepticism. Instead he believes that

Arabia itself, including its climate and weather, has a *real* existence, and can be a source of *real* inspiration. He has been able to charge local customs with meaning: the discovery, real in the Orient as elsewhere — but in the Orient undoubtedly so — that faith in the providentiality of God's creation is not an error.

Islam's Connection with Christianity

In *Thalaba* the beliefs and customs of the Islamic Orient are a survival of the ancient life and faith of the Bible. In this Southey followed several orientalists, who discovered in the modern Arabs a living image of ancient biblical characters and manners. This 'modernization' of the past seems to have satisfied a special religious thirst in him. Islam, as he found from his early youth, possessed many elements of conformity with Christianity, such as piety, simplicity, hospitality and stoicism. His emphasis on these 'connected' themes, as he put it in his preface to the poem, makes *Thalaba* an important work, not only from a literary, but also from a spiritual, point of view.[67]

This point can easily be confirmed from a close reading of the notes. They not only provide explanations of allusions in the text, but (and herein lies Southey's originality) they also express his sense of the relationship between Christianity and Islam. For example, we have seen his comment on a line spoken by Thalaba's mother, whose resignation to the will of God is immediately connected to a biblical quotation. Here is the note to the mother's statement, 'He [God] gave, he takes away!' (I, stanza 4): 'The Lord gave, and the Lord taketh away; blessed be the name of the Lord. — Job, i, 21.'[68] Travel works, useful to Southey in so many ways, also provided him with much material to support this connection. Bruce's travels in Egypt and Africa, Volney's descriptive account of his tour in the Levant, and Niebuhr's travels in the

Arabian peninsula all insist on the biblical authenticity of the scenes they witnessed. Niebuhr sees valleys, 'so common in Arabia, which, when heavy rains fall, are filled with water, and are then called *wadi*, or rivers, although perfectly dry at other times of the year'.[69] In *Thalaba*, this becomes a 'vernal brook', over which his hero passes in his journey through the desert. But the note Southey furnishes to this image is a quotation from the Bible which he combines in the notes with that of Niebuhr: 'My brethren have dealt deceitfully as a brook, and as the stream of brook they pass away — Job, vi, 15.'[70]

Once again, he finds in the Arab world reassurances that the Bible was after all about real people whose descendants can be visited today. His approach in this regard reaffirms his contention that there is in the Orient a direct access to a 'primitive' ground of spiritual life where things happen and are felt in ways more closely related to biblical events and feelings than would be possible in modern Europe.

As the ancient Scottish figure, Ossian, and the Highland peasants and crofters appealed to the early Romantics as quintessentially Romantic figures, so the modern Arab may be recognized as Southey's Romantic hero. His simplicity and rustic piety, and the peacefulness of his desert life, with none of the complexities and corruptions of urban life in Europe, seemed to Southey to express the integrity and purity of biblical times. His description of Moath and Oneiza provides an example:

Nor rich, nor poor, was Moath; God hath given
Enough, and blest him with a mind content.
No hoarded gold disquieted his dreams;
But ever round his station he beheld
Camels that knew his voice,
And home-birds, grouping at Oneiza's call,
And goats that, morn and eve,

> Came with full udders to the Damsel's hand.
> [III, stanza 21]

Moath's manner of life — his constancy, his acceptance of his state, his tent, clothes, belongings and animals — recalls that of biblical figures and European mountaineers. Southey's note quotes travellers' reports confirming the Arab's freedom from social pretension and snobbery, and the natural strength to be drawn from a simple life. Volney, for example, writes:

> We must not . . . when we speak of [the chiefs of] the Bedouins, affix to the words Prince and Lord, the ideas they usually convey; we should come nearer the truth, by comparing them to substantial farmers, in mountainous countries, whose simplicity they resemble in their dress, as well as in their domestic lives and manners. A Sheik, who has the command of five hundred horse, does not disdain to saddle and bridle his own, nor to give him his barley and chopped straw. In his tent, his wife makes the coffee, kneads the dough, and superintends the dressing of the victuals. His daughters and kinswomen wash the linen, and go with pitchers on their heads, and veils over their faces, to draw water from the fountain. These manners agree precisely with the descriptions in Homer, and the history of Abraham, in Genesis.[71]

In another note, Southey explicitly relates the 'Hyke', the modern Arab garment called a *haik*, to the Bible. Shaw, who is quoted to explain the lines, 'So in his loosen'd cloak/The Old Man wrapt himself,' describes the importance of the use of a girdle to fix the *haik*, which could be as long as six yards. 'This,' Shaw concludes, 'shows the great use there is for a girdle in attending any active employment; and in consequence thereof, the force of the Scripture injunction alluding thereunto, *of having our loyns girded*.[72] Similarly, Chenier, another oriental traveller, is quoted as stressing: 'The Moor is wrapped up in [the *haik*] day and night; and of this haik is the living model of the drapery of the ancients.'[73] Interestingly enough, Southey finds these accounts sufficiently justifiable to quote the following biblical verse:

> If thou at all take thy neighbour's raiment to pledge, thou shalt deliver it unto him by that the Sun goeth down.
>
> For that is his covering only, it is his raiment for his skin: wherein shall he sleep? — Exodus, XXII, 26, 27.[74]

Other travellers' accounts emphasize the Arabs' generosity and modesty, qualities all too rarely encountered in the courts and professions of Europe. What is specifically notable is Southey's awareness of the irony that the very people looked down upon as primitive pagans in the west are much closer to the biblical spirit than the modern Christians so complacent about their social superiority.

Even specifically Islamic manners and customs found favour in Southey's poem. For example, this is how he represents an Arab guest drinking a cup of tamarind juice: 'When raising from the cup his moisten'd lips,/The stranger smiled, praised, and drank again' (II, stanza 34). Praising Allah during and after the drinking is a religious custom widely practised in modern Islamic countries. The equally typical salute of peace, and the spreading of the skin, also find their way into the poem:

> Anon the Master of the tent,
> The Father of the family,
> Came forth, a man in years, of aspect mild.
> To the stranger approaching he gave

The friendly saluting of peace,
And bade the skin be spread.
Before the tent they spread the skin,
Under a Tamarind's shade,
That, bending forward, stretch'd
Its boughs of beauty far.
[stanza 32]

The modesty and hospitality of this style of life, reflected in the almost bathetic simplicity of the writing, are consolidated by the note, which is extracted from *Description of the East* (1743–45) by Richard Pococke:

> An Arab Prince will often dine in the street before his door, and call to all that pass, even beggars, in the usual expression, *Bismillah*, that is, in the name of God; who come and sit down, and when they have done, give their *Hamdellilah*, that is, God be praised; for the Arabs, who are great levellers, put every body on a footing with them, and it is by such generosity and hospitality that they maintain their interest.[75]

Southey's interest in such details is a good deal more than infatuation with oriental landscape or even than curiosity in sociological practices. It is a recognition of a principle regulating human relations that is much more satisfactory than western competitiveness or ambition, namely: brotherhood. It expresses and confirms his 'pantasocratic' tendencies.

In fact, the links between biblical and Islamic life can be found at every level in *Thalaba*. To take a final example, Southey alludes to a biblical passage prohibiting the use of ornaments: 'In that day the Lord will take away the bravery of their tinkling ornaments about their feet, and their cauls, and their round tires like the morn . . . The chains, and the bracelets, and the mufflers, the bonnets, and the ornaments of the legs — (Isaiah, iii, 18).'[76] As frequent quotations and references show, Southey was very well aware of how widespread was the use of personal ornaments in the Orient. He must have been struck by the affinities between the Koran and the Old Testament when he found in the Koran a very similar condemnation of ornaments. Of the faithful women, it says: 'And let them not make a noise with their feet, that their ornaments which they hide may therefore be discovered.'[77] It is remarkable to find that Sale's comment on this Koranic injunction refers to the very same passage in Isaiah:

> By shaking the rings, which the women in the East wear about their ankles, and are usually of gold and silver. The pride which the Jewish ladies of old took in making a tinkling with these ornaments of their foot, is (among other things of that nature) severely reproved by the prophet Isaiah.[78]

These passages surely suggest more than a coincidence in Southey's reading in the Koran. The idea of an affinity between the Bible and the Koran dominates *Thalaba* to such an extent that Southey came to believe that Islam and Christianity shared a common source, and that biblical ethics could combine with what he often called 'the morality of the Koran' into a single force for regenerating the moral order of the world.

The scenes in *Thalaba* which describe Islamic devotion and worship are treated with admiration and respect. Figures like Thalaba, Oneiza, Zeinab and Moath are not only descendants of biblical ancestors; they are also in touch with the simplicity and divinity of nature. Consider the following passage:

> 'Tis the cool evening hour:
> The Tamarind from the dew

Sheathes its young fruit, yet green.
Before their tent the mat is spread;
The Old Man's solemn voice
Intones the holy Book.
What if beneath no lamp-illumined dome,
Its marble walls bedeck'd with flourish'd truth,
Azure and gold adornment? sinks the word
With deeper influence from the Imam's voice
Where in the day of congregation, crowds
Perform the duty-task?
Their Father is their Priest,
The Stars of Heaven their point of prayer,
And the blue Firmament
The glorious Temple, where they feel
The present Deity.
[III, stanza 22; my italics]

These pastoral devotions, explicitly distinguished from the grand rituals of the mosque with the apparatus of priesthood, affected even the agnostic travellers on whose reports Southey depended. The simple Arabs were in tune with a much greater temple than any created by architects and builders: the tranquillity of nature, not the pomp of divine service; the dome above their heads is that of heaven itself. The passage as a whole strongly suggests spiritual universality rather than sectarianism, and quietly affirms an omnipotent monotheism. From this point of view, Islam becomes a living part of the great religions of the world. Making the 'stars of Heaven [as] their point of prayer' is no mistake on the part of Southey; he knows, as other passages confirm, that Mecca is the direction towards which Muslims pray. But this phrase also contains an allusion to popular traditions concerning Al-Beit Al-Mamour, which are explained in the notes. Quoting D'Ohsson, Southey writes: 'The [Câba] is the point of direction, and the centre of union for the prayers of the whole human race, as the Beith-Mamour is for those of all the celestial beings.'[79] The point of this complex phrase is clear: it is not to Mecca that Southey makes us look, but to the great creation itself, and to the universal aspects of Islam.

Conclusion

To conclude we may ask: how did Southey regard Islam? Southey's attitude was more than positive, but he deliberately avoided explicit commendation. He must have been sufficiently aware of the example of George Sale, whose excellent translation of the Koran and the sympathies he expressed towards its religion earned him the label 'half-Mussulman'. Southey's achievements were disguised by his adoption of Islam as a means rather than as an end, but the fact remains that he found no difficulty in accommodating his own views to Islamic traditions, which he took seriously on their own terms.

In fact Southey is not merely an apologist for Islam, as (to his own dismay) he might have seemed to be while writing *Thalaba*, and even the unfinished sequence *Mohammed*. He made an intelligent attempt to convey the spirit and principles of the Islamic faith as it really exists. Although his greater aim — the blending of the great religions — was impossible to achieve, his imagination was able to conceive the possibility of some sort of universal doctrine combining their morality.

Among the motifs Southey, like Landor before him, found in Islam was that of retribution. This is clearly expressed in his narrative as a whole, in which the destruction of evil in exchange for the bliss of paradise is the central theme. As we have seen, Islam's 'submission' to the will of God requires a moral recognition of God's hell and paradise, the places where all deeds and things come to a final judgement, and where the mystery of this world, of good and evil, life and death, is in some sense revealed. In his poem, especially on the subject of retribution, Southey adopts the Islamic emphasis on divine punishment not only as a valid corrective but also as a source of moral fulfilment.

Despite his admiration for this type of resignation, which he once described as Islam's 'only virtue',[80] Southey's attitude remained somewhat ambivalent. For him, Islam lacks the doctrine of redemption through forgiveness. Although his Muslim hero becomes progressively more Christian than Islamic as he approaches the end of his quest, he clearly remains attached to the notion of a final judgement. In one of his letters, Southey somewhat lamely declares: 'Free-will, God, and final retribution solve all difficulties.'[81] He echoes the Koranic concept that hell and paradise embody a resolution to the mystery of life. Roderick (Southey's less famous hero) describes the concept of hell and paradise as a 'heavenliest harmony' that 'Reduce the seeming chaos' of life.[82] Without paradise or hell, all human activities, and existence itself, would appear meaningless. Death cannot be 'the termination of our existence'. If so, Southey writes, 'I should wish rather to have been born a beast, or never to have been born at all.'[83] Without reward or retribution, he further asserts, 'this world would be a mystery too dreadful to be borne . . . our best affections and our noblest desires mere juggle and a curse'.[84]

Thus his use of the Islamic theme of temporal and celestial retribution, which hangs over those who do injustice to themselves and to others, adds freshness, high relief and force to the renovative morality that constituted his deepest response to the revolutionary last decade of the 18th century. This made *Thalaba* a more moralizing poem than its immediate predecessors — Beckford's sensational *Vathek* and Landor's political *Gebir*. Southey's vision of the other-worldly torments lacked the grandeur and sublimity of Beckford's magnificent Halls of Eblis; nor did he maintain Landor's essential realism in dealing with conquest and colonization. But *Thalaba*'s engagement with Islam at every level was altogether more serious and more informed, and it produces a moral stance that is in some ways more original, and, perhaps, more prophetic.

Chapter 3

Thomas Moore's *Lalla Rookh* and the Politics of Irony

IN writing *Lalla Rookh*, Thomas Moore intended to make his poem a landmark in the oriental tale genre of his time. The success just achieved by such prominent Romantics as Byron and, before him, Beckford, Landor and Southey, prompted Moore's spirit of emulation. He wrote in his *Memoirs*, 'I shall now take to my poem, and do something, I hope, that will place me above the vulgar herd of both wordlings and of critics.'[1] But his achievement in *Lalla Rookh*, fascinating as it is in its oriental concerns and colouring, seems to have fallen short of the 'real' success predicted by him and by his publishers, who paid him the unprecedented sum of 3000 guineas on delivery of the manuscript. The poem ran through a number of editions; but how effective and influential it really was in literary circles remains a matter for investigation, on which this chapter will seek to cast some light.

About his own poem, Moore does not appear to have said much of great interest. He wrote that it was more than a mere narrative' it was meant 'to form a store house, as it were, of illustrations purely Oriental',[2] — that is, to inform as well as to entertain. With the other Romantics, he had been captured by the idea of the East from an early age. As an adult he was therefore naturally drawn to oriental material as a means of tackling contemporary religious and political issues, such as freedom of worship and Irish national independence. And as he became more and more interested in the East, he not only greatly enlarged his store of knowledge, particularly from travel books, but also found in this material subtler means of expressing increasingly complex ideas.

Moore's claim to oriental verisimilitude is controversial. It was known that his information about oriental culture, beliefs and customs was derived from more than 80 works dealing with the Orient; but what he represented in his poem was less the image of eastern life for its own sake than a development of his own cultural and personal preoccupations. Yet Moore is certainly right when he says of *Lalla Rookh*:

> . . . my own chief work of fiction ('Lalla Rookh') is founded on a long and laborious collection of facts. All the customs, the scenery, every flower from which I have drawn an illustration, were inquired into by me with the utmost accuracy; and I left no book that I could find on the subject unransacked. Hence arises that matter-of-fact adherence to Orientalism for which Sir Gore Ouseley, Colonel Wilks, Carne, and others, have given me credit.[3]

Thus in the poem every oriental allusion is supported by a quotation from d'Herbelot, Bruce, Thevenot, Savary or Niebuhr among others. But what seems equally clear is the existence of a hidden, or at least another, purpose. The offhand or incidental way in which he refers to 'that matter-of-fact adherence to Orientalism' strongly suggests that such adherence was not his main intention. This purpose is 'hidden' in the sense that the poem nowhere directly acknowledges that the Orient has an allegorical function invoking political and cultural ideas much closer to home than the Levant or India.

We have seen that the covert allegorical or symbolic use of oriental local colour is a general practice in many Romantic orientalists. Despite the presence of occasional footnotes making connections between the eastern story and contemporary European politics, morality or religion, English Romantic poets seemed reluctant to admit their use of the Orient as a mask either concealing, or making it easier to develop, ideas too radical or too alien for the average literary opinion of the time. It is as if they constructed in their oriental romances a more comfortable environment for their ideas than their readers, left to themselves, could have provided.

How, then, was Moore's work received in the literary reviews of the time? Generally with applause for the precision and accuracy of its oriental colouring. The *British Review*, however, attacked Moore, as well as Byron, for their alleged portrayal of the 'dirt and debauchery' associated with 'the Mahometan world' as consistently attractive. 'The great mistake of which these poets take advantage is this: where so much is made of corporeal delights, and the various gratifications of sense; where we hear of nothing but of groves and of baths and fountains, and fruits and flowers, and sexual blandishments, we are too apt to figure to ourselves a paradise of sweets . . .'[4] The reviewer goes on to stress the worthlessness of the attempt by Moore and his predecessors to glamorize a culture in which 'man tramples upon man in a series of cruel oppressions down to the drooping wretchedness of the squalid populace, who have neither the reason nor rights of men'.[5]

In a different view, the *Literary Panorama* finds *Lalla Rookh* 'sufficiently dull', the reason being that 'it is laboured without producing any effect'.[6] These reviews are striking for their failure to detect, or even suspect, the political implications of *Lalla Rookh*, and in particular the political satire it attempts. The *British Review* concludes its critique with a dismissal of the poem as a work based on 'the fictions of Oriental extravagance, and proceeds without moral, or purpose, or plan . . . in a tissue of flowery language, amorous description, and rambling vehemence'.[7] Apparently, Moore was far from displeased at the failure of the reviewers to discover his real intention, for he devoted a good deal of ingenuity to covering his tracks.

The only reviewer not taken in by Moore's tactical deviousness was the formidable editor of the *Edinburgh Review*, Francis Jeffrey. His review detected plain evidence in the poem of Moore's commitment to Irish liberty. Of 'The Fire-Worshippers', which ostensibly deals with the struggle of the indigenous Persians against the Muslim occupants, he wrote:

> Perhaps there are a few passages of general declamation, even in this poem, coloured by what some may think party rather than natural feelings; but they are of rare occurrence, and may easily be forgiven to a poet who belongs to a country where pride has long struggled with oppression, — where religion has been given as a reason against the diffusion of political privileges, — and where valour guards liberties which the bravest are not permitted to enjoy.[8]

But Jeffrey recognizes that such passages of explicitness are 'rare', and that for the most part Moore's political and moral concerns are diffused in or covered by the Islamic fables. What did Moore gain by adopting the indirect method? Perhaps he sought to avoid the danger of persecution or hostility for holding unorthodox political views. Or, more significantly, maybe he aimed to clear a narrative space in which to develop new and strong ideas in relative freedom from the restrictions of prevailing prejudices. Or finally, the adoption of a specifically Islamic allegory might, because of the genre's extraordinary vogue with the reading public, ensure the widest circulation for the hidden ideas it carried. In the fashion for the oriental narrative as a vehicle for morality, established in the 18th century by such works as Dr Johnson's *Rasselas* and Goldsmith's *The Citizen of the World*, *Lalla Rookh* represents its ultimate form. But it also carries Moore's Irish allegories. Not only the fashion but also the man was projected by the poem; Moore's political spirit found its expression in the East, as he once expressed it.[9] Yet his literal fidelity to the material was such that many European critics thought the poem was written by an oriental. Some Persians were even quoted as having taken Moore to be a native of Persia.

Moore's deeper personal convictions find their way much more easily into *Lalla Rookh* than in his other works. In the *Irish Melodies*, for example, Irish material is visible in the episodes of Irish history and the heroic Irish figures. But this material, being explicit, has needed to be diluted to make it acceptable to English tastes. Moore compromises by offering it as a form of local colour and fashionable patriotism. Whatever political attitudes the *Irish Melodies* may express, they remain too vague and oscillating to be effective. This is not the case with *Lalla Rookh*: there may be no direct reference to Irish affairs in the poem, but its commitment to national independence is beyond question.

Moore was undoubtedly aware of the success achieved by those Irish writers who had found in Macpherson's

'Ossianic' fragments an inspiring model of imaginative freedom. 'For them,' as Robert Welch says, 'Gaelic past was associated with authentic imaginative power and energy. Almost immediately, of course, the idea took form that Irish literature should somehow assist in the great work of achieving some sort of political independence for Ireland.'[10] The *Irish Melodies* reveal the extent to which Moore followed this path, though the indefiniteness of Welch's 'somehow' indicates how far Moore lacked real direction. But another model superimposed itself on that of the undefined Ossianic nationalism. Byron's oriental tales, written and published during the time Moore was producing his oriental narratives, showed Moore with what success oriental material could be put to the service of a passion for liberty. Certainly Byron himself recognized and acknowledged Moore's decision to migrate eastward, so to speak, as 'the only poetical policy'.[11]

'The Veiled Prophet of Khorassan' as a Political Allegory

That *Lalla Rookh* is Moore's political allegory may be seen from a close examination of the two narratives which deal respectively with tyranny and colonialism: 'The Veiled Prophet of Khorassan' and 'The Fire-Worshippers'. Both exhibit to a remarkable degree how Moore is able to use Islamic material to define and express complex, even ambiguous, views.

The 'veiled prophet' of the title of the first narrative is Hakim Ibn Hisham, known in Islamic history by the name of 'Al Mokanna' of Khorassan, from a veil he used to wear on his face (*mokanna* in Arabic meaning 'veiled'). He lets it be believed that this veil, which in fact masks his hideous repulsiveness, is needed to protect his subjects from the dazzling brilliance of his countenance. In general terms, he conveniently represents for Moore the power of despotism, which depends on systematic mystification for its effects. More particularly, as will be argued later, Mokanna may be seen as standing for Napoleon Bonaparte. He has an authority that he owes to his powers of mystification and manipulation. This is how he is presented at the beginning of the poem:

There on that throne, to which the blind belief
Of millions rais'd him, sat the Prophet-Chief,
The Great MOKANNA. O'er his features hung
The Veil, the Silver Veil, which he had flung
In mercy there, to hide from mortal sight
His dazzling brow, till man could bear its light.
[p 9][12]

But this impressiveness is a disguise hiding a ghastly reality. Here is how he takes leave of the narrative:

Upon that mocking Fiend, whose Veil, now rais'd,
Show'd them, as in death's agony they gaz'd,
Not the long promis'd light, the brow, whose beaming
Was to come forth, all conquering, all redeeming,
But features horribler than Hell e'er trac'd
On its own brood; — no Demon of the Waste,
No church-yard Ghole, caught lingering in the light
Of the blest sun, e'er blasted human sight
With lineaments so foul, so fierce as those
The' Impostor now, in grinning mockery, shows . . .
[p 106]

The horror itself has some kind of perverse impressiveness. Mokanna is more than a human monster; he is plainly the 'enemy of mankind' — a satanic figure. Moore's analysis of despotism has several levels, from the moral to the political, from the psychological to the religious. These strata are not conducive to simplicity and directness of judgement.

The plot of 'The Veiled Prophet' is simple. It is interwoven in one of Moore's most complex streams of rhetorical narration. The success achieved by Mokanna in his rebellion against the Islamic state of the Calif Al Mahdi attracts many people, especially the young, who are drawn by his slogan 'Freedom for the World'. Azim, a Muslim officer who has spent some time as a captive in Greece, hastens to enlist in Mokanna's revolution. Before long, however, he discovers that Mokanna has been using his rebellion to satisfy a perverted lust for power and domination. But Azim is unable to convince his beloved, Zelica, to flee with him from Mokanna's influence. This innocently pious maid had signed a darkly religious contract to become Mokanna's 'bride' in hope of a place in his paradise as the wife of her 'brave youth', whom she had believed to have died in captivity. Mokanna's plot is to use Zelica, on whom he bestows the title, 'Priestess of the Faith', to seduce Azim into becoming an officer in his army. But Azim is not taken in; he resists temptation and joins the army which Al Mahdi has mobilized for the overthrow of Mokanna. At the end of a savage battle, the defeated Mokanna flees to his palace in Neksheb, where he leaps into a bath of liquid fire. Azim breaks into the palace and is met by a figure wearing Mokanna's veil. The figure hurls itself on his lance, and reveals itself to be his own beloved. The rest of his life Azim spends in prayer by Zelica's grave; and in the end he is blessed by a vision in which angels tell him that God has forgiven her.

The story is full of ambiguities arising from Moore's acutely imaginative commitment to his orientalism. His interest in oriental revolt and tyranny for its own sake necessarily puts him at a distance from European analogues such as the French Revolution and the Napoleonic conquest. This distance allows him the room to define a nuanced and subtle judgement, relatively free from the political prejudices of his readers or the political pressure of immediate events.

In this it seems probable that the influence of Voltaire can be detected — and particularly the Voltaire of the play *Mahomet.* In that work, Voltaire uses the character of the Muslim Prophet to satirize religious fanaticism as a form of tyranny, showing how the emotional devotion of the Prophet's followers could be misused for the fulfilment of personal despotism. Moore, on the other hand, shows a much greater interest in the accuracy of historical fact than his predecessor, who admits to inaccuracies in his preface to the play. Moore was able to discover that Muhammad could not be regarded as a simply despotic figure, and that Islamic material could be used in modes more complex than moral satire.

Moore's reading of Voltaire must have been thorough and extensive, for there are many similarities in their literary stance towards despotism. But Moore excelled the great Frenchman in several respects. Apart from his historical precision and oriental verisimilitude, he presents a genuine analysis of human nature. He attends to the origins and causes of despotism rather than to its manifestations, and to the psychological and religious factors that condition the growth of tyranny.

If Voltaire's 'Mahomet' was a religious impostor, Mokanna is Moore's symbol of tyranny both religious and temporal. Nevertheless Moore's despot is himself a 'prophet', if a self-proclaimed one. Mokanna has a double role — as a false prophet, and as a political dictator. The first role manifests the religious and emotional side of despotism whereas the second represents the political and materialistic side. In both we can sense the figures of Napoleon and George III — the latter being certainly a tyrant with respect to Ireland. That Moore had in mind the English Protestant domination of his Catholic countrymen is suggested by his interest in the links between religious and political tyranny.

Moore's protagonist is a universal figure who represents tyranny in both obvious and obscure dimensions. For example, Moore attributes Mokanna's success in establishing himself as a political and religious despot to the 'blind belief' of those who listen to him. This common characteristic of oriental despotism we have already identified in the writings of Landor and Southey, but Moore's diagnosis of Mokanna's despotism produces new insights into the nature of tyranny.

Mokanna's silver veil is supposed to 'hide from mortal sight/His dazzling brow, till man could bear its light'. This light is thought to be a holy effulgence similar, according to some Islamic sources, to that which Moussa (Moses) had acquired by coming into the presence of God:

> For, far less luminous, his votaries said,
> Were ev'n the gleams, miraculously shed
> O'er Moussa's cheek, when down the Mount he trod,
> All glowing from the presence of his God.
> [p 10]

The question therefore emerges: what is the connection in this narrative between tyranny and religion, between the political and the spiritual?

Moore's reference to Moses is based on a passage from d'Herbelot's account of the doctrines of Mokanna, which he reproduces in his notes to the poem:

> Sa doctrine étoit que Dieu avoit pris une forme et figure humaine depuis qu'il eut commandé aux Anges d'adorer Adam, le premier des hommes. Qu'après la mort d'Adam, Dieu étoit apparu sous la figure de plusieurs prophètes, et autres grands hommes, qu'il

avoit choisis, jusqu'à ce qu'il prit celle d'Abu Moslem, Prince de Khorassan [i.e. Mokanna], lequel professoit l'erreur de la Tanassukhiah, ou Metempsychose; et qu'après la mort de ce Prince, la Divinité étoit passée, et descendue en sa personne.

[p 343]

(His doctrine was that God had assumed a human figure and face since he had ordered the angels to adore Adam, the first of men. That after the death of Adam God had appeared in the form of several prophets and other great men whom he had chosen, until he had taken on that of Abu Moslem, Prince of Khorassan, who professed the error of Tanassukhiah, or Metempsychosis; and that after the death of this Prince, divinity had passed and descended into his person.)

D'Herbelot does not make clear whether Mokanna actually believes this doctrine or whether he is simply using it to his own ends, that is, whether he is a megalomaniac or a cynic. But he strongly suggests that the ways of political despotism and of religious fanaticism are not as distinct as they might seem. Moore of course does distinguish between true faith on the one hand, and perversion and exploitation of faith on the other, yet his transformation of d'Herbelot's prose into poetry still produces no straightforward effect. Mokanna has just boasted of his power to 'track the flame' of the individual soul through its successive incarnations 'as through a torch-race'. Moore now makes him enlarge the idea of metempsychosis into an apostolic, even divine, succession:

'Nor think 'tis only the gross Spirits, warm'd
With duskier fire and for earth's medium form'd,
That run this course; — Beings, the most divine,
Thus deign through dark mortality to shine.

Such was the essence that in Adam dwelt,
To which all Heav'n, except the Proud One, knelt:
Such the refined intelligence that glow'd
In Moussa's frame; — and, thence descending, flow'd
Through many a Prophet's breast; — In Issa shone,
And in Mohammed burn'd; till, hastening on,
(As a bright river that, from fall to fall
In many a maze descending, bright through all,
Finds some fair region where, each labyrinth past,
In one full lake of light it rests at last!)
That Holy Spirit, *setting* calm and free
From lapse or shadow, centres all in me!'
[pp 15–16]

A number of complex associations flow into this passage: metempsychosis, man made into the image of God, Persian doctrines of the power of light, and Old Testament and Islamic mystic traditions. This weight of association is given further focus by the clarity of Moore's rhetoric. The notion of a divine descent is sustained through a running image that blends light and water (the 'torch-race' as a 'stream'), which culminates in the idea of a 'bright river' which makes its way, still 'bright', through the maze of nature and the world until it falls into the 'lake of light'. Moreover, it is powerfully suggested that this light gets even stronger as it flows from prophet to prophet finally to reach Mokanna: it 'dwelt' in Adam, 'glowed' in Moussa, 'shone' in Issa, 'burn'd' in Muhammad, and loses all 'lapse or shadow' in Mokanna. Mokanna thus receives an awe-inspiring inheritance, his 'light' being made up at once of 'the Holy Spirit', which is clearly as much a Christian as an Islamic identification of the light that 'deigns through dark mortality to shine', which bears the stamp of Zoroaster, and the calm and free luminousness characteristic of the Islamic vision of Gabriel, recognized by the Koran as the Holy Spirit.

Similarly, Mokanna also brings to fulfilment prophecies of the coming of the just Messiah — the Judaeo-Christian saviour, the Messiah of the esoteric Persian belief whose light will eventually overcome darkness, and the manifestation of the Islamic Mahdi. But more than this, the final couplet suggests that all these avatars are confounded in Mokanna, for he represents the Second and Final Coming. If Mokanna is ultimately an ambiguous figure, it is because he seems to possess the very powers he seeks to mystify and destroy.

Mokanna's Wordly Paradise

Mokanna's power over his subjects is omnipotent. He appeals to the deepest feeling of his followers, and to sustain their fanaticism he promises them a paradise full of delights, physical and spiritual, providing an image of the future joys in the luxuries of his own palace and garden. We have seen how this is a traditional pattern in Romantic narratives, where worldly paradises are represented as devices and temptations by tyrants. But Mokanna is different from, say, Shedad or Aloaddin, for he seeks to destroy Islam *by the path of Islam*. His paradise is not a substitute for God's paradise, or a mocking defiance of the divine reward. It is rather an anticipation of the eternal paradise promised by Allah to the faithful. This makes Moore's despot a unique prototype: one who adopts religious means against religious ends.

The earthly paradise in which Mokanna lives is therefore a model of the Islamic heaven. The perversion lies in the fact that it is Mokanna, not Allah, who dispenses it. The faithful know very well that true paradise is to be found in the next world, not this one, and that terrestrial paradises, however seductive, must be impious frauds. Yet the apparent authenticity of Mokanna's paradise creates an ambiguous reaction even in the true faithful. When Zelica is summoned to attend Mokanna in his place of prayer, her response is one of horror, arising out of the familiar ecstasy of the Muslim faithful:

Sad and subdued, for the first time her frame
Trembled with horror, when the summons came
(A summons proud and rare, which all but she,
And she, till now, had heard with ecstasy,)
To meet Mokanna at his place of prayer . . .
[p 28]

Memories of her love for Azim, repressed after her fatal oath of allegiance to Mokanna, awaken in her a sense of Mokanna's impiety. She finds him in his palace of pleasure, but Moore's description of the scene carefully distinguishes it not only from a Christian piety that could not allow itself to envisage paradise in Islamic terms, but also from a Muslim piety that regards this world as only a preparation for future delights.

Upon his couch the Veil'd Mokanna lay,
While lamps around — not such as lend their ray,
Glimmering and cold, to those who nightly pray
In holy Koom, or Mecca's dim arcades, —
But brilliant, soft, such lights as lovely maids
Look loveliest in, shed their luxurious glow
Upon his mystic Veil's white glittering flow.
Beside him, 'stead of beads and books of prayer,
Which the world fondly thought he mused on there,
Stood vases, filled with Kishmee's golden wine,
And the red weepings of the Shiraz vine;
Of which his curtain'd lips full many a draught
Took zealously, as if each drop they quaff'd,
Like Zemzem's Spring of Holiness, had power
To freshen the soul's virtues into flower!
[pp 30–31]

Moore finely suggests Zelica's growing reservations by distinguishing Mokanna's sensuous excesses from the images of a chaste and modest worship of God: from the lamps, 'glimmering and cold' for those who 'nightly' pray in 'holy Koom' (in Iran) or in 'Mecca's dim arcades'; from the 'beads and books of prayer' and 'Zemzem's Spring of Holiness' (the miraculous well at Mecca) — all Islamic elements associated with religious practice.

It is important to recognize that Moore does not fail the conception of paradise as expressed in the Koran, especially in its emphasis on sensual beauty, satisfaction and tranquillity. Over and over again, the paradise Mokanna offers his followers evokes Islamic paradisal images, such as houris, wine and peacefulness. On the brink of his final defeat at the hands of Azim, this is how Mokanna addresses his soldiers:

> To-night — yes, sainted men! this very night,
> I bid you all to a fair festal rite,
> Where — having deep refresh'd each weary limb
> With viands, such as feast heav'n's cherubim,
> And kindled up your souls, now sunk and dim,
> With that pure wine the Dark-ey'd Maids above
> Keep, seal'd with precious musk, for those they love . . .
> [p 102]

The repeated emphasis on wine, both here and in the previous quotation, for example, is not parodic or satirical. As a proof of his Islamic precision, Moore annexes a verse from the Koran, Chapter 83, that reads: 'The righteous shall be given to drink of pure wine, sealed; the seal whereof shall be musk.'[13] Moore also alludes to a famous passage in the Koran dealing with the houris of paradise: 'Therein [in paradise] shall be agreeable and beauteous damsels . . . Having fine black eyes; and kept in pavilions from public view.'[14] Moore exploits without reserve this image in terms of which he introduces the dwellers of the 'Haram's curtained galleries' in Mokanna's palace:

(Creatures so bright, that the same lips and eyes
They wear on earth will serve in Paradise,)
There to recline among Heav'n's native maids,
And crown th' Elect with bliss that never fades! —
Well hath the Prophet-Chief his bidding done;
And every beauteous race beneath the sun,
From those who kneel at Brahma's burning founts,
To the fresh nymphs bounding o'er Yemen's mounts;
From Persia's eyes of full and fawn-like ray,
To the small, half-shut glances of Kathay;
And Georgia's bloom, and Azab's darker smiles,
And gold ringlets of the Western Isles;
All, all are there; — each Land its flower hath given,
To form that fair young Nursery for Heaven!
[pp 11–12]

This bravura passage is not without malice, needless to say: the association of the Calvinist term 'elect' with this nubile 'Nursery' is far from innocent. Yet we have here much more than a simple case of the orthodox Christian view of the Muslim heaven, known traditionally as 'Mohammedan libertinism', and which caused many a Christian to regard Islam as the religion of carnality and sacrilege; much more, too, than that later, better informed Christian scepticism which repeatedly raised the question of why the Arab Prophet promised to provide in the next life what he had shunned as evil and immoral in this life. By making Mokanna speak the language of the Koran, Moore was not essentially satirizing Islam from a Christian perspective. He was defining a special problem for his characters, which could be called the problem of 'premature bliss' — the assumption that the conditions of heaven were operative on earth. This allowed him, of course, to deepen his diagnosis of tyranny; but it also allowed him to attend to the psychological conflicts in his characters — especially in Azim and Zelica.

An example is provided in the episode from Part II of the poem, in which Azim is tempted to join the ranks of Mokanna's army. The venue selected for this episode is a part of the despot's earthly paradise, which works on Azim's senses like Spenser's Bower of Bliss, beautiful but treacherous, with its fragrant summer night, its enchanting music, its 'lightsome maidens', dancing and singing with exquisite art. At first the seduction scene, resembling what we have seen in Southey's *Thalaba*, seems magical. As Azim thinks of his lost love Zelica,

> . . . still nearer on the breeze
> Come those delicious, dream-like harmonies,
> Each note of which but adds new, downy links
> To the soft chain in which his spirit sinks.
> He turns him tow'rd the sound, and far away
> Through a long vista, sparkling with play
> Of countless lamps, — like the rich track which Day
> Leaves on the waters, when he sinks from us;
> So long the path, its light so tremulous; —
> He sees a group of female forms advance . . .
>
> [p 56]

But one of these maidens sings him a sad song of homesickness, and the spell of the gaiety is broken; and despite more direct assaults, including a love-song and a gallery of voluptuous pictures, he cannot cease to long for Zelica. Indeed, Moore's handling of this episode is so subtle that it is worth pausing over an example.

The pictures of sensual delight are ambiguous in that the desire they awaken is both a temptation and an inspiration. They depict three incidents found in the Koran and in Islamic tradition, the first subject being the 'gay voluptuous wandering' of King Solomon with Bilqis (Queen of Sheba), who teaches him 'that to be blest is to be wise'. Then comes the second, which deals with the amorous love between Joseph and Zuleikah, wife of Potiphar:

There hung the history of the Genii-king,
Traced through each gay, voluptuous wandering
With her from Saba's bowers, in whose bright eyes
He read that to be blest is to be wise; —
Here fond Zuleika woos with open arms
The Hebrew boy, who flies from her young charms,
Yet, flying, turns to gaze, and, half undone,
Wishes that heaven and she could *both* be one!
[p 365]

These lines perfectly capture the Islamic awareness that sexuality is as much a promise as a danger, as the belief in houris in paradise serves to legitimize, at least in part, the institution of the harem on earth.

The same ambiguity is fully preserved in the third episode, which deals with the Prophet Muhammad's special relations with Mary, his Coptic wife:

And here Mohammed, born for love and guile,
Forgets the Koran in his Mary's smile; —
Then beckons some kind angel from above
With a new text to consecrate their love!
[p 365]

It is therefore not surprising that the erotic temptations of the earthly paradises (more Islamic, and therefore more 'realistic' than in Southey, where the feeling is more Christian) only serve to strengthen Azim's longing for Zelica.

That 'once adorned divinity' finally appears. But when

she does, the effect is tragic; she reveals, behind the veil, 'That wreck of beauty's shrine' (p 67) and 'the withering blight,/That sin and sorrow leave whene'er they light' (p 69). Azim has turned away from the paradise of pleasure precisely because it has awakened in him a longing for something higher than animal pleasure; and when that appears in the form of Zelica, it reveals itself to have been utterly and irretrievably destroyed by her love for him, which, generating a longing for paradise out of passionate desire for an absent lover, has delivered her into the hands of Mokanna. Mokanna has hideously intermingled and confused the order of heaven and the order of earth. The result renders life unintelligible for Azim and Zelica. Her refusal to break her oath to Mokanna makes a virtue of her crime (her association with him), while Azim's refusal to relinquish her makes a crime (his association with evil power) of his virtue. Victims of Mokanna's ambiguity, they have no way out.

Mokanna as Eblis

Summoned by Mokanna to 'share his orison', Zelica, deeply damaged by her commitment to him, enters 'sad and subdued' his garden oratory. Deep in a reverie, Mokanna fails to notice her, and betrays himself in a monologue that serves to define him, in full Romantic style, as a satanic tyrant:

> . . . with fiendish laugh, like that which broke
> From Eblis at the Fall of Man, he spoke: —
> 'Yes, ye vile race, for hell's amusement given,
> Too mean for earth, yet claiming kin with heaven;
> God's images, forsooth! — such gods as he
> Whom India serves, the monkey deity; —
> Ye creatures of a breath, proud things of clay,
> To whom if Lucifer, as grandams say,

Refused, though at the forfeit of Heaven's light,
To bend in worship, Lucifer was right! —
Soon shall I plant this foot upon the neck
Of your foul race, and without fear or check,
Luxuriating in hate, avenge my shame,
My deep-felt, long-nurst loathing of man's name! —
Soon at the head of myriads, blind and fierce
As hooded falcons, through the universe
I'll sweep my darkening, desolating way,
Weak man my instrument, curst man my prey!
[pp 31–32]

This outburst brings together a number of satanic motifs: derisive contempt against man for his weakness (his transience and materiality — 'breath' and 'clay') outrageously mingled with his pretensions (his claims of kinship with God and heaven); destructive envy, the product of humiliated pride, directed against man's relative favour in God's eye; the rejection of religious truth and faith as superstition ('as grandams say'); and so on. This is obvious enough; what is not so obvious is what the Islamic sources bring to this satanism. It seems clear that Moore is alluding explicitly to the Koran:

> And remember when we said unto the angels, Worship Adam; and they *all* worshipped him except Eblis, *who* said, Shall I worship him who thou hast created of clay? *And* he said, What thinkest thou, *as to* this *man* whom thou hast honourd above me? Verily, if thou grant me respite until the day of resurrection, I will extirpate his offspring, except a few. God answered Begone, *I grant thee respite*: but whoever of them shall follow thee, hell shall surely be his reward; an ample reward for your demerits.[15]

Mokanna is virtually a reincarnation of Eblis himself,

reproducing his attitudes and his conduct, especially in regarding man as a rival and a competitor. But the oriental context allows Moore to make a subtler point. Mokanna, like Eblis, is deeply contemptuous of man for being made in the image of God. He dismisses this doctrine as mere mimicry, calling God 'the monkey deity' (namely, the Indian god Hanuman), and contrasting his own proud, destructive independence by attributing to himself an alternative animal image — the 'hooded falcon'. Yet the irony is that, in his contempt for imitation, Mokanna is himself the most imitative of all beings, becoming virtually the double of Eblis as he is depicted in the Koran. Eblis's claim that 'light', from which he was created, is superior to man's 'clay' is given a new force by Mokanna. Mokanna's lines suggest a new dimension to Satan's rebellion against God. In particular they underline the inferior rationality of man, whose naivety persuades him of his superiority to Satan, on the illusory grounds that 'clay' is better than 'fire'. These issues are quite plainly defined in the Koran itself, particularly in the account of the creation of man, upon which Moore himself elaborates in his notes, on the authority of Sale:

> The earth (which God had selected for the material of his work) was carried into Arabia, to a place between Mecca and Tayef, where, being first kneaded by the angels, it was afterwards fashioned by God himself into a human form, and left to dry for the space of forty days, or, as others say, as many years; the angels, in the mean time, often visiting it, and Eblis, (then one of the angels nearest to God's presence, afterwards the devil) among the rest; but he, not contented with looking at it, kicked it with his foot till it rung; and knowing God designed that creature to be his superior, took a secret resolution never to acknowledge him as such.[16]

Through Mokanna, it seems, Moore is satirizing these traditions.

While it cannot be denied that Moore's treatment of Mokanna gives him a certain satanic magnificence, Moore's attitude to religious dogmatism and fanaticism is generally ironic. His description of Mokanna's despotism implies a contempt for religious zeal and fanaticism which he finds at the root of all kinds of despotism. How closely political tyranny and religious fanaticism are linked in Moore's mind may be seen from the last lines of Mokanna's soliloquy (quoted above). Placed at the head of 'myriads' of destructive beings, Mokanna becomes not only a re-enactment of Eblis's destruction of Adam's 'vile race', but a full-scale destructive being in his own right. Another passage from the Koran describes how the Prophet Muhammad, being outnumbered in one of his battles against the infidels, receives from God the help of 'myriads of troops'[17] under the Archangel Gabriel. Mokanna's evil is on the same scale, and he belongs to the same cosmic scene. In the Koran, God also speaks of Eblis in military terms. Thus he says to Eblis: 'whosoever of them [Adam's race] shall follow thee, hell shall be your reward . . . and entice to vanity such of them as thou canst, by thy voice; and assault them on all sides with thy *horsemen* and thy *footmen*' (my italics).[18] That Mokanna's followers are naturally thought of as a demonic army simply confirms the association of political and religious excess.

Koranic associations do not merely help to define the nature of tyranny; they also serve to bring out the gullibility and superstition that make tyranny possible. Although fully prepared to make use of miracles, or 'alleged miracles', Mokanna pours a contempt on human credulity that expresses Moore's own attitude to that defect:

> Ye too, believers of incredible creeds,
> Whose faith inshrines the monsters which it breeds;

Who, bolder ev'n than NEMROD, think to rise,
By nonsense heap'd on nonsense, to the skies;
Ye shall have miracles, aye, sound ones too,
Seen, heard, attested, everything — but true.
[p 33]

Like Voltaire, who uses the despot to define and satirize gullibility, Moore uses Mokanna to satirize human weakness and blindness, which creates the very despotism that oppresses them. This paradox is magnificently focused in this passage by the Islamic imagery. The 'believers' who 'breed' superstitious 'creeds' are themselves despotic. They are compared, though in Moore's usual ironic and duplicitous style, to the biblical and Islamic figure of Nimrod, who, as we have seen, is referred to in the Koran as wanting, like Egypt's pharaoh, to build his own tower to excel God's sovereignty. But Mokanna's 'believers' are even 'bolder' than Nimrod as they attempt to rise to heaven, not on structured towers, but, 'By nonsense heap'd on nonsense.' There could be no severer attack on human credulity.

The complexity of Moore's attitude to Mokanna is to be seen in the fact that his radical religious cynicism, which is a satanic trait, in part carries Moore's endorsement. The fact that Moore is ostensibly attacking Islamic excesses should not stop us from applying the attack more generally. In this passage one may wonder whether Moore's target is Islam or Christianity, or religious credulity in general:

Your preaching zealots, too inspir'd to seek
One grace of meaning for the things they speak;
Your martyrs, ready to shed out their blood,
For truths too heavenly to be understood:
And your State Priests, sole vendors of the lore,
That works salvation; — as, on Ava's shore
Where none *but* priests are privileg'd to trade

In that best marble of which Gods are made.
[p 33]

The last three lines allude to a religious practice in Ava, where marble objects are made and sold as images of the Birman deity, Gaudma. According to Syme, the Birmans 'are suffered, and indeed encouraged, to buy figures of the deity ready made'.[19] Yet how distinct is this malpractice from the sale of relics and indulgences in Christianity? Not even the famous parody of the Islamic paradise promised to the faithful can be dismissed as something confined to mere 'paganism':

Houris for boys, omniscience for sages
And wings and glories for all ranks and ages.
Vain things! — as lust or vanity inspires,
The Heav'n of each is but what each desires,
And, soul or sense, whate'er the object be,
Man would be man to all eternity!
[p 34]

Self-indulgent and self-deceived as the details may be ('houris', 'omniscience', 'wings'), the fundamental point is that paradise is the product of lust or desire, and not an independent realm of holy joy. The rhetorical power which Moore gives to Mokanna is in fact justified by the authority and conviction of his cynicism. In this Mokanna has all the sublimity of the Romantic outlaw: he lives his hatred and enacts his contempt.

Mokanna's full ambiguity is revealed in his treatment of his followers, and of Zelica in particular. She is taken in by him; but her gullibility is presented as a nobler thing than his cynicism. It serves to show up his limitations. For what draws her to him is a rejection of the world that is provoked by the loss, permanent as she thought, of Azim. It is out of an unselfish religious feeling that she commits herself to Mokanna. This he exploits in his usual vein, presenting himself as an inspired prophet. The greater his cynicism, the more strongly her innocence stands as a reproach to him.

His reaction to Zelica's resistance serves to disclose to her his true nature. During his first audience with her, he begins by invoking images of piety and virtue, addressing her as the 'light of the Earth'. But he quickly begins to exploit the ambiguity in the word of 'love', describing her as one who 'turn'st religion's zeal/So close with love's, men know not which they feel.' His language then becomes openly licentious, and he exploits the fashionable diction of the oriental love poetry known as *gazzel*, describing her eyes, her cheeks, her lips ('which have magic in their pressure') as an 'advance' to 'heaven'. When that partly fails, he recoils into straightforward threats, reminding her of the sacredness of her oath and the consequences of breaking it (imaged in the hellish charnel-house where it was taken). By an obvious irony, Mokanna's attempted seduction of Zelica shows how dependent he is on what he denies. He himself claims that power and victory have no meaning without the full enjoyment of beauty, of which Zelica is the ideal. She is the '*one*, to make the victory sure':

> One who in every look joins every lure;
> Through whom all beauty's beams concenter'd pass,
> Dazzling and warm, as through love's burning glass
> Whose gentle lips persuade without a word,
> Whose words, e'en when unmeaning, are adored,
> Like inarticulate breathings from a shrine,
> Which our faith takes for granted are divine!
>
> [p 37]

And the reason for this all-consuming craving and desire is nothing but his own hidden hideousness, which he finally reveals to her in a perverted assertion of brute power.

The climax is typical of Moore's use of the shock tactic of self-disclosure (another being Zelika's revelation of the effects of grief and guilt on her face when she later unveils before Azim). It is possible that this is a deliberate parody of a convention in oriental literature dealing with mystical and ritualistic practice in which a spiritual experience concludes in a moment of disclosure. But in this case what Mokanna reveals to Zelica is that, in submitting herself to him, she has bound herself to the devil — a link that hell itself cannot 'burst'. If Mokanna cannot enjoy her body, he can possess her soul. But the irony is that he can do the latter because she has what he lacks — a religious respect for the sacredness of an oath, which is, of course (as her refusal, later, to escape with Azim shows), the sole reason for Mokanna's power over her.

Mokanna as Prophet

Important aspects of Mokanna suggest links with stereotyped representations of Muhammad as impostor. Yet Moore's commitment to traditional orientalism produces a curious, though perverted, result: he makes Mokanna re-enact incidents in the life of the Muslim Prophet himself.

One of the most striking of such episodes occurs at the climax of the narrative. Having been defeated in a two-day encounter with the calif's army, thanks to the outstanding efforts of Azim, who turned the tide of battle against the Khorassani tyrant, Mokanna makes a last stand on the far side of the river Oxus in the citadel of Neksheb, and exhorts his troops for the last time:

'Glorious defenders of the sacred Crown
I bear from Heav'n, whose light nor blood shall drown
Nor shadow of earth eclipse; before whose gems

The play pomp of this world's diadems,
The crown of Gerashid, the pillar'd throne
Of Parviz, and the heron crest that shone,
Magnificent, o'er Ali's beauteous eyes,
Fade like the stars when morn is in the skies:
Warriors, rejoice — the port, to which we've pass'd
O'er Destiny's dark wave, beams out at last!
Victory's our own . . .'

[p 94]

The phrase, 'the pillar'd throne/Of Parviz', makes an unmistakable allusion to the life of the Prophet Muhammad, which a note by Moore underlines:

> There were said to be under this Throne or Palace of Khosrou Parviz a hundred vaults filled with 'treasures so immense that some Mahometan writers tell us, their Prophet, to encourage his disciples, carried them to a rock, which at his command opened, and gave them a prospect through it of the treasures of Khosrou.' — *Universal History*.[20]

But Moore must have consulted more than the *Universal History*: he must also have had access to lives of the Prophet Muhammad, written during the 17th and 18th centuries by Prideaux and others, which presented the Muslim Prophet as a shameless fraud. But the quotation from the *Universal History* refers to an actual incident that took place in the year 13 of Hijrah (AD 604) when the Muslims in Medina were surrounded by the infidel armies, from which they were separated by a ditch they had dug around the city. According to the more reliable Islamic reports, the Prophet was working on a big rock in the ditch when three flashes appeared in the surroundings. One of these the Prophet interpreted to his people as a sign that Persia and its treasures would, as the triumph of Islam proved a decade later, pass into Muslim hands. The incident undoubtedly served to raise the Muslims' morale at this critical moment. Moore's elaboration of his story makes it clear that Mokanna imitated not only the military but also the prophetic aspects of Muhammad's career. His harangue to his followers concludes:

> Victory's our own — 'tis written in that Book
> Upon whose leaves none but the angels look,
> That Islam's sceptre shall beneath the power
> Of her great foe fall broken in that hour,
> When the moon's mighty orb, before all eyes,
> From Neksheb's Holy Well portentously shall rise!
> [p 94]

But this particular prophecy does not only associate Mokanna with Muhammad, it also *dissociates* him from the Arab Prophet; for here it is, of course, Mokanna, the Persian renegade, who predicts the downfall rather than the triumph of Islam, and goes on to suffer a final defeat rather than a victory. This irony makes it clear that Mokanna is less an attack on Islam than a bad imitation or parody of it.

The passage, as elsewhere in 'The Veiled Prophet', is rich in allusions to Islamic doctrines, such as the 'Book of Fate', and the angels that have access to the book's 'leaves' and to the 'Holy Well'. But Moore's genius is shown in the use to which he puts these allusions. Here he introduces them only so as to make them give way to occult Persian doctrines. The image of light has a special significance of Persian gnosticism. (It also signifies, for Moore, political liberty, as can be seen from his political poems on Ireland, and as will become clear when we discuss 'The Fire-Worshippers'.) Here it is associated with the allusion of the 'moon's mighty orb' rising out of the well which Mokanna fabricates as an emblem of freedom to break 'Islam's sceptre'.

This 'shining orb' is another device used by Moore to regulate the complex relationship of Mokanna to Muhammad. The latter had been asked by infidels to show them a specific miracle as evidence of his prophetic powers; in response he had split the moon into two halves. It is unlikely that Moore would have overlooked the connection between this incident and Mokanna's trick as reported in d'Herbelot (p 95):

> Il amusa pendant deux mois le peuple de la ville Nekscheb, en faisant sortir toutes les nuits du fond d'un puits un corps lumineux semblable à la Lune, qui portoit sa lumière jusqu'à la distance de plusieurs milles.
>
> (For two months he entertained the people of Nechsheb by causing to rise out of a well every night a luminous body resembling the moon which cast its light to a distance of several miles.)[21]

Moore adds that this earned Mokanna the nickname 'Sazendèhmah', or the Moon-Maker. The Prophet Muhammad is identified by Islamic tradition as the 'one who caused the moon to split into two halves' as a cosmic miracle to his people. But here again it is the contrast rather than the parallel with Muhammad that matters. Mokanna's wizardry is clearly a device to impose a specious authority.

> And they beheld an orb, ample and bright,
> Rise from the Holy Well, and cast its light
> Round the rich city and the plain for miles . . .
> Instant from all who saw the' illusive sign
> A murmur broke — 'Miraculous! divine!'

The Gheber bow'd, thinking his idol star
Had wak'd, and burst impatient through the bar
Of midnight, to inflame him to the war!
While he of Moussa's creed saw, in that ray,
The glorious Light which, in his freedom's day,
Had rested on the Ark, and now again
Shone out to bless the breaking of his chain!
[p 95]

Not only is this light specious in its cause but also in its effect, for it becomes all things to all men: to the Gheber and the Jew it merely reflects back their own creed to themselves. It provokes not a new realism and a new determination, but a crazy megalomaniac defiance of inevitable destruction. And when they launch their attack, they are 'like a diminutive mountain-tide' hurling itself into 'the boundless sea'.

The function of associating Mokanna with Muhammad is to deepen the ambiguity of Moore's protagonist. For Mokanna's defiance of Islam is, on the one hand, a defiance of something that is essentially fundamental (at least in the eyes of the Christians), but on the other also of something that is authentic (at least when Islam is compared to the claims of the tyrant rebel). To put the matter more generally, Moore is himself, in part, sceptical of religious creeds; and to the extent to which he embodies this scepticism, the veiled prophet cannot be dismissed as a merely negative figure. Moore's treatment of the theme of oriental despotism permits him to focus a major issue of European politics — the emergence of secular autocracy out of the French Revolution. His portrayal of Mokanna in all its ambiguity cannot fail to evoke Napoleon Bonaparte. Like *Thalaba*, the first poem in *Lalla Rookh* offers an attack on the fanaticism that accompanied the outbreak of the French Revolution and the gullible hero-worship that made possible the Napoleonic phenomenon, which could 'with baleful lustre blind the brave and free', and which 'dazzle[d] Europe into slavery'.[22] Let us first consider the way in which Moore wrote about Napoleon in 1815:

> What do you think now of my supernatural friend, the Emperor? If ever a tyrant deserved to be worshipped it is he. Milton's Satan is nothing to him for portentous magnificence — for sublimity of mischief. If that account in the papers be true, of his driving down in his carriage like lightning towards the royal army embattled against him, bareheaded, unguarded, in all the confidence of irresponsibility — it is a fact far sublimer than any that fiction has ever invented, and I am not at all surprised at the dumb-founded fascination that seizes people at such daring. For my part I could have fancied that Fate herself was in that carriage . . . What desperate weather! all owing to Bonaparte.[23]

It is remarkable how many of the elements that have gone into the creation of Mokanna are reproduced here: first his demonic power, half-jokingly ('my supernatural friend' who can control the 'weather'), then his visible splendour ('his portentous magnificence'), then his power to enforce a superstitious reverence ('deserved to be worshipped'), then the dazzling energy of a reckless courage, conveyed in the image of 'lightning' which evokes a 'dumb-founded fascination', and finally the Romantic awe before the 'sublimity of mischief' of 'Milton's Satan'. All the essentials of the conception of Mokanna are represented.

Two major traits which Napoleon may be said to share with Mokanna deserve further examination: his political astuteness and his military genius. As a politician, Napoleon was a product of the French Revolution and shared, at least in part, its ideology of liberation. It was in the name of these new standards that he made his appeal to the ardent spirits of the age, which had become increasingly impatient under the old ruling monarchies. Such followers are well represented in Azim, who has all the youthful idealism of revolutionary Europe:

And now, returning to his own dear land,
Full of those dreams of good that, vainly grand,
Haunt the young heart; — proud views of human-kind,
Of men to Gods exalted and refin'd; —
False views, like that horizon's fair deceit,
Where earth and heav'n but *seem*, alas, to meet! —
Soon as he heard an Arm Divine was rais'd
To right the nations, and beheld, emblaz'd
On the white flag Mokanna's host unfurl'd,
Those words of sunshine, 'Freedom to the World'. . .
[pp 13–14]

That these ideals were regarded by Moore as illusions ('vainly grand', 'false views', 'fair deceit') does not make them insignificant. Such a Napoleonic slogan as 'Freedom to the World' is grand enough to kindle support, yet it is too vague to give it direction. Thus it easily becomes a manipulative device. And it emphatically has the desired effect:

At once his faith, his sword, his soul obey'd
The' inspiring summons; every chosen blade,
That fought beneath that banner's sacred text,
Seem'd doubly edg'd, for this world and the next;
And ne'er did Faith with her smooth bandage bind
Eyes more devoutly willing to be blind,
In virtue's cause; — never was soul inspir'd
With livelier trust in what it most desir'd,
Than his, the' enthusiast there, who kneeling, pale
With pious awe, before that Silver Veil,
Believes the form, to which he bends his knee,

Some pure, redeeming angel, sent to free
This fetter'd world from every bond and stain,
And bring its primal glories back again!
[p 14]

It might seem at first that the enthusiasm Mokanna inspired in his followers goes quite beyond Napoleon's, in that it clearly has a religious dimension. Yet the restoration of the world's 'primal glories' is not a programme entirely out of line with that of Napoleon, who sought to break the mould of artificial social privilege not merely in France, but on an international scale, from America to Russia.

However wicked and ruthless a despot he is, Mokanna speaks the language of a liberator, and, like Napoleon, he behaves in the style of celebrated freedom fighters. But this brings us to my second point — the virtues of military leadership shared by both figures. Mokanna's address to his soldiers, like Napoleon's famous speeches to his army of Italy, shows that he understands what motivates military courage:

'But these,' pursued the Chief, 'are truths sublime,
That claim a holier mood and calmer time
Than earth allows us now — this sword must first
The darkling prison-house of Mankind burst,
Ere Peace can visit them, or Truth let in
Her wakening day-light on a world of sin!
But then, celestial warriors, then, when all
Earth's shrines and thrones before our banner fall;
When the glad Slave shall at these feet lay down
His broken chain, the tyrant Lord his crown,
The Priest his book, the Conqueror his wreath.'
[pp 16–17]

Here again is the unmistakable allusion to the French Revolution, and to Napoleon's dependence, as he sought to expand his empire, on slogans invoking freedom and equality. But what is new is Moore's remarkable emphasis on, and enactment of, the power of *rhetoric* as the basis of military energy:

And from the lips of Truth one mighty breath
Shall, like a whirlwind, scatter in its breeze
That whole dark pile of human mockeries; —
Then shall the reign of mind commence on earth,
And starting fresh as from a second birth,
Man, in the sunshine of the world's new spring,
Shall walk transparent, like some holy thing!
[p 17]

Human eloquence ('lips', 'breath') has the elemental force of nature ('breeze', 'whirlwind'): the power to overthrow and destroy what is old and worn out; and to define, express and establish reason ('reign of Mind') in a great seasonal rebirth: 'the world's new spring'. At this level it is scarcely possible to distinguish the power of the sword from the power of the word. In this respect, Moore is quite different from his predecessors Landor and Southey; nor is this irresistible eloquence limited to the military figures.

Physical prowess on the battlefield is treated in a more conventional way, and detailed elaboration is scarcely necessary. Mokanna's conviction and daring are such that his mere presence in the line of battle is a source of inspiration to his followers. In the great two-day battle against the calif, he shows himself to be inexhaustible in his energy and power of example:

. . . the Silver Veil
Is seen glittering at times, like the white sail
Of some toss'd vessel, on a stormy night,
Catching the tempest's momentary light!

And hath not *this* brought the proud spirit low?
Nor dash'd his brow, nor check'd his daring? No.
Though half the wretches, whom at night he led
To thrones and victory, lie disgrac'd and dead,
Yet morning hears him with unshrinking crest,
Still vaunt of thrones, and victory to the rest . . .
[p 97]

And this would have earned him his victory had it not provoked in Azim, now possessed by his desire for vengeance and fighting for the other side, even more remarkable feats of military leadership. What is more interesting than Mokanna in victory is Mokanna in defeat. Forced to retire with the remainder of his followers, he hurls his small band forward in insane defiance on the calif's enormous army. It is clear that he will never give up and that his will can never be broken. His conduct after his defeat is magnificent; it displays his strength of personality in a way that victory never could achieve, for failure is a much greater test on one's resources than success. But it is only his end that shows what is really behind his — and perhaps Napoleon's — energy. It is a satanic vanity. Such is this vanity, in fact, that it does not permit him to submit to a simple death:

'For *me* — I too must die — but not like these
Vile, rankling things, to fester in the breeze;
To have this brow in ruffian triumph shown,
With all death's grimness added to its own,
And rot to dust beneath the taunting eyes
Of slaves, exclaiming, 'There his Godship lies!'
No — cursed race — since first my soul drew breath,
They've been my dupes, and *shall* be, ev'n in death.
Thou see'st yon cistern in the shade — 'tis fill'd
With burning drugs, for this last hour distill'd; —
There will I plunge me, in that liquid flame —

Fit bath to lave a dying Prophet's frame! —
There perish, all — ere pulse of thine shall fail —
Nor leave one limb to tell mankind the tale.'
[pp 107–8]

His capacity to dominate, to defy, to scorn, to boast, to mystify is at no time less impaired than when he destroys himself. Nor on any other occasion is he more ambiguous, for it is at this moment that his egoism, which provokes Moore's moral contempt, and his energy, which prompts his imaginative delight, reach their summit.

'The Fire-Worshippers' and National Independence

Lalla Rookh is much concerned with tyranny. It is the theme of its two major narratives. But the two approach the matter in different ways. In 'The Veiled Prophet of Korassan' the emphasis is on the tyrant, and therefore on a multi-level exploration of the nature and origin of his tyranny. But in 'The Fire-Worshippers' the emphasis is on the *tyrannized*. The tyrant conqueror is scarcely portrayed directly; the force of his influence is registered on the reaction of the people whom he subjects. If the former story is concerned with the causes, the latter deals with the effects of tyranny. The story is set in Persia, or Iran, in the seventh century, when that country was being conquered by the Arabs. Iran is ruthlessly held down by the Emir Al Hassan, who has a beautiful daughter, Hinda. The Iranian resistance is embodied in a group of guerrilla patriots under the leadership of a passionately idealistic youth, Hafed. While on a venture to assassinate the Muslim emir, Hafed encounters and falls in love with Hinda, as she falls in love with him, their love surviving the disclosure of each other's identity. Hafed's mountain retreat is betrayed to the Arabs by a treacherous member of the Persian band; the emir, preparing an extraordinary assault, sends Hinda back to Arabia by sea. Her ship is captured by Hafed, who takes her to his fortress, where she warns him of the impending attack and pleads with him to flee with her. Hafed refuses, sending her back to her homeland so that he may seek martyrdom in a last-ditch stand. After a veritable massacre, Hafed's band is overwhelmed, and he immolates himself on a funeral pyre. Witnessing this from her ship, Hinda in turn casts herself into the sea.

Al Hassan, then, is a political and military colonialist. His behaviour produces a dark form of tyranny in which a whole nation is condemned to suffering and degradation. That this is a theme that preoccupied Moore can be seen from his return to it in the other minor narratives. In 'Paradise and the Peri', for example, he refers to Sultan Mahmood of Gazna, the Muslim invader of India in the 11th century, thus:

Land of the Sun! what foot invades
Thy Pagods and thy pillar'd shades —
Thy cavern shrines, and Idol stones,
Thy Monarchs and their thousand Thrones?
'Tis he of Gazna — fierce in wrath
He comes, and India's diadems
Lie scatter'd in his ruinous path. —
His bloodhounds he adorns with gems,
Torn from the violated necks
Of many a young lov'd Sultana;
Maidens, within their pure Zenana,
Priests in the very fane he slaughters,
And chokes up with the glittering wrecks
Of golden shrines the sacred waters!

[pp 127–8]

Even in this weak writing, one can see that military invasion involves much more than the acquisition of land. It means the destruction of an entire culture, both social and religious. In that particular narrative, the last survivor of his race, a young Indian warrior, meets the conqueror, who offers him, out of admiration for his valour, life, freedom and favour. In silent contempt, the young man lets loose his last arrow against his victor. It misses its target, and he is killed. This act of patriotic independence is its own reward. The gesture may seem futile, but it proclaims the survival of the spirit of the conquered race, even in irreversible defeat.

The Peri, a spiritual being who seeks admission to paradise, collects a drop of this martyr's blood in the hope that it will serve as a passport to heaven. Though it does not, the drop is received by the angel guarding the Gates of Paradise with the words: 'Sweet is our welcome of the brave/Who die thus for their native land' (p 130). These lines echo the predominant tone of Moore's *Irish Melodies*, which in part glorify the martyrs of Irish independence. The case for regarding 'The Fire-Worshippers' as dramatizing an analogue of Ireland under the English seems, though circumstantial, so powerful as to be conclusive.

Moore's own relationship to Irish politics is quickly summarized. He came from a Catholic Dublin family, whose members were interested in politics, as Robert Birley notes, at a highly dangerous time.[24] As a young man he became a close friend of Robert Emmet, and endangered his place at Trinity College by refusing to collaborate with an inquiry. He was unable to participate in the 1798 rebellion, which cost Emmet his life, because of illness. Thereafter his career took him to England, and although, even after he had long been famous, he supported O'Connell and the Repealers, he did not involve himself actively in Irish politics. It would seem that his patriotic convictions were strong enough to produce a poem, but not bold enough to make the poem explicit.

Further evidence in confirmation of the political analogy in the poem is to be found in the introductory pages added by Moore to the 1841 edition of *Lalla Rookh*. After completing 'The Paradise and the Peri', he began to feel that the oriental material was in itself too 'slow in touching my sympathies' and began to 'despair of their ever touching the hearts of others'. He goes on:

> But at last — fortunately, as it proved — the thought occurred to me of founding a story on the fierce struggle so long maintained between the Ghebers, or ancient Fire-worshippers of Persia, and their haughty Moslem masters. The cause of *tolerance was again my inspiring theme*; and the spirit that had spoken in the melodies of Ireland soon found itself at home in the East.[25] [My italics]

But Moore had earlier hinted at the analogy. In the notes affixed to the first edition, he quoted one of his earlier models:

> Voltaire tells us that in his Tragedy 'Les Guèbres,' he was generally supposed to have alluded to the Jansenists. I should not be surprised if this story of the Fire-Worshippers were found capable of a similar doubleness of application.[26]

Here was a clear, if veiled, hint to his earliest readers that they should be alert to the allegorical possibilities of his story.

That the parallel between Ireland and Iran remains wholly implicit, moreover, is not only a consequence of Moore's political caution. It also has to do with his wish to be accurate in his representation of Islamic life and history. In an earlier note, he writes:

> Objections may be made to my use of the word Liberty in this, and more especially in the story that follows it, as totally inapplicable to any state of things that has ever existed in the East; but though I cannot, of course, mean to employ it in that enlarged and noble sense which is so well understood at the present day, and, I grieve to say, *so little acted upon*, yet it is no disparagement to the word to apply it to that national independence, that freedom from the interference and dictation of *foreigners*, without which, indeed, no liberty of any kind can exist, and for which both Hindoos and Persians fought against their Mussulman invaders with, in many cases, a bravery that deserved much better success.[27] [My italics]

Such a passage makes it quite clear that, if Moore seeks an analogy (here with respect to the meaning of the term 'liberty'), it is one which has to be faithful to local history, manners and ideology; and it will exist only at the level of resemblance. This is not to say that cautionary considerations did not also prevail. As we have seen, he had to make sure that the sale of the poem would justify the huge investment his publisher Longman was putting into it.

Why, if he wished to establish an Irish analogue, did Moore pick on Iran, and on the Ghebers in particular? It is certainly possible to see in the Ghebers' doomed revolt a shadow of the 1798 Irish rebellion, and, in the fate of its dashing heroic chieftain, Hafed, an echo of Robert Emmet. Consider the following passage identifying Hafed as Hinda's lover:

> And who is he, that wields the might
> Of Freedom on the Green Sea brink,
> Before whose sabre's dazzling light

The eyes of Yemen's warriors wink?
Who comes, embower'd in the spears
Of Kerman's hardy mountaineers? —
Those mountaineers that truest, last,
Cling to their country's ancient rites,
As if that God, whose eyelids cast
Their closing gleams on Iran's heights,
Among her snowy mountains threw
The last light of his worship too!

[p 190]

At first sight it may seem that Moore's use of local colour is not very exact, to say the least. For example, Hafed's sabre with its light that dazzles the Yemenis (warriors from Arabia Felix), is in fact a standard Arabic, not a Persian, metaphor. It is used by Amru Alkais, for instance, one of the authors of 'The Arabic Odes', better known as *Mualakat*, to which Moore refers in his notes: 'When the bright scimitars make the eyes of our heroes wink.'[28] Moore was not very discriminating in his distribution of the Islamic material as he freely transformed an image from one context to another without apparent concern. This example even shows how the oriental image serves a serious purpose for Moore. He wishes to cluster about the figure of Hafed a whole set of fire images, not only because it gives him military glamour, but because it defines his role as leader of the fire-worshippers, with the sun as its central symbol, whose evening rays, in a finely turned image, gleam last on the mountains which are the final refuge of its worshippers. The sabre, flashing like the sun, proclaims that it has been drawn in what is for the Ghebers a holy war.

Moore's main purpose is to develop the idea of colonial conquest in terms of a contrast of cultures, and more particularly of religions. If in 'The Veiled Prophet of Khórassan' religion is treated in relation to the psychology of power, in 'The Fire-Worshippers' it is handled in relation to the sociology of identity. This is an important dimension of the narrative. The following passage evokes Persia's greatness before the Arab invasion:

And see — the Sun himself! — on wings
Of glory up the East he springs.
Angel of Light! who from the time
Those heavens began their march sublime,
Hath first of all the starry choir
Trod in his Maker's steps of fire!
Where are the days, thou wondrous sphere,
When Iran, like a sun-flower, turn'd
To meet that eye where'er it burn'd? —
When, from the banks of Bendemeer
To the nut-groves of Samarcand
Thy temples flam'd o'er all the land?
Where are they? ask the shades of them
Who, in Cadessia's bloody plains,
Saw fierce invaders pluck the gem
From Iran's broken diadem,
And bind her ancient faith in chains . . .

[p 187]

Persia's ancient religion was Zoroastrianism, reformed by Zoroaster as early as 700 BC into an intensely ethical dualism that was virtually a monotheistic doctrine, inculcating a lofty morality, and having as its central ritual the worship of fire, thought to represent the divine essence and the source of life. In his eternal conflict with darkness (Ahriman), this supreme divinity (Mazdar) was assisted by Mithra, an ancient Arian god of light, thought of as the sun, or the eye of God himself. This passage evokes this divinity through his strides ('march sublime') of fire in the daily journey of the sun, to which ancient Persia turns as naturally as the sunflower, and whose temples 'flame', both in ardour of spirit and in literal ritual. It is this whole system of reverence and ritual which Moore presents to be destroyed by Islam, a religion and ideology which appears, to the conquered, as follows:

Hard, heartless Chief, unmov'd alike
Mid eyes that weep, and swords that strike; —
One of that saintly, murderous brood,
To carnage and the Koran given,
Who think through unbelievers' blood
Lies their directest path to heaven; —
One, who will pause and kneel unshod
In the warm blood his hand hath pour'd,
To mutter o'er some text of God
Engraven on his reeking sword.

[p 162]

Al Hassan's pitilessness in his suppression of Iran is attributed to his religious fanaticism, which does not admit of self-doubt, and to the nature of his religious beliefs, which hold that the killing of the infidel is a holy act that makes murder a blessing and the murderer a saint. The rhetoric equates 'murderous' with 'saintly', 'carnage' with 'the Koran' and 'reeking sword' with 'text of God' (the latter an allusion to the Islamic practice of engraving a Koranic text on the sword blade).

This hostile depiction of Islam, ostensibly attributed to the old fire-worshippers, simultaneously represents the Christian prejudice against Islam and Islam's justification of conquest. More precisely, the old religion of Zoroaster is aligned with old Catholicism, being the older form of Christianity, while Islamic Arabia and Protestant England are paralleled. It seems clear that the power of this passage is fed by a private conviction of feeling in Moore, for which the oriental material is at once the pattern and the symbol.

Moreover, Moore is very sensitive to the distortions and falsifications to which the master religion is prone. From the vantage point of ideological conquest, it is very easy to turn the defeated alien into an inhuman monster, be he Papist or Zoroastrian. When Hinda meets Hafed incognito, she sees only a man; but when he has to identify himself, he does so ironically in the descriptive terms applied to him by the victors, and pre-eminently by her father, concluding, however, in a reassertion of his faith and pride:

'. . .Yes — *I* am of that impious race,
Those Slaves of Fire, who, morn and even,
Hail their Creator's dwelling-place
Among the living lights of heaven!
Yes — *I* am of that outcast few,
To Iran and to vengeance true,
Who curse the hour your Arabs came
To desolate our shrines of flame,
And swear, before God's burning eye,
To break our country's chains, or die!'

[p 178]

The full implications of the dismantling of a political construct by the simplicity of love (a Landoresque theme, no doubt) will be traced in the following section. Here we must take note of the extent to which Moore has conceived his attack on the tyranny as imperialism in terms of the repression, as well as the suppression, of a whole form of life.

That this form of life should be specifically oriental is something to which Moore has given much attention. First of all, Hafed expresses an intensity of reactive hatred that has to be explained, in part at least, in cultural terms. It is an expression of masculine and racial honour, the attack on the nation being construed as an attack against the self.

Hafed had met Hinda because he had forced an entry into Al Hassan's tower in order to assassinate him:

Yes, Emir! he who sealed that tower,
And, had he reach'd thy slumbering breast,
Had taught thee in a Gheber's power
How safe ev'n tyrant heads may rest —
Is one of many, brave as he,
Who loathe thy haughty race and thee;
Who, they know the strife is vain,
Who, though they know the riven chain
Snaps but to enter in the heart
Of him who rends its links apart,
Yet dare the issue, — blest to be
Ev'n for one bleeding moment free,
And die in pangs of liberty!

[pp 188–9]

Furthermore, as this passage indicates, the Persian patriot is animated by a fatalism that accepts the value of revolt even if 'the strife is vain'. To Moore, the Arab domination of Iran was a historical fact, with the altars of Mithra permanently replaced by the worship of Allah. (He viewed the British occupation of Ireland in a similar perspective, and with a similar, though distinctly less heroic, combination of acceptance and dissent.) But these lines are imbued with a mood of oriental resignation, especially characteristic of the Persian Ghebers, and which paradoxically accounts for their readiness to resist unto death. Their sole aim and passion seem to be to achieve martyrdom, and, in a phrase suggestive of an erotic analogy, to 'die in pangs of liberty'.

This is quite borne out by the climax of the action in which Hafed, faced by innumerable odds, decides to sacrifice himself and his band. Before the ultimate confrontation he addresses his men thus:

'Tis o'er — what men could do, we've done —
If Iran *will* look tamely on,
And see her priests, her warriors driven
Before a sensual bigot's nod,
A wretch who shrines his lusts to Heaven,
And makes a pander of his God!
If her proud sons, her high-born souls,
Men, in whose veins — oh last disgrace!
The blood of Zal and Rustam rolls, —
If they *will* court this upstart race,
And turn from Mithra's ancient ray,
To kneel at shrines of yesterday! —
If they *will* crouch to Iran's foes,
Why, let them — till the land's despair
Cries out to Heaven, and bondage grows
Too vile for ev'n the vile to bear!
Till shame at last, long hidden, burns
Their inmost core, and conscience turns.'
[pp 197–8]

He begins with contempt for the religion and moral values of the conqueror, pride in the lineage and nobility of his own religious traditions, and shame that his nation seems reconciled to accept the alien power and give up its identity. He is making clear to his men that he expects no victory or even a practical result (he envisages at best an oppression so intolerable that even the 'vile' will be forced to react). What he offers, in effect, is a religious rite of atonement, resembling the ancient oriental fatalism that seems to remind us of the passive resistance of many liberation movements. Moreover, if this rite is properly performed, it will sanctify a spot of Iranian earth for the nation as a whole, and keep alive its sense of its future:

'. . .When Hope's expiring throb is o'er,
And ev'n Despair can prompt no more,

This spot shall be the sacred grave
Of the last few who, vainly brave,
Die for the land they cannot save!'

[pp 198–9]

This fatalism is, however, transformed in a characteristic oriental turn into a revenge longing to glut itself on slaughter, whether given or received. There is no passivity, patience or submissiveness, nothing of the lamb to the slaughter, in this band, no trace of the meekness associated, in different ways, with Christianity or Buddhism. Just before the final encounter, Hafed declares that such 'tameness' would be an 'inglorious sacrifice':

Shall we die tamely? die alone?
Without one victim to our shades,
One Moslem heart, where, buried deep,
The sabre from its toil may sleep?
No — God of Iran's burning skies!
Thou scorn'st the' inglorious sacrifice.
No — though of all earth's hopes bereft,
Life, swords, vengeance still are left.
We'll make yon valley's reeking caves
Live in the awe-struck minds of men,
Till tyrants shudder, when their slaves
Tell of the Ghebers' bloody glen.

[p 255]

Moore's political message is obvious; the 'pangs of liberty' eventually have to take the form of blood-bath.

But although the carnage envisaged may seem to such as Moore typically oriental, its long-term effects are true wherever a nation, such as Poland (where *Lalla Rookh* was very popular) or Ireland itself, finds itself in a state of historical subjugation. The words that Moore applies to Hafed could equally refer to Robert Emmet:

Yet shall his death-hour leave a track
Of glory, permanent and bright,
To which the brave of after-times,
The suffering brave, shall long look back
With proud regret . . .
[p 244]

The victorious nation glorifies itself in public monuments of stone. The defeated nation can only make monuments of the places where its patriots have fallen:

This rock, his monument aloft,
Shall speak the tale to many an age;
And hither bards and heroes oft
Shall come in secret pilgrimage,
And bring their warrior sons, and tell
The wondering boys where Hafed fell . . .
[p 244]

More is involved than personal immortality. It is only by keeping a tradition of resistance alive, even under impossible conditions, that the spirit of nationhood can be perceived.

Even so, the issue for Moore is the stain that colonial tyranny brings rather than the logistics of military action. Although the memory of Hafed's sacrifice will awaken the desire for vengeance in future generations, what this sacrifice does first of all is to atone for and purify the disgrace and humiliation of enslavement. In that sense, Hafed's martyrdom is more religious than political. Yet the fact remains that it is also a clarion call to the new generation to cut the throats of the oppressors in a style that seems scarcely compatible with the spirit of the 'pilgrims' and the 'wonder' of the acolyte. The boy warriors are required to

. . .Swear them on those lone remains
Of their lost country's ancient fanes,
Never — while breath of life shall live
Within them — to forgive
The' accursed race, whose ruthless chain
Hath left on Iran's neck a stain
Blood, blood alone can cleanse again!
[p 244]

On the other hand, Hafed prepares himself for his suicide by ritualistic fire with the fervour and even the ecstasy of a Christian martyr (Issa, we have already seen, is the Islamic name for Christ):

Such are the swelling thoughts that now
Enthrone themselves on Hafed's brow;
And ne'er did Saint of Issa gaze
On the red wreath, for martyrs twin'd,
More proudly than the youth surveys . . .
[p 245]

Yet even here the Christian note is not allowed to predominate for long. To die on a pyre lit by the sacred fire of the altar is no agony for the Ghebers, if one is to judge by historical precedent: 'The Ghebers say that when Abraham, their great Prophet, was thrown into fire by order of Nimrod, the flame turn'd instantly into a bed of roses, where the child sweetly reposed.'[29] Moore takes his passage from Tavernier. But it is only a variant of the Koran's account of the same incident: 'And when Abraham was cast into the burning pile, we said, O fire, be thou cold, and a preservation unto Abraham.'[30] 'Having miraculously lost its heat,' Sale then comments, quoting Islamic authors, 'the pile changed to a pleasant meadow.'[31] This oriental tradition is beautifully turned into poetry. The pyre which Hafed will embrace has been heaped up 'of every wood of odoriferous breath' by his comrades, and stands ready 'to fold in radiant death' the survivors.

> The few, to whom that couch of flame,
> Which rescues them from bonds and shame,
> Is sweet and welcome as the bed
> For their own infant Prophet spread,
> When pitying Heav'n to roses turn'd
> The death-flames that beneath him burn'd!
>
> [p 245]

At this point 'The Fire-Worshippers' rejoins 'The Veiled Prophet of Khorassan' in its combination of the religious and the political. But once again we find that this attempt, characteristic of the other Romantic orientalists we have examined, produces an effect of profound ambiguity. For the final immolation of Hafed is an act of purification, ultimately sacrificed in a halo of rose-leaves and wood-scent, that is also a preparation for the emotional release of bloody violence and vengeance in years to come.

Love and Patriotism

Romantic love constitutes a major element of *Lalla Rookh*. It occupies a central place in all its four poems; and in the two major narratives, but especially in 'The Fire-Worshippers', it forms an essential part of their political purpose. To understand its overall function, we need to address the question of how it is affected by the perspective of orientalism. For, after all, its main symptom — that it produces passionate unselfishness in the lovers, who are prepared to sacrifice everything, including themselves, for the other's good — is not unlike romantic love as understood in the West.

For the West, it was generally believed that, in an oriental climate, love was simpler, more passionate and more sensual than in the fogs of the north. This notion was strengthened by Islamic polygamy and the institution of the harem. It is, however, essential to understand that, for Moore, oriental love preserved a clear distinction between *pleasure* and *love*. This is the whole point of the final poem of *Lalla Rookh*, trivial as it has seemed to some readers. 'The Light of the Haram' is made up mostly of lyrics — odes and songs. In Cashmere, during the feast of the roses, the Sultan Selim discovers that his favourite, Nourmahal, has suddenly and inexplicably vanished. In his attempt to find consolation for her absence, he hears two women sing: a young and seductive Georgian girl, who celebrates endless voluptuousness in perpetually renewed novelties; and a veiled Arab maiden who celebrates the eternal joys of reciprocal fidelity, in the incorruptible desert far from the luxury of courts and tents. Selim, deeply moved by the second, longs all the more deeply for Nourmahal; whereupon the veiled maiden reveals herself to be the very same, so demonstrating the conquering power of the patient love of a faithful woman. In a similar vein, Azim of 'The Veiled Prophet' is exposed to all the exquisite seductions of Mokanna's harem, but remains unmoved by them, and therefore free from the evil power of the tyrant, because of his love for Zelica, which survives all the vicissitudes of separation, and indeed the ravages wrought by the baleful influence of Mokanna.

It is therefore in the context of reciprocal love that Moore develops his erotic orientalism. This orientalism is marked by three characteristics derived from his general impression of Islamic woman. First, when innocent and ignorant, she is much more voluptuous, has much more animal grace and inner fire than her western counterpart. Secondly, she is much less domesticated, much less easily thought of as a mother and wife, in fact is less *socialized*, than western women. She is far closer to 'nature' in the Rousseauan sense of being less contaminated by worldliness and artifice. Thirdly, whatever the devotion of her lover, he always remains her master: once she falls in love with him, she yields up her mind and heart without restraint or qualification — to the point, indeed, of not wishing to survive his death or infidelity.

These points will be substantiated shortly in a discussion of Zelica and Hinda; first we must note another important qualification on Moore's part. In the first of the two 'interlude' poems, 'Paradise and the Peri', love in the higher sense is given an intermediate place in the scale of values. The Peri is required to find what in the world below is most acceptable to heaven in order to gain admittance. Not even the last drop of blood of the last defeated patriot refusing the mercy of his conqueror is good enough, nor is the expiring sigh of a maiden who has sacrificed herself by ministering to her lover dying of the plague. It is only the tear of a repentant sinner moved by the prayer of an innocent child that opens paradise for the Peri. In the perspective of this story, selfless love is superior to patriotism but inferior to religion. Not that love is in any way reduced in importance; but it is experienced essentially from the woman's point of view. Zelica flings herself on to the point of Azim's spear in the conviction that to perish at his hand is ultimate fulfilment; Hinda drowns herself in response to her lover's death by fire. And here the Peri's bride, reckless of any danger to herself, seeks out her infected lover who has hidden himself from her — 'She, who would rather die with him,/Than live to gain the world beside!' — and embraces him, saying:

> 'Oh! let me only breathe the air,
> The blessed air, that's breath'd by thee,
> And, whether on its wings it bear
> Healing or death, 'tis sweet to me!. . .'
>
> [p 136]

Her love possesses her so completely that even the breath of death becomes the breath of life to her. Now, since love is mainly the domain of women, as love of country and love of God is the domain of men, it follows that there will exist a tension or ambiguity in the relation between women and men. For Moore, as for Byron, even the higher type of love cannot be the whole of experience for a man, though it may be a necessary condition for full political, military and religious experience. Moore makes a clear distinction between the roles of men and women in the Orient: the lover is also a master, and the mistress is also a servant.

Western romantic love is often adulterated by a 'metaphysical' element, or an idealism that sometimes amounts to a superstition; but the Islamic version, as Moore conceives it, is born of this earth and has its being in it, whatever its destination after death. It follows that its relation with patriotism and religion can be much more sharply defined. For the lover, it is marked by ambiguity. On the one hand, it brings a new energy and passion to his pursuit of his duty, whatever it may be; on the other, it interferes with it. This ambiguity is fully exhibited in 'The Fire-Worshippers'. But it is anticipated in 'The Veiled Prophet', particularly in the fate of Azim.

Zelica is possessed by a love that is her strength and her weakness. It is so intense that she cannot survive the prolonged uncertainty of her separation from Azim while he is held a prisoner in Greece; she concludes that he is dead, that she must now hope to recover him only in the next world, and that Mokanna himself offers the straightest path to this reunion. But she is too stricken by her feelings to notice how sinister Mokanna's plans are until it is too late — that is, until she is irreversibly bound to him by an oath which contradicts the very piety that makes it impossible for her to break it. Love as 'life' has driven her into the arms of corruption, and as 'purity' has entangled her in damnation. In the strictest sense of the word, the good has been *perverted* by its very vitality. Once she has made her commitment to Mokanna,

> Though health and bloom return'd, the delicate chain
> Of thought, once tangled, never clear'd again.
> Warm, lively, soft as in youth's happiest day,
> The mind was still all there, but turn'd astray . . .
> [p 21]

In her relationship with Azim, therefore, a similar contradiction manifests itself. She has been cut off from him because of the very strength of her attachment to him. She cannot, of course, obey her satanic master in seducing the youth; she can only serve him by refusing to go with him — by leaving him. Henceforth her love can only take a negative form; and it is not surprising that, at the last, the veil behind which (like her master) she conceals her ravaged features is what brings her to her fate upon her lover's spear, as he seeks to exterminate the tyrant. To be killed by Azim seems to her the only way in which her fidelity to him, and her atonement for her sinful contract with Mokanna, can find its ultimate expression. From Azim's point of view, Zelica's possession by Mokanna can only heighten his political resolve, which is to rid the earth of the monster. Driven to superhuman feats of valour by avenging love, he turns the battle decisively against Mokanna, and leads the final assault on his citadel. But, as the outcome of the narrative demonstrates, what thrusts his fury to its goal (the killing of his demonic 'rival') is what necessarily disappears from him as he fulfils it.

By far Moore's most significant treatment of the relation between romantic love and patriotism is in 'The Fire-Worshippers'. In that poem he uses romantic love to give depth to the patriotic impulse in the figure of Hafed. Hinda is brought up in a characteristically cloistered way by her father, the colonial satrap Al Hassan. She has been taught to admire him, and to fear and hate the Ghebers; but we see that this indoctrination is purely external and superficial. She is left to 'bloom' naturally in the emir's coastal tower, 'An image of Youth's radiant Fountain/Springing in a desolate mountain!' (p 165). In her 'truth and tenderness and grace' she is an unexpected and miraculous product of her 'ungentle race' — a living proof that nature, which has been allowed to manifest itself in her unmolested, is essentially good. Her innocence is the product of her isolation:

> Oh what a pure and sacred thing
> Is Beauty, curtain'd from the sight
> Of the gross world, illumining
> One only mansion with her light!
> Unseen by man's disturbing eye.
>
> [p 165]

As an unspoilt creature, she generates her own soft light, to which Hafed's own nature, as a mountaineer who worships the light of the sun, inevitably and abruptly responds. She falls in love with the man whom society and politics declare to be her mortal enemy, as he does with her, the daughter of the tyrant of his people. Nothing could display more plainly the existence of a common humanity, coextensive with nature, that transcends the artificial barriers erected by man. Nothing could demonstrate more plainly the strength of this common humanity than their love's survival of the discovery of who and what they are.

We have already noticed how, in identifying himself, Hafed parodies the epithets ('slave', 'outcast', 'impious', and so on) by which he is known to the conqueror. One of the functions of love is to *deconstruct* such ideological fabrications. This the main thrust of the narrative makes abundantly clear. When Hinda is sent back by her father by sea to Arabia, so that she may not witness the final destruction of the Ghebers, she is captured by the dreaded Gheber chieftain, and feels she has fallen into the hands of a monster of evil:

> He whom her soul was hourly taught
> To loathe, as some foul fiend of sin,
> Some minister, whom Hell had sent
> To spread its blast, where'er he went,
> And fling, as o'er our earth he trod,
> His shadow betwixt man and God!
>
> [p 223]

She is taken blindfolded into the Gheber mountain stronghold; and when the bandage is removed from her eyes, she sees before her the reality behind this construct — Hafed, her ardent and protective lover. Far from being agents of the devil, the Ghebers are humane and — unless provoked — an unaggressive group of people. One cannot help believing that Moore, the native Irishman who made good in England, was especially receptive to the signs of caricature and distortion in the colonial British attitude to his own people.

This deconstructive process extends well beyond the events of the narrative itself. Contemplating the gallant band of freedom fighters, Moore exclaims against the application of pejorative epithets to patriotic resistance:

> Rebellion! foul, dishonouring word,
> Whose wrongful blight so oft has stain'd
> The holiest cause that tongue or sword
> Of mortal ever lost or gain'd.
> How many a spirit, born to bless,
> Hath sunk beneath that withering name,
> Whom but a day's, an hour's success

Had wafted to eternal fame!
As exhalations, when they burst
From the warm earth, if chill'd at first,
If check'd in soaring from the plain,
Darken to fogs and sink again; —
But, if they once triumphant spread
Their wings above the mountain-head,
Become enthron'd in upper air,
And turn to sun-bright glories there!
[pp 189–90]

In such a passage, written at the time of the full tide European reaction expressed in the Congress of Vienna, and which sought to vilify the great political upheavals of the turn of the 19th century, Moore comes very close to expressing revolutionary sympathies. The deconstruction of an ideological distortion is always a radical act.

In 'The Fire-Worshippers', however, both sides offer a hostile version of each other, but in this respect the victim has the advantage over the aggressor, in that his hostility is necessarily more soundly based. Accordingly, when the lovers fall for each other, it is Hinda who relinquishes her people's view of the Ghebers; Hafed does not alter his view of the Arabs at all. This distinction is reinforced by the oriental conception of gender differences, which makes man the dominant sex whose interests must be served by the woman. The moment she loves Hafed, Hinda abandons all her former beliefs and associations to a single all-dominating commitment to her lover, which can extend to the declaration that, should they need to expiate the sin of loving, they would pray — 'Thou, for *my* sake, at Alla's shrine,/And I — at *any* God's, for thine!' There can therefore be no conflict between them. His will prevails, or rather does not need to prevail since, by the mere fact that it is *his* will, it is already *hers*. The conflict is not between the two of them, but in the love they both serve. In their second meeting, Hinda indulges in the dream that they could be 'wafted off to seas unknown',

> And we might live, love, die alone!
> Far from the cruel and the cold, —
> Where the bright eyes of angels only
> Should come around us, to behold
> A paradise so pure and lovely!
>
> [p 173]

And she asks him the pointed question: 'Would this be world enough for thee?' Her lover's mournful look in reply makes her uneasy; and almost immediately she learns the truth of what he is. So that, in their final encounter in the mountain stronghold of the Ghebers, she pleads with him to escape with her in 'the bark that brought [her] hither' — 'Go where we will,' she declares,

> Through good and ill, through storm and shine,
> The world's a world of love for us!
> On some calm, blessed shore we'll dwell,
> Where 'tis no crime to love too well . . .
>
> [p 246]

This dream — which is the dream of love for both of them — he has to renounce in the name of his love of country. After a moment of weakness and tears, 'a dangerous cloud/Of softness', he turns his back on her to blow the great sea-horn to summon his men to 'the tremendous death-die cast'. If a paradise exists in which their love can find happiness, it will not be found in this world. His duty to Iran is inviolate.

In its effects, romantic love is therefore in radical conflict with love of country. Yet, from love, patriotism receives a generosity and grandeur which by itself it would lack. As far as Hinda is concerned, love awakens a range of sympathies previously unknown to her. Before meeting Hafed, she would listen to her father's tales of bloodshed 'unlistening and aloof . . . unaw'd, unmov'd,/While Heav'n but spar'd the sire she loved.' Indeed, she

> Slept like a lake, till Love threw in
> His talisman, and woke the tide,
> And spread its trembling circles wide.
>
> [p 201]

This enlarges her concerns beyond her merely filial fears for her father:

> And bitterly, as day on day
> Of rebel carnage fast succeeds,
> She weeps a lover snatch'd away
> In every Gheber wretch that bleeds.
>
> [p 201]

As far as Hafed is concerned, the effect of love is less obvious but more profound. His love for Hinda is, in its origins, at one with his love for his country. It therefore enforces the Romantic doctrine that the thirst for personal and national liberty is a force of nature and that political ideals are nourished by elemental powers. To some extent, the Ghebers' sun worship has already established this perspective on their political struggle; but Hafed's love for Hinda awakens in him an ardour of devotion and commitment that attunes his ambitions with life itself.

They are, of course, suited to each other as lovers, and even prepared for each other before their meeting. There is, for all the modesty of Hinda's upbringing, something wild, free and unconventional about her nature, that must appeal to Hafed's adventurous and passionate faith in liberty. Similarly, there is in Hafed an enforced natural heroism to which Hinda's unquestioning admiration of her father's martial qualities ('Thou know'st him not — he loves the brave . . . . He tells me . . ./A hero shall my bridegroom be . . .') make her very receptive. Hafed therefore believes that, had she 'been born a Persian maid', 'Iran's cause' and hers would have been 'one'. But this is too simple. Because they belong, like Romeo and Juliet, to mortally opposed camps, their love is much more intense, daring — in short, romantic; and although in one sense this division ultimately sets love and patriotism at odds, in a deeper sense, by introducing a common element of dangerous living both to love and to patriotism, it reveals a more profound accord. The relation between these two motifs is fraught with moral ambiguity. So, in the same ambivalent vein, the image of Hinda that never wholly leaves Hafed's mind as he fights his last battle, brings at once a sense of loss and pain, but also a sense of resolution and valour. She is 'His heart's pure planet, shining yet/Above the waste of memory,' at once emphasizing and transcending the 'waste', and causing and justifying his final martyrdom.

The Oriental Landscape

As with the other Islamic narratives being examined, *Lalla Rookh* depends very heavily on the evocation of the oriental picturesque — that is to say, on extended or incidental descriptions of natural background. Much of the magic of the Orient consists in the environment of weather, climate and landscape. This setting is obviously drawn, not on direct experience (for of our poets only Byron witnessed the scenes he described), but as the elaboration of a pre-existent model or ideal, elaborated from traditional literature. This model was extremely potent, and obviously answered a fundamental need in the Romantic age. In very general terms, the oriental landscape was necessarily a landscape of distance, in which the impurities and defects of actuality could not be perceived, and which therefore offered no resistance to the dreams of wish fulfilment. It was also an ideal landscape, that is, a landscape of the mind rather than one that was lived in. It should be noted that not even the most authentic sources — the records and narratives of travellers in the Orient — reproduced the perspective of the *native* Arab, for whom, presumably, the act of living in his own environment was no more *special* than for the native Englishman in his. The traveller passed through — to him — unexpected, surprising and strange scenes, and for that very reason the scenes were designed to awaken wonder. Therefore we come to the third general characteristic: that this distant, hence ideal, setting was also specific and particular. The taste was not just for any exoticism, it was for an Islamic one, firmly located in the Levant or the Middle East, and associated with a distinctive civilization.

Each of the poets with whom we are concerned treated this convention in his own way. We have seen something of Landor's harmonious and classical version, still in touch with the composition of a Poussin landscape; we have also noticed Southey's more earnest biblical settings, evocative of nomadic tribes and folk cultures, and tinged with touches of gothic terror as projected by Beckford. Moore's is quite different from these. Take one sample — the opening paragraph of 'The Fire-Worshippers':

'Tis moonlight over Oman's Sea;
Her banks of pearl and palmy isles
Bask in the night-beam beauteously,
And her blue waters sleep in smiles.
'Tis moonlight in Harmozia's walls,
And through her Emir's porphyry halls,
Where, some hours since, was heard the swell
Of trumpet and the clash of zel,

Bidding the bright-eyed sun farewell, —
The peaceful sun, whom better suits
The music of the bulbul's nest,
Or the light touch of lovers' lutes,
To sing him to his golden rest!
All hush'd — there's not a breeze in motion;
The shore is silent as the ocean.
If zephyrs come, so light they come,
Nor leaf is stirr'd nor wave is driven; —
The wind-tower on the Emir's dome
Can hardly win a breath from heaven.
[pp 161–2]

The distancing, idealizing and exotic elements blend effortlessly in this style. First we notice the smoothness, harmony and facility of the versification: the rhymes return with a suave variation; the metre, never less than exactly correct, blends unobtrusively with the shape and movement of the phrases and sentences; the musical effects of alliteration and assonance are handled with consummate ease. A peaceful melodiousness is evoked by 'The music of the bulbul's nest/Or the light touch of lovers' lutes . . .' The gentle repetition of the open vowel in 'music' and 'lutes', or the slight variation in sameness of 'touch' and 'lovers'; or the subtle weave of consonants in 'bulbul', 'light', 'lovers' and 'lutes', all produce a sweetness of texture that reinforces the local meaning, but is also characteristic of Moore's style, whatever it describes. And this confers on the writing as a whole a beauty that is invariably inoffensive and predictable. The exotic note is struck at regular intervals: instead of the more familiar ones ('Oman's Sea', not the 'Persian Gulf', 'Harmoza', not 'Gombaroon'); or the sound effect ('trumpet' tempered by the more unusual 'zel', 'lute' modified by the 'bulbul', or nightingale); but this is never allowed to get out of hand. No intimate, distinctive or surprising fact about the Near East is provided; the Orient flows down the stream of the 'beauteous' natural imagery: the moonlight, the pearls and palms, the blue waters, the recent sunset, the porphyry halls, the silence, the breathlessness. One is not surprised to learn that some of the early readers and reviewers of *Lalla Rookh* thought its extreme atmosphere 'over-sweet'. One reviewer wrote: 'We are so cloyed before we come to the end of Mr Moore's quarto volume, with these stimulating sweets, as to be ready almost to wish ourselves in a garden of leeks and onions to relieve our senses, that we may not 'Die of a rose in aromatic pain!'[32] Some readers went even further. For example, Victor Jacquemont, a naturalist who travelled for the Paris Museum of Natural History, criticized Moore's ecstatic description of the scenery through which had passed Lalla Rookh's cavalcade. 'Thomas Moore is not only a perfumer, but a liar to boot,' he wrote in his *Letters from India*. 'I am now pursuing the same route that Lalla Rookh formerly did; and I have scarcely seen a tree since I left Delhi.'[33] Nor are these reservations confined to the landscape. The reviewer in the *British Review*, for example, returns to the charge thus: '. . . those miserable Turks and Greeks and Persians and Albanians make a figure only in the sickly pages of our Epicurean poets; there is scarcely an individual among them whom an Englishman of cleanly habits could endure by his side.'[34] The racial snobbery of such a remark is evident enough; but it does mark the degree of idealization — of abstraction and removal from realism — implicit in Moore's poetry. Yet it would be unjust to see in Moore's writing nothing but confectionery. Moore is perfectly aware, in the passage under discussion, that the tranquillity of the scene is in ironic contrast with the clash and tension between the native Iranians and the conquering Arabs. Nor is this a point we learn by discovering the context — by reading, for example, the lines that follow the set piece: 'Ev'n he, that tyrant

Arab, sleeps/Calm, while a nation round him weeps . . .' (p 162).

We become aware, as we read, that the apparent harmoniousness of the landscape conceals serious undercurrents. A simple example is the emphasis on the music — the 'swell of trumpet' and the 'clash of zel', which suits the aggression of military conquest, associated with a palace, in contrast with the 'peaceful sun' associated with the country, and with natural music (the song of the nightingale) or at least the music of the arts of peace ('lovers' lutes'). There is even a subtle hint, in the quiet presentation of the sun image ('bright-eyed sun' immediately followed by 'peaceful sun'), that the sun is more significant than it appears. It is a symbol of what is suppressed, or at least denied, in Iran, for the Iranians are sun-worshippers. Even more subtle is the image that closes the description. It is certainly the most interesting of the 'orientalist' details: 'The wind-tower on the EMIR's dome/Can hardly win a breath from heaven' (p 162).

Moore cannot forbear underlining the authenticity of this detail of the tower in a note from de Bruyn: 'At Gombaroon and other places in Persia, they have towers for the purpose of catching the wind, and cooling the houses.'[35] Ironically, it is a superb image of complete atmospheric stillness; but it is also a striking and picturesque evocation of a foreign climate and human adaptation to it. Beyond this, moreover, it calls on an awareness of the tower as a symbol and mark of oriental despotism. (We find the same association of the tower with despotism in *Vathek*.) And finally it suggests, through the emphasis on the word 'heaven', how far its owner and inhabitant, the emir, is removed from the grace and approval of God, despite his claim of the opposite. In fact, from the perspective of the emir's silent and breathless tower we can now read the whole natural description in political terms. The trumpet and the zel have dismissed the sun and fallen silent. The whole atmosphere is living in silence: but it is a *created* silence. The invading army has 'hushed' the scene, and driven into flight the life of liberty. We are witnessing an *imposed* silence. The political passage, describing the subjection of the Iranian people, is no mere novelty, but grows naturally out of what precedes it.

Moore, at his best, uses landscape description as a flexible, suggestive language of morality and politics. But he can also use it to evoke the poignancy of the human condition. The second episode of 'Paradise and the Peri', for example, opens with a description of the Nile paradise. This deploys Moore's usual display of manicured props. The Peri, having had her drop of patriotic blood rejected, goes in quest of a yet more precious object, and finds herself near 'Afric's Lunar Mountains' (the Mountains of the Moon are in modern Uganda, not in Abyssinia — though Moore's mistake could not have been easily detected at the time), near 'the spring of the new born Giant' (the Nile river or 'that Egyptian tide') deep in 'solitary woods'. She then restlessly visits the famous ruins of the 'sepulchres of Kings' and 'warm Rosetta's vale' echoing with dove calls, where she finds moonlight upon the wings of pelicans on Lake Moeris, 'fruits of gold' (oranges) in abundance, date trees (compared to languid maids drooping into their beds), the lapwing flitting through 'ruin'd shrines and towers', and the 'purple-winged Sultanas' sitting on a column. But again, by an uncomplicated irony, this is the landscape of disease and death: the 'Demon of the Plague' is infesting the region, more destructive than the 'desert Simoom'. Unlike Southey, who also took his account of the simoom from Bruce, Moore does not evoke this awe-inspiring phenomenon for its own sake, but to illustrate the devastating effect of the plague. Similarly, he draws on the accounts provided by Jackson and Bruce of oriental plagues and hyenas, partly to define the Orient, but mostly to give flesh to his moral conception. The heaps of corpses are so foul that they sicken vultures and only attract the 'blue-eyed' hyenas. The Peri recognizes a fallen world, and an original sin more Christian than Islamic:

> 'Poor race of men!' said the pitying Spirit,
> 'Dearly ye pay for your primal Fall —
> Some flow'rets of Eden ye still inherit,
> But the trail of the Serpent is over them all!'
> [p 133]

The harmonious beauty of the landscape is therefore profoundly flawed; its growth and fertility are diverted to destructive and corrupting ends; the plague is not merely a *negation* of the landscape, but a perversion of it. The youth sickens and dies, not because of any transgression on his part, but because of the damage suffered by nature — that is, by the very condition of life. Yet the original Eden is not wholly lost. The maiden who loves the dying youth, his 'betrothed bride', is herself an agent of health and beauty ('a young envoy sent by Health'); and her natural impulse to cherish him in his last moments prompts her to expose herself to the deadly infection. And although she, too, dies (her expiring sigh being collected by the questing Peri), one feels that, through her voluntary act, the original landscape achieves a kind of victory over its perverted condition.

The idea of true love as the manifestation of redemptive or uncorrupted nature is, as the final section of this chapter describes in more detail, the central theme of *Lalla Rookh.* It triumphs, too, in 'The Veiled Prophet' — though there nature itself is manipulated and corrupted by the evil powers of Mokanna. The gardens of the tyrant have all the beauty of the Nile paradise, except that their attraction is deliberately deployed to seduce and subject Azim. As in *Thalaba*, it is an *artificial* paradise, a theatre set in which all the arts of sexual seduction are exhibited, as the scene moves from outdoors and the park to indoors and the chamber, and from music and dance to voluptuous shows and puzzling pictures. But what saves Azim in this corruption deadlier even than the Egyptian plague is not nature as female beauty, but fallen nature in the form of the ravaged Zelica, who heroically renounces her lover so as to keep him whole and pure. Thus, even in its corrupted version (Zelica in the service of Mokanna), true love may achieve a redemptive function.

In such depictions of oriental landscape and climate, the Romantic poets in general, and Moore in particular, were faithful to a generalized account, halfway between an artificial convention and the actual reports of European travellers. In other words, these oriental scenes had enough local colour to convey some of the flavour of Islamic life, but were too undifferentiated and unspecified to become realistic. When literary material is in this intermediary state, it becomes malleable to the author's deeper values, political or moral, and easily turns into a symbolic code. For all the poets we are dealing with, their generalized view of the Orient offers them a simplified alternative to the unsatisfactory complexities of European life. In the case of Moore, oriental landscape becomes symbolic of the true values of life in that it contrasts with the artificial setting of the city and the palace. In short, it forms a new language, as it were, to express that romantic primitivism that was once and for all made fashionable by Rousseau in his rejection of the insincerity of the salon in favour of the simplicity of the chalet.

Two examples of this elementary codification will suffice to make clear what is involved. The first is 'The Fire-Worshippers', which has a political orientation close to Moore's heart. In this poem it is obvious that he associates the cities of the plain with Arabic tyranny, and the mountains of Persia with the pride and independence of Iran. (Other earlier Romantics located the untamable spirit of national liberty in the Scottish Highlands or the Swiss Alps.) The expressive power of mountains is, for Moore, such that he alters geography to suit his own purposes. He confesses in his note that the mountain stronghold of the Ghebers is his own creation, for the '"stupendous chain"... does not extend quite so far as the shores of the Persian Gulf', according to the information provided by Kinnier's *Persian Empire*, but 'form the boundary of the Persian and Turkish empires. It runs parallel to the river Tigris and Persian Gulf, almost disappearing in the vicinity of Gombaroon.'[36] In the poem, however, 'A rocky mountain, o'er the sea/Of Oman beetling awfully' constitutes an essential part of the theme at hand:

A last and solitary link
Of those stupendous chains that reach
From the broad Caspian's reedy brink
Down winding to the Green Sea beach.
Around its base the bare rocks stood,
Like naked giants, in the flood,
As if to guard the Gulf across;
While, on its peak, that braved the sky,
A ruin'd Temple, tower'd, so high
That oft the sleeping albatross
Struck the wild ruins with her wing,
And from her cloud-rock'd slumbering
Started — to find man's dwelling there
In her own silent fields of air!

[p 194]

Beneath this great peak, deep caverns are invaded by the 'stormy wave'; and the whole landscape is so frightening that the 'bold' among the Arabs regard it with superstitious terror. But here we need to realize that it is not the reader who is meant to experience the fear (unlike the case of *Vathek*, which is designed to thrill and appal); rather is the reader gradually made aware, as we have seen, that the fearful prejudice that turns human beings into monsters is an ideological construct. The dwellers of these mountains are human beings in the full sense. If the passage does convey a sense of supernature within nature, it is essentially because of the human qualities these rugged retreats symbolize. These mountains — the 'towers sublime', rising above a 'deep and wizard glen' — embody an elemental nature which finds an echo in the elemental thirst for independence that has taken possession of the Ghebers. Moreover, it is a *defiant* virtue, as implacably resistant to invaders as the natural obstacles themselves. The tradition of gothic landscape has been put to the service of a recognizable, indeed admirable collective human passion. But this passion is not merely political. The descriptive set piece continues:

No eye could pierce the void between:
It seem'd a place where Gholes might come
With their foul banquets from the tomb,
And in its caverns feed unseen.
Like distant thunder, from below,
The sound of many torrents came;
Too deep for eye or ear to know
If 'twere the sea's imprison'd flow,
Or floods of ever-restless flame.
For, each ravine, each rocky spire
Of that vast mountain stood on fire . . .
[pp 195–6]

The contrast between the height of the peaks and the depth of the glens creates a landscape of such extremes that one might be tempted to imagine it as the residence of 'Gholes'. It might have *seemed* such a place, but it was obviously not the home of corpse-eating fiends. Here one form of orientalism is rejected in favour of a more historical one: the fact (as accepted by Moore) that the Ghebers built their temples over subterranean fires:

Still did the mighty flame burn on
Through chance and change, through good and ill,
Like its own God's eternal will,
Deep, constant, bright, unquenchable!
[p 196]

In short, the landscape literally bears within itself a *religious* revelation in symphony with itself. Gothic melodrama expresses, in the final analysis, the romantic pantheism always lurking beneath the depictions of the natural sublime in the poetry of the time. The landscape gives considerable complexity to what would otherwise be political and religious commonplaces.

The second example of landscape as code is shown, in a simpler and more straightforward style, in the modest final poem of *Lalla Rookh*, 'The Light of the Haram'. Here again we encounter the association of true value (in this case, true love) with pastoral landscape, as against urban and princely magnificence. The Georgian maiden's song in favour of sensual pleasure is challenged by the masked Arabian maid's lyric:

'Fly to the desert, fly with me,
Our Arab tents are rude for thee;
But, oh! the choice what heart can doubt,
Of tents with love, or thrones without?'
[p 313]

She evokes the wilderness in images that are given a piquant new slant by the use of oriental imagery: if the rocks are rough, the yellow acacia flowers there; if the sands are bare, the silvery-footed antelope acts as the courtier. This is the true context for a lover based on faithful reciprocity. Thus the three main themes of *Lalla Rookh,* as adumbrated in 'Paradise and the Peri' — patriotism, love, religion — all find their deepest expression in the language of oriental landscape.

Orientalism and Ambiguity

This chapter has placed some emphasis on Moore's deployment of oriental material in variously ambiguous ways. I conclude by arguing that he felt ambiguously towards Islam itself, and that he built this ambiguity into the framework of his narrative.

The ambiguities of Moore's attitude to Islam may be brought out most vividly by contrasting the Muslim satrap Al Hassan in 'The Fire-Worshippers' with the unnamed warrior who is the main figure of the concluding episode of 'Paradise and the Peri'. Al Hassan, of course, is a tyrant, as such figures often are in the western imagination. In the tales of Byron and, more particularly, Shelley, the extremism of oriental tyranny is such that human characteristics are virtually ruled out of the characterization. In Shelley's *The Revolt of Islam,* for example, Sultan is a sadist and an absolute tyrant. Moore's tyranny, in contrast to theirs, receives broader and more realistic treatment — no doubt because, as an Irishman, his view of tyranny was better informed than that of the two liberal English aristocrats. So Moore makes us imagine Al Hassan's domestic life and arrangements, particularly in his relation to his daughter.

But what is most striking about Al Hassan is that his tyranny arises out of his religious fanaticism. He and his army are described as a 'murderous brood' whose 'saintliness' makes them all the more ruthless and terrifying. They regard their invasion of Iran as a holy war, justified by the Koran; and they believe that 'through unbelievers' blood/Lies their directest paths to heaven.' The following passage develops this idea with some subtlety; Al Hassan is described thus:

One, who will pause and kneel unshod
In the warm blood his hand hath pour'd,
To mutter o'er some text of God
Engraven on his reeking sword; —
Nay, who can coolly note the line,
The letter of those words divine,
To which his blade, with searching art,
Had sunk into its victim's heart!
[pp 162–3]

These lines strikingly evoke the spiritual joy (which Moore regards as perverted) to be found in holy killing. The blood Al Hassan spills is no reason for divine pity, but an expression of divine vengeance declared by the divine text inscribed in the blade of the sword, thus justifying the act of killing; the 'truth' is therefore literally driven into the unbeliever's heart. To be sure, Moore follows this frightful passage with a comment that suggests that Al Hassan is distorting (though not necessarily hypocritically) the ethics of the Koran, and that the true God will ultimately turn His judgement on him:

Just Alla! What must be thy look,
When such a wretch before thee stands
Unblushing, with thy Sacred Book, —
Turning the leaves with blood-stain'd hands,
The wresting from its page sublime
His creed of lust, and hate, and crime?
Ev'n as those bees of Trebizond, —
Which, from the sunniest flowers that glad

With their pure smile the gardens round,
Draw venom forth that drives men mad!
[p 163]

There is a strong implication here that the Koran is a sacred book on a level with the Bible; and that the extraction (with its implications of 'forced reading') of militaristic bloodshed as a virtue from 'its page sublime' is a perversion. But the concluding image drawn from Tournefort, of the Trebizond bee drawing from the 'sunniest flowers' venom to madden men, does not help matters; for if the 'sublime pages' are presented by those flowers, then they can nourish the viciousness of the wicked quite as easily as the virtue of the good. For Moore, Islam, like any other creed, can be both a sublime religion and a ruthless faith. The argument that it was the Irish content of Moore's allegory that drove him to this ambiguity is unconvincing. The identification of Al Hassan with that opponent of Catholic emancipation, George III, is not precise, especially given the British king's character and state of mind at the time; if there is any analogy, it is only of the most general kind. Islam is not a cipher for Christianity, where Moore, given his own views, would be *forced* to regard holy killing as perverted hypocrisy; it generates and contains its own ambiguities.

If Al Hassan underlines one side of the ambiguity, the 'unnamed warrior' brings out the other. This warrior is not a fanatical zealot like Al Hassan; but he has believed in analogous ways, if at a personal level, for, like the Byronic hero, in his eye can be read

Dark tales of many a ruthless deed;
The ruin'd maid — the shrine profan'd —
Oaths broken — and the threshold stain'd
With blood of guests! — *there* written, all,
Black as the damning drops that fall

From the denouncing Angel's pen,
Ere Mercy weeps them out again!
[p 144]

So his conversion to the innocent virtues of 'Mercy', 'Pity', 'Peace' and 'Love', which the sight of the guileless purity of the child brings about, can be regarded as representing the shift from the Koran as 'bloodshed manual' to the Koran as 'book of love'. To see the extent of this turn, we have to regard the boy as an embodiment of a most beautiful and peaceful natural landscape Moore ever imagined — a version, in fact, of that unfallen Eden or paradise associated with 'Syria's land of roses' and 'sainted Lebanon', the 'unclouded skies of Peristan' and the 'wild bees of Palestine' (p 141).

. . . a child at play,
Among the rosy wild flowers singing,
As rosy and as wild as they . . .
[p 143]

The boy's 'unclouded, joyous gaze' meets the 'lurid glance' of the 'unnamed warrior' without a tracc of impurity. And at that moment evening falls:

But, hark! the vesper call to prayer,
As slow the orb of day-light sets,
Is rising slowly on the air,
From Syria's thousand minarets!
The boy has started from the bed
Of flowers, where he had laid his head,
And down upon the fragrant sod
Kneels, with his forehead to the south,
Lisping the' eternal name of God
From purity's own cherub mouth,
And looking, while his hands and eyes

Are lifted to the glowing skies,
Like a stray babe of Paradise,
Just lighted on that flowery plain,
And seeking for its home again!
On, 'twas a sight — that Heav'n — that child —
A scene, which might have well beguil'd
E'en haughty Eblis of a sigh
For glories lost and peace gone by!
[p 145]

The feeling of this passage is Islamic, but again in a generalized way. The whole landscape, as the sun sets, exhales its prayer upwards, like rising fragrance. The child kneeling among the flowers is only the focus of a process that wholly reconciles heaven and earth, ritual ('minarets') and spontaneity ('lisping'), in a typically Romantic vision of redeemed or prelapsarian nature. In Moore, Islam draws its substance less from the Koran than from the image of the Near Orient as a pastoral paradise, the original side of Eden. *Purity*, a general virtue, and not a doctrine or an ethic, is the keynote. But this note is sounded in a standard motif of orientalism — the image, as common in painting as in literature, of the oriental dusk, the Muslim fall of day. In *Thalaba*, we encounter Southey's incorporation of Bruce's beautiful depiction of the Muslim ritual sunset prayer. In *Lalla Rookh*, Moore elaborates it in terms that reflect with great exactitude the details of Islamic piety (the call to prayer from the minarets, the kneeling with the forehead 'upon the fragrant sod', and towards the south — i.e. Mecca). His orientalism is more precise than Southey's or Landor's, or even Byron's, but it derives its vitality from the same set of conventions.

As a religion, Islam's appeal to Moore and the other Romantics was in its universality and pantheism. The 'unnamed warrior' weeps for the loss of innocence; the 'warm, meek' tear that flows down his cheek in the glow of sunset, is finally bathed in a light more lovely 'than ever came from sun or star', for it gains the Peri admission to paradise. The Peri then compares this tear to the *Nukta*, or 'the miraculous Drop which falls in Egypt precisely in St John's Day, in June, and is supposed to have the effect of stopping the Plague'.[37]

> '. . . Oh! is it not thus, thou man of sin,
> The precious tear of repentance fall?
> Though foul thy fiery plagues within,
> One heavenly drop hath dispell'd them all!'
>
> [p 146]

The emphasis on *penitence* is Islamic orthodoxy; but the redemption it carries, that is, the recovery of natural piety and natural purity, is essentially Romantic.

Although ostensibly, then, Moore contrasts genuine or holy Islamic faith from perverted superstition, the fact remains that the depiction of the positive aspect does not wholly make up or balance the negative aspect, and his attitude to the ideology of the Orient, so to speak, remains ambiguous. The local or specific ambiguities we have noticed in the course of this chapter are then caught up in a more general ambiguity, which is, in its turn, reproduced in the celebrated formal device which proved controversial when the work was first published: the narrative prose frame to the four poems which gives its name — 'Lalla Rookh' — to the whole.

Inspired, no doubt, by the example of *The Arabian Nights*, Moore devised a framework of explanation and commentary to the poetic narratives. In this the actual telling or singing of the stories plays an active part in advancing the plot. The prose narrative concerns the journey of an Indian princess, Lalla Rookh, daughter of Arungzebe, from Delhi to Cashmere, where she is to be wedded, by parental arrangement, to the son of Abdalla, King of Bucharia. This matrimonial trip, described stage by stage, through varying landscapes, is made more interesting by the recitals of a very handsome young poet, Feramorz, and by the criticism of her most conceited chamberlain, Fadladeen, who fancies his own literary judgement and erudition.

At an elementary level, the narrative frame exists to motivate the telling of the stories. Thus 'The Veiled Prophet' is told to entertain the bored princess; 'Paradise and the Peri' likewise, though 'in a lighter and humbler strain'. The narrative of 'The Fire-Worshippers' is prompted by the tower of a ruined fire-temple seen on the journey, and the 'Light of the Haram' by the fact that it concerns the Sultana Nourmahal of the Royal Gardens which the travellers have reached. But these are very modest devices. The real function of the framing narrative is to record two opposing responses to Feramorz's — and Moore's — poetry.

The first of these responses is the Chief Nazir Fadladeen's, whose role is to puncture the mood of hothouse lyricism generated by the poetry of the orient, and to dispel its historic claims and affirmations. He is surely not impressed by 'The Veiled Prophet', and produces a comically reductive summary of it (p117):

> The chief personages of the story were, if he rightly understood them, an ill-favoured gentleman, with a veil over his face — a young lady, whose reason went and came, according as it suited the poet's convenience to be sensible or otherwise; and a youth in one of those hideous Bucharian bonnets, who took the aforesaid gentleman in a veil for a Divinity. 'From such materials,' said he, 'what can be expected? — after rivalling each other in long speeches and absurdities, through some thousands of lines as indigestible as the filberts of

> Berdaa, our friend in the veil jumps into a tub of aquafortis; the young lady dies in a set speech, whose only recommendation is that it is her last; and the lover lives on to a good old age, for the laudable purpose of seeing her ghost, which he at last happily accomplishes and expires . . .'

We delight in this sort of writing because of its skill as a pastiche of untalented and pedantic criticism; but it is much more than that. We respond to its *validity*, not merely its *absurdity*. It represents a *possible* reaction to Feramorz's unremitting intensities, and affords the reader some badly needed comic relief. Fadladeen's attack on the versification (on Moore's famed metrical fluency) has a much cruder effect: if it 'appeared to him, in the uneasy heaviness of its movements, to have been modelled upon the gait of a very tired dromedary' (p 118), he is, needless to say, plain wrong, even if the epithet 'very tired' may strike home in that Moore freely confessed that his inspiration flagged when he was writing *Lalla Rookh*.

Fadladeen's criticism of the other three poems is in the same vein. Of the lighter 'Paradise and the Peri', he exclaims: 'And this . . . is poetry! this flimsy manufacture of the brain . . . The lax and easy kind of metre in which it was written ought to be denounced . . . as one of the leading causes of the alarming growth of poetry in our times' (p 149). Again, despite its patent absurdity, this offers us the release of an alternative perspective. 'The Light of the Haram' he labels as 'a rapid dream', which might easily represent the verdict of certain moods in the reader. His scorn for 'The Fire-Worshippers', however, is less telling, for Moore is more seriously committed to the political theme. (Ironically, Francis Jeffrey, whom Fadladeen is meant to represent — or intimidate, as it were — did not condemn, but applauded the political spirit of the poem in the review already cited.) Fadladeen adopts the stance of the political censor (in terms of the political allegory, the stance of the authoritarian 'English' official convinced that any political idea produced in Ireland is an abomination needing to be stamped out). His plot to report Feramorz to her future husband at the journey's end is, of course, overturned by the discovery of the true identity of Lalla Rookh's anonymous poet; and he becomes the victim of comic, or even farcical, justice. But despite the loss of face, the comic irreverence he has introduced remains alive, and presents a surprising and refreshing new perspective.

There are, however, two critics, not one, in this frame narrative, and *two* 'readings' of the poem. The second critic is, of course, Lalla Rookh herself. Hers is the criticism of the heart, and her response is warm and spontaneous. To her, the poetry she hears is the sincere expression of the poet's feelings. She is the Romantic critic as opposed to the sterile Augustan know-all, and her literary judgement declares itself in the most telling way possible — she falls in love with the poetry and the poet. Brought up in a society in which the poet is a paid domestic, she pays no attention to the entrance of Feramorz into her father's hall until she sees his Krishna-like beauty, and above all, until she hears him speak. 'She now, for the first time, felt that shade of melancholy, which comes over the youthful maiden's heart, as sweet and transient as her own breath upon a mirror' (p 78). This she feels after witnessing a girl on a river bank sending downstream floating lamps which seem symbolic of human transience. Her sense of the world has become poetical: but that is because she has fallen for a poet. Her defence of Feramorz against Fadladeen's strictures reflects the same emphasis: 'In short,' she declares, 'it is quite cruel that a poet cannot wander through his region of enchantment, without having a critic for ever, like the Old Man of the Sea, upon his back!' (p 121). Her criticism dispenses with criticism. After hearing 'Paradise and the Peri', she is so hopelessly in love that she resolves to have nothing more to do with her poet. But circumstances conspire against her, and she finds herself listening to 'The Fire-Worshippers', a story of tragic separation between lovers who embody her own feelings, for her approach to Cashmere must sunder her permanently from all hopes of happiness. 'The time was now fast approaching when she must see him no longer, — or see him with eyes whose every look belonged to another; and there was a melancholy preciousness in these last moments, which made her heart cling to them as it would to life' (p 274). This repeats, at a more natural level, the heroic suffering of the tale she has just heard. And then, finally, she hears 'The Light of the Haram' with its defence and definition of true, as against epicurean, love, and with its covert promise of better things in its story of the reconcilement of a lovers' quarrel. And, as every reader must have guessed, the promise is fulfilled, for Feramorz turns out to be the chosen husband waiting for her on the throne of Bucharia.

This conclusion might be seen as a complete vindication of the sort of criticism — and the conception of poetry — represented by *Lalla Rookh*, and, by the same token, of the idealized orientalism which the four narratives, each in its own way, plainly endorse. But if that is all there were to Moore in *Lalla Rookh*, the poem would be a much more conventional, limited and unintelligent work. But *Lalla Rookh* is improved by the fact that the disrespectful voice of an alternative criticism is not silenced, and that the Islam that remains threatening or fanatical to Christian prejudices is not flushed out of the text, but continues to offer resistance to conventional sentimentality and exercise a secret appeal to Romantic realism. In a word, *Lalla Rookh* is saved by its ambiguity.

Chapter 4

Byron's 'Turkish Tales' and Realistic Orientalism

QUESTIONS of genius aside, there is one crucial element that distinguishes Byron from the other Romantic narrative poets who are the subject of this study — the fact that he had direct experience of the Orient. The experience of his travels to Albania, Greece and Turkey, which were the ultimate destination of his 'grand tour' (2 July 1809 to 14 July 1811), cannot be exaggerated, both for what they contributed to his general outlook, and for their influence on the so-called 'Turkish Tales' that will, with the relevant parts of Canto II of *Childe Harold's Pilgrimage*, largely written during the tour itself, form the material of this chapter. These include *The Giaour* (May 1813), *The Bride of Abydos* (December 1813), *The Corsair* (February 1814), *Lara* (August 1814; though not set in the orient, it is included because of its connection with *The Corsair*), and *The Siege of Corinth* (January 1816).

It would be wrong, however, to assume that Byron escaped the effects of literary orientalism, and went to Athens and Constantinople with a mind empty of conceptions and attitudes towards Islamic life. As a boy, he had been the full beneficiary of a classical education, which was to have profound effects on his view of Greece. But he had also started to read early in orientalist literature proper — a fact for which we have his own testimony. Isaac Disraeli quotes him as saying:

> Knolles — Cantemir — De Tott — Lady M. W. Montagu — Hawkins's translation from Mignot's History of The Turks — the Arabian Nights — All travels or histories or books upon the East I could meet with, I had read, as well as Rycaut, before I was *ten years of old*. I think The Arabian Nights first.[1]

Even if Byron is exaggerating his precociousness, the range and depth of his reading cannot be doubted. To this evidence may be added an entry from a memorandum book, quoted by Moore and attributed by him to 1807:

> I have read Knolles, Sir Paul Rycaut, and Prince Cantemir, besides a more modern history, anonymous. Of the Ottoman history I know every event, from Tangralopi and afterwards Othman I. to the peace of Passarwitz, in 1718, — the battle of Cutzka, in 1739, and the treaty between Russia and Turkey in 1750.[2]

Byron's reading in this material has been repeatedly examined by scholars, including S. C. Chew, W. C. Brown and H. S. C. Wiener.[3] To these should be added Bernard Blackstone for his remarkable study, 'Byron and Islam: the triple Eros'.[4]

Blackstone usefully reminds us that Persian poetry in translation was available to Byron — notably a number of translations of Hafiz before 1807, and Stephen Weston's *Specimens of Persian Poetry* (1805), which seems to have been widely known. It seems difficult to believe, however, that Byron could have read Paul Rycaut's *The Present State of the Ottoman Empire* (1668) before the age of 10, even though Rycaut was something of a sensationalist, whose accurate observations of Turkish society and politics were laced with exotic accounts of sex and violence. Blackstone makes an elaborate and rather strained, but not wholly implausible, case for the influence of Stephen Weston's *Moral Aphorisms in Arabic, and a Persian Commentary in Verse, translated from the Originals, with Specimens of Persian Poetry* (1805), which Byron is alleged to have read on his arrival at Trinity, perhaps on the advice of E. D. Clarke (the Cambridge orientalist and author of six volumes of *Eastern Travels*, published 1810–23, which allegedly opened Byron's eyes to the virtues of 'pagan' love. More generally, the influence on the 'Turkish Tales' of George Sale's translation of the Koran (1734), which, he once stated, 'contained the most sublime poetry',[5] is very well known, as is that of the now familiar Sir William Jones, d'Herbelot's *Bibliothèque orientale*, Richard Knolles's *General Historie of the Turkes*, Beckford's *Vathek* (and especially Henley's notes) and Jonathan Scott's elaborate introduction to *The Arabian Nights*.

There is little point in dwelling on the subject of Byron's debt to travellers in the Near Orient, a subject that has been thoroughly investigated, but we may pause briefly over Byron's relationship with Lady Mary Wortley Montagu, who certainly coloured Byron's perception of the Near East. In his letter to his mother of 28 June 1810, from Constantinople, Byron takes Lady Mary to task in general terms: 'by the bye, her Ladyship, as far as I can judge, has lied, but not half so much as any other woman could have done in the same situation.'[6] And he reproves her later (by mistake she had compared St Paul's to the New Mosque, not Santa Sophia): 'Of Constantinople you will find many correct descriptions in different travels, but Lady Mary errs strangely when she says "St Paul's would cut a figure by St Sophia".'[7] We see here an ample example, even if misguided, of Byron's passion for correcting misconceptions about the East.

But this wish to check word against thing presupposes that he has absorbed the literature he is testing in this way. In any event, such a desire to dispel misinformation and prejudice he would have learnt from Lady Mary herself. Her famous and fascinating letters from Turkey express a strong tendency to correct error and to represent the positive side of Turkish life, culture and religion. She repeatedly expressed contempt towards her predecessors, travellers who lacked objectivity and impartiality, and who complacently regarded themselves as 'qualify'd to give exact accounts of the Customs, Policys and Interests of the Dominions they have gone through post, when a very long stay, a diligent Enquiry, and a nice observation are requisite even to a moderate degree of knowing a Foreign Country, especially here, where they are naturally very reserv'd'.[8] In this quality of open-minded attention to cultures other than her own, Lady Mary undoubtedly anticipated Byron, who, as we see from his praise of her, admired her for her daring and almost Romantic openness. She herself praised it in others. When, for example, she met the 'fair' Fatima, she was impressed by her curiosity 'after the manners of other countries and has not the partiality for her own, so common to little minds'.[9]

There was one area of Turkish life about which Lady Mary would have had privileged information not directly available to Byron. Of all the travellers who wrote about Turkey, she was the only one to have had access to Turkish harems, which, of course, provided her with a wealth of information about Muslim women. Indeed, the subject of women occupied a major portion of her letters home. Her main objectives are different from those of other travellers: veracity and truth. Her motto in these letters, 'nothing seems to me so agreeable as truth',[10] must have impressed the young poet whose later correspondence from Greece and Turkey establishes beyond doubt his zeal for the same truth, which he preferred to call 'costume'. Returning to her theme of veracity in travellers, for example, Lady Mary writes:

> They never fail give you an Account of the Women, which 'tis certain they never saw, and talking very wisely of the Genius of the Men, into whose Company they are never admitted, and very often describe Mosques, which they dare not peep into. The Turks are very proud, and will not converse with a Stranger they are not assur'd is considerable in his own Country. I speak of the Men of Distinction, for as to Ordinary Fellows, you may imagine what ideas their Conversation can give of the general Genius of the people.[11]

In particular, she sought to combat the idea that Muslim women were more enslaved by men in the Islamic East than in the Christian West. Admittedly, she seems to have limited herself to visiting ladies and wives of high-ranking officials. But these seemed no less free, and in certain respects freer, than Englishwomen of her own rank. Reporting a conversation with a Turkish scholar, Ali Bey, she writes sardonically, even facetiously: 'I have frequent disputes with him concerning the difference of our Customs, particularly the confinement of Women. He assures me there is nothing at all in it; only, says he, we have the advantage that when our Wives cheat us, no body knows it.'[12]

What is most striking about Lady Mary's response to oriental women is her own freedom from conventional prudery and hypocrisy. Her account of a visit to Fatima, the kahya's lady, for example, is an implicit condemnation of English narrow-mindedness and puritanism which would have had an enormous appeal to Byron. It requires a sustained quotation to savour the full effect of her emotional independence:

> I was met at the door by 2 black Eunuchs who led me through a long Gallery between 2 ranks of beautiful young Girls with their Hair finely plaited almost hanging to their feet, all dress'd in fine light damasks brocaded with silver. I was sorry that Decency did not permit me to stop to consider them nearer, but that Thought was lost upon my Entrance into a Large room, or rather Pavilion, built round with gilded sashes which were most of 'em thrown up; and the Trees planted near them gave an agreeable Shade which hinder'd the Sun from being troublesome, the Jess'mins and Honey suckles . . . encreas'd by a white Marble fountain playing sweet Water in the Lower part of the room . . . Her fair Maids were rang'd below the Sofa to the number of 20, and put me in Mind of the pictures of the ancient Nymphs. I did not think all Nature could have furnish'd such a scene of Beauty. She made them a sign to play and dance . . . Nothing could be more artful or more proper to raise certain Ideas, the Tunes so soft, the motions so Languishing, accompany'd with pauses and dying Eyes, halfe falling back and then recovering themselves in so artful a Manner that I am very positive the coldest and most rigid Prude upon Earth could not have look'd upon them without thinking of something not to be spoke of.[13]

There can be no doubt that this combination of exoticism with ambiguous, often naive, hedonism; of irreverence, the wish to shock the conventional; and realism, the attempt to strike a blow against idealistic pretence, would have held the strongest possible attraction for Byron.

Finding also in her the example of a truth teller, he would have followed it partly because the truth matters, whatever it be, but especially because the *truth of the Orient* was precisely what English ethics would ignore or misrepresent. Most of all, Byron, like Lady Mary, was offended by the English *complacency* that felt London to be the centre of the world. We need take only two examples, both suggesting less that Islam is right than that Christianity is wrong to regard itself as superior to other religions.

The first is a note in *The Giaour* where the poem alludes to the alleged Islamic 'creed' concerning the soullessness of women:

Oh! who young Leila's glance could read
And keep that portion of his creed
Which saith that woman is but dust,
A soulless toy for tyrant's lust?
[lines 487–90][14]

The soul of Leila 'beamed forth' so plainly from her gaze that the doctrine of the soullessness of women would not be credited. Byron, however, says in his note that this idea is 'a vulgar error: the Koran allots at least a third of paradise to well-behaved women; but by far the greater number of Mussulmans interpret of their own way, and exclude their moieties from heaven'.[15] Byron would certainly have found in Sale's 'Preliminary Discourse' to his edition of the Koran the observation 'that there are several passages in the Koran which affirm that women, in the next life, will not only be punished for their evil actions, but will also receive the rewards of their good deeds . . . and that in this case God will make no distinction of sexes'.[16] In support of this, the following text can be cited from the Koran: 'God has promised to believers, men and women, gardens beneath which rivers flow, to dwell therein for aye; and goodly places in the gardens of Eden.'[17] In a later reference to the immortality of women's souls, Byron quite naturally expresses the informed view. Of Zuleika in *The Bride of Abydos* he writes:

> And oft her Koran conned apart;
> And oft in youthful reverie
> She dream'd what Paradise might be —
> Where woman's parted soul shall go
> Her Prophet had disdain'd to show.
> [II, lines 103–7]

This passage relies on many popular Islamic sources and western commentaries which interpreted Muhammad's reluctance to promise women what he had promised to their men as a device to avoid arousing the latters' jealousy. The existence of the female soul is not denied, though its *exact* destination is unknown. But the aspect for us to note is that Byron's commitment to Islamic accuracy, or his hostility to English inaccuracy, is so strong that even when his poetry scores a legitimate dramatic effect, he feels the need to point out that this effect is based on a mistaken notion.

The second example is no more than a reminder of Byron's explicit principles in this respect. In his correspondence with his publisher, John Murray, Byron frequently asks him to check or confirm facts. 'Look out in the Encyclopedia article *Mecca* whether it is there or at *Medina* the Prophet is entombed,' he wrote to Murray.[18] The next day he wrote again:

> Did you look out? is it *Medina* or *Mecca* that contains the *holy* sepulchre? — don't make me blaspheme by

> your negligence — I have no book of reference or I would save you the trouble. I *blush* as a good Mussulman to have confused the point.[19]

On more than one occasion he finds himself getting impatient with Murray's prejudices. Once, when Murray apparently cast doubt on an existing link between Islam and the Bible, Byron referred him to such authorities as Jones and d'Herbelot, and Henley in his notes to *Vathek*.[20] He repeated the caution in another letter:

> I send you a note for the *ignorant*, but I really wonder at finding *you* among them — I don't care one lump of Sugar for my *poetry* — but for my *costume*, and my *correctness* on those points (of which I think the *funeral* was a proof) I will combat lustily.[21]

We shall have reason to return to this notion of 'costume'. For the moment we know enough to see that the criteria of truth from reading, and of truth from experience, cannot be taken independently of each other, for the ideal of accuracy and respect of foreign cultures was one that Byron had learnt from his reading, not least from Lady Mary Wortley Montagu's correspondence.

Byron's Voyage

Given our relative ignorance of what Byron really did during his tour of Greece and Turkey, especially after his companion Hobhouse's return to England, it would be easy to decline to assess how far actual experiences and adventures provided the material of the 'Turkish Tales'. It seems clear that *The Giaour*, for one, was based on an incident in which Byron was perhaps more personally involved than even the highly coloured account of Lord Sligo (one of Byron's friends from Cambridge) suggested.

Lord Sligo, arriving in Athens in Byron's absence, discovered that Byron had successfully saved the life of a young woman on the way to execution for adultery (by drowning in a sack). Byron acknowledged, with some embarrassment, his friend's report, notably in a letter to Professor E. D. Clarke, in which he wrote that 'the Athenian account of our adventure (a personal one) which certainly first suggested to me the story of the Giaour . . . is not very far from the truth'.[22] It is also possible that *The Bride of Abydos* was inspired by personal adventure in the East. 'I had a living character on my eye for Zuleika,' he wrote to John Galt.[23] More significantly, in his journal entry of 14 November 1813, he refers to '*Zuleika*' (i.e. *The Bride of Abydos*):

> but what a romance could equal the events —
>
> 'quæque ipse . . . vidi,
> Et quorum pars magna fui.'
>
> (I myself saw these things . . . and I bore great part in them).[24]

It is also possible that the character of Seyd in *The Corsair* was inspired, like the figure of Giaffir in *The Bride of Abydos*, by Byron's meeting with Ali Pasha, who had made himself absolute ruler of Albania and western Greece. He would also certainly have heard of the exploits of such pirates as Lambro Katzones, which would have served to suggest the atmosphere of Conrad's island refuge. As for *The Siege of Corinth*, it was based on an episode in the wars between the Ottoman Empire and the West that took place in 1715, and which Byron could have picked up orally during his sojourn in the Orient (he visited Corinth in 1810), for there was no account in print until 1856 (in Finlay's history of Greece). A Turkish army of 70,000 men overwhelmed the contingent of 600 Venetians defending the city, and massacred them after a magazine full of ammunition exploded. Thus it seems as if these apparently imaginative tales do have a foundation of fact; though much more important, of course, is the local colour which Byron was able to apply with great effect as a result of his prolonged stay in the region (and to which a separate section is devoted below).

More significant for our purpose than external events and incidents must be the question of Byron's contact with and interest in the religion of Islam itself. In his paper[25] Blackstone argues vigorously, and with considerable detail (much of which is speculative), in favour of a much deeper involvement on Byron's part than has hitherto been accepted. The fundamental question was posed by no less a figure than Annabella, Lady Byron, herself, when she wrote:

> He often spoke of a mysterious necessity for his return to the East, and vindicated the Turks with a spirit of nationality, admiring above all their complete predestinarianism. He would say "The East — ah, there it is," . . . and he has two or three times intimated to me that he abjured his religion there. In the autumn in London, he said with a shudder of conscious remembrance, "I was very *near* becoming a Mussulman." He preferred the Turkish opinions, manners & dress in all respects to ours. This idea of his conversion to their faith having occurred to me at Halnaby, derived some confirmation from his composing at Seaham that part of the Siege of Corinth which relates to Alp's assumption of the Turban . . .[26]

It would obviously be quite wrong to deduce from those remarks that Byron had undergone a conversion to Islam, especially in the light of his declaration in 1818, reported by Isaac Disraeli, that he 'often thought of turning Mussulman while in Turkey, and regretted *not having done so*'.[27] Yet this testimony of sympathy, amounting to identification, is impressive. That Byron has 'lost' his own religion there can be little doubt. On the other hand, one cannot be sure how close he came to an actual conversion — for two reasons. First, it is quite possible that he exaggerated his 'lawlessness' and 'paganism' to shock his straight-laced wife, who unintentionally would provoke mischief in such a character as her husband. Secondly, Byron's treatment of Alp does not seem sufficiently inward or sympathetic to justify identifying Alp's apostasy with any hidden desire on Byron's part. Yet the question of Byron's relationship with Islam must be faced.

As I have already indicated, the strongest case so far has been made by Blackstone, who begins by claiming that Byron's relationship (such it was) with Ali Pasha was much more significant than is generally credited. Ali was a bandit chief who had raised himself to being the absolute ruler of the lands on the eastern shore of the Adriatic, and had entertained Byron in the hopes, it seems, of fostering links with the English against the French. In a letter from Byron to his mother (12 November 1809) a full account is provided of Ali's court inland at Tepalene; and this is fleshed out in a more studied style in *Childe Harold's Pilgrimage*, Canto II, stanzas 38–71. The actual encounter with Ali is described in stanzas 55–66. According to Blackstone, Ali is believed to be a member of the Bektashi order of Sufism, who represented a radical break with Islamic orthodoxy. In his letters to his mother, Byron claimed that Ali had 'told me to consider him as a father'.[28] Blackstone exaggerates his case when he speculates that, by the word 'father', Ali had actually meant 'baba', which could translate as 'father' *and* 'spiritual guide' in sophist terms, and that Ali offered Byron an initiation to become a Bektashi adept. Furthermore, Blackstone rules out any counter-evidence on the basis that, since such adepts were vowed to silence, Byron's reticence, indeed *silence*, in this matter is a confirmation of its truth. On such principles, one will find *any* evidence, *anywhere*, and for *any* conviction. But there can be no doubt that Byron had plenty of opportunity to see dervishes for himself, and perhaps participated in their traditional whirlings, to which allusions abound in his works. We also know that he and Hobhouse saw several performances by whirling dervishes in Athens and Constantinople.

These various dervishes belong to the sect known in Islam as Sufism, which turned Muslims away from the world towards a direct adoration of God, which relieved the adept of desire, and made his goal the reunion with the source of life, life itself being regarded as an emanation from God. This reunion was achievable through a ritual using the images of music, wine and love to signify their relation to God, envisaged as pure ecstasy. To what extent a temperament like Byron's (whether vowed to silence or not) could have accepted such a combination of asceticism and exaltation must surely remain in doubt. Blackstone suggests that the heroines of the 'Turkish Tales' are 'of the nature of the allegorical mistresses or youths of Sufi poetry, symbolising noesis, mystical realization'.[29] It is true that Leila's gaze arouses in the Giaour a love that 'lift[s] from earth our low desire' while 'Heaven itself descends to Love' (*The Giaour*, lines 1134, 1136). But this does not require the explanation of sophism. Such metaphysical love is not absent from the tradition of western love poetry, though it may well have received stimulus from contact with the East. Nor can it be denied that Byron had inherited more than his share of Calvinist guilt and self-division, that these anxieties are deeply etched into the narrative of the 'Turkish Tales', and that they may have received reinforcement by contact with Islamic Sufism. But to go much beyond these speculations, and to propose allegorical interpretations of the tales on the basis of a hidden cipher of Sufism, or to explain Byron's marriage to Annabella as the desperate gamble of an 'adept' who had lost the 'noetic' and was seeking compensating stability in the 'domestic', seems just as bizarre.

The central stanzas (55–66) of Canto II of *Childe Harold*, devoted to Ali Pasha's capital and court, provide a clear enough statement of the appeal Islam made to the young Byron:

> Childe Harold saw, like meteors in the sky,
> The glittering minarets of Tepalen,
> Whose walls o'erlook the stream; and drawing nigh,
> He heard the busy hum of warrior-men
> Swelling the breeze . . .
>
> [II, stanza 55]

Here is struck the note of exotic fierceness which he continued to associate with Islamic civilization: the combination of uncompromising religious passion and military virtues which he identified as the qualities of nature. Tepalene is a focal point for all the races and nations of the East (stanzas 56–8): 'The Turk — the Greek — the Albanian — and the Moor,' are given unity by two sounds: 'the deep war drum' (stanza 57) and 'the Muezzin's call' (stanza 59); and they live life between the two extremes contained in Ramazan, the Islamic month-long lent: fasting and feasting (stanza 60). As for Ali himself, at once sinister and profound, wielding the 'lawless law' of the tyrant whose word is death, ravaged by age ('crimes . . . have marked him with a tiger's tooth' — stanza 63), yet with 'an agèd venerable face' throwing 'milder radiance' (stanza 62) — he seems an embodiment of that fierce freedom from the hypocritical restraints and compromising insincerities that the Romantics after Rousseau associated with life in the urban West. At least at the simplest level one can begin by saying here that 'Islam' made it possible for Byron to give a hard, authentic edge to one of the central impulses of Romanticism. The move from Ossian and the Highlanders to Ali and the Albanians was, in Byron's sense, a move from literature to life, from words to deeds, and from illusions to realities. It is not surprising, therefore, that his return to London, fashion, fame and fortune left him feeling at least as dissatisfied and alienated as stimulated and enhanced.

The Experience of the Orient

One of the major differences between Byron's orientalism and that of his predecessors or contemporaries lies in the use to which he put his reading. For Landor, Southey and Moore, literature was a means of generating more literature. And although they all made serious efforts to achieve documentary accuracy, these efforts were justified in terms of moral or political objectives that ultimately applied to Western Europe, and particularly to England. Despite the immense vogue for oriental material, these writers did not merely indulge the fantasies of their readers, but tried to turn them to literary and social advantage.

Byron's reading, however, as events turned out, was a preparation for a direct encounter with reality. His visit to Albania, Greece and Turkey was most certainly not that of a naive traveller, absorbing neutrally and passively impressions, facts and events. By the time of the tour, he was immensely impressionable, but with a mind already well stored with information and expectations, particularly with regard to Greek civilization. Perhaps for that very reason, the reality of the Islamic Orient, especially landscape and climate, and manners and forms of life, made an enormous impact on him. This impact, as this chapter will attempt to show, was interpreted by the values and preconceptions that Byron took with him to the Orient; but it also influenced and modified them so profoundly that it is not irrelevant to distinguish Byron from his rivals by invoking the phrase 'realistic orientalism'. My purpose now is to bring into focus the latent problem that lies behind this study as a whole: the problem of the tension implied in the phrase itself — *orientalism* pulling it *towards* the realm of free fantasy and dream, *realistic* drawing it *towards* the testing ground of history, politics and verisimilitude. The conflicting impulses of indulgence and discipline, of reverie and truth (the cardinal polarities of Romanticism), are, I believe, given a novel expression in the oriental narratives of the period; but they achieve an unusual integration in Byron's 'Turkish Tales'.

The Oriental Landscape

The natural setting provided for the 'Turkish Tales' is much more than a background. It has a special significance both for what it is in itself and for the way in which it defines the central preoccupation of the tales.

The landscape of the eastern Mediterranean, like the cultures it nurtured, never lost for Byron a quality of *revelation*. This means that he always saw and remembered it from the perspective of an Englishman brought up under northern mists and rain, and that it always seemed to him to represent the 'real'. In one sense, of course, England is real: it exists, it possesses all the characteristics of actuality. But it is also imperfect and muffled, further away from paradise. As Byron himself acknowledged: 'With those countries . . . all my really poetical feelings begin and end.'[30] This feeling of coming home, as it were, is everywhere implicit. It becomes explicit in many passages. For example, there is the description of the sunset and moonrise over the Morea which Byron wrote 'on the spot in the Spring of 1811' for the *The Curse of Minerva*, and which was transformed into the opening of Canto III of *The Corsair*:

> Slow sinks, more lovely ere his race be run,
> Along Morea's hills the setting sun;
> *Not, as in Northern climes, obscurely bright,*
> But one unclouded blaze of living light!
> [lines 1–4; my italics]

And again,

> But lo! from high Hymettus to the plain,
> The queen of night asserts her silent reign.
> *No murky vapour, herald of the storm,*
> Hides her fair face, nor girds her glowing form.
> [lines 33–6; my italics]

Nor are the sun and the moon merely free from the imperfections of the British climate; in the Mediterranean they illuminate what they were meant to shine on, that is, a version of paradise. The yellow beam that the setting sun throws 'O'er the hushed deep . . . /Gilds the green wave, that trembles as it glows' (lines 5–6). Similarly, moonlight is designed to 'play' 'With cornice glimmering', while 'the white column greets her grateful ray, . . . /Her emblem sparkles o'er the minaret' (earth answering heaven) on 'the sacred Mosque' and the 'turret of the gay Kiosk' (lines 37–44). In short, heaven and earth (literally in the case of the minaret) seem made for each other in ways unimaginable in the countries of the north. The opening of *The Bride of Abydos* only confirms this. Its initial question, 'Know Ye the land . . . ?' is a deliberate allusion to Goethe's famous 'Kennst du das Land . . .',[31] in which he celebrates precisely the same discovery. It is 'the Land of the cedar and vine/Where the flowers ever blossom, the beams ever shine': ''Tis the clime of the east — 'tis the land of the Sun —' (line 16).

The idea of the East as being in the neighbourhood of paradise (though it cannot be theological paradise, for it has a 'real' worldly existence) is developed in ways that emphasize vitality and energy. Byron's landscapes are never static, but always flowing, always in movement. The opening section of Canto I of *The Corsair* locates the pirate band's affirmation of independence and liberty in the context of the sea:

> 'O'er the glad waters of the dark blue sea,
> Our thoughts as boundless, and our souls as free . . .
> Ours the wild life in tumult still to range
> From toil to rest, and joy in every change.'
>
> [lines 1–8]

There seems to be a perfect concord between the restless grandeur of the sea and the passionate energy of man. Here, too, this virtue is contrasted with the vice of more civilized and tamer societies: the 'luxurious slave!/Whose soul would sicken o'er the heaving wave' (lines 9–10) is banished, as is the 'vain Lord of wantonness and ease' (line 11). Outlaws — to use Byron's suggestive phrase — 'snatch the life of life' (line 25); the law-abiding citizen is too 'craven' and 'feeble' ever to experience the exultation which only risk can purchase. These outlaws also differentiate themselves in the death they face:

> Let him who crawls enamoured of decay,
> Cling to his couch, and sicken years away;
> Heave his thick breath, and shake his palsied head;
> Ours — the fresh turf, and not the feverish bed.
> While gasp by gasp he falters forth his soul,

Ours with one pang — one bound — escapes controul.
[lines 27–32]

In this view, death itself becomes a proclamation of exultant independence which, rooted in nature ('the fresh turf'), 'escapes controul' with, paradoxically, 'one bound' of superabundant life.

This quality of movement and reciprocal responsiveness is characteristic even of the apparently calmer and less dramatic landscapes. The opening section of *The Giaour* evokes the Mediterranean (here, Greek) — nature as a harmony of echoing elements. The isles of Greece, as seen from a mainland height in the expanse of sea, 'lend to loneliness delight' (line 11); the tides that lave 'these Edens of the eastern wave' (line 14) reflect mountain peaks; the breeze 'wakes and wafts the odours' (line 20). This principle is summarized as follows:

For there the Rose, o'er crag or vale,
Sultana of the Nightingale,
The maid for whom his melody —
His thousand songs are heard on high,
Blooms blushing to her lover's tale;
His queen, the garden queen, his Rose,
Unbent by winds, unchill'd by snows,
Far from the winters of the west,
By every breeze and season blest,
Returns the sweets by nature given
In softest incense back to heaven;
And grateful yields that smiling sky
Her fairest hue and fragrant sigh.
[lines 21–33]

The image of the nightingale (*bulbul*) singing to the rose (*gûl*) is a trope of Persian poetry. Coleridge quotes a stanza from Sir William Jones's translation of Mesihi:

Come, charming maid! and hear thy poet sing.
Thyself the rose and he the bird of Spring:
Love bids him sing, and Love will be obey'd.

and a stanza from Fitzgerald's translation of Omar Khayyám:

. . . The Nightingale cries to the Rose
That slow cheek of hers to incarnadine.

We have already encountered the idea in Thomas Moore:

Oh! sooner shall the rose of May
Mistake her own sweet nightingale.[32]

And we will encounter it again in *The Bride of Abydos*:

. . . the gardens of Gúl in her bloom;
Where . . . the voice of the nightingale never is mute.
[lines 8–10]

This, then, is a thoroughly literary device, which becomes nothing less than a symbol of orientalism. But what does Byron make of it? He reanimates it, or restores its literal force, by associating it with the vividness of the living landscape (differentiated from 'the winters of the west'), which receives the breath of heaven ('wind'), and for that very reason returns its breath to heaven ('perfume'); and which gives the nightingale his reason for singing and receives in exchange its brighter colour.

This kind of vividness, which constitutes Byron's 'oriental realism' (a blend of literature and experience), by no means requires symbolic developments — quite the contrary. The image of the nightingale singing to the rose contains the idea of the lover singing to his beloved, and thus, as Jerome McGann has noted, the landscape of

Greece becomes linked, even identified, with Leila, the heroine of *The Giaour*, who is destroyed by the two men contending for her.[33] What the *political* implications of this situation are we shall examine in due course. But here it must be made clear that it shows Byron not to be an idealist in the usual sense.[34] His notion of paradise is pitched not in the ideal realm, but in the actual region of the Mediterranean. This means that earth and heaven are not simply opposites: earth rises some way towards the conditions of heaven, as heaven descends some way towards the condition of earth. And if this is true of nature, it must equally be true of love, for Leila belongs to her environment and partakes of the qualities of nature. Whatever there may be of transcendence in Byron is rooted in experience; the idea of supernature is firmly anchored in the idea of nature. If the view that Byron was not a mystic in any sense is correct, then Blackstone's claim that Byron may have made a Sufist (i.e. mystic) commitment while in the East, and that his unhappiness when he returned to England can be explained in terms of his failure to live up to this commitment, must be open to considerable doubt. Byron's debt to Islam was something much more open and direct.

The realistic paradise constituted by the landscape of the Islamic Mediterranean contains human actions that are the reverse of paradisal (namely, satanic). This is a paradox which Byron insists on again and again. It is a major motif of *The Giaour*:

Strange — that where Nature lov'd to trace,
As if for Gods, a dwelling-place,
And every charm and grace hath mixed
Within the paradise she fixed —
There man, enamoured of distress,
Should mar it into wilderness . . .
Strange — that where all is peace beside

There passion riots in her pride,
And lust and rapine wildly reign
To darken o'er the fair domain.
[lines 46–51, 58–61]

The point is clearly established that the love which nature inspires (there is a sinister progression from 'enamoured' to 'passion' to 'lust' to 'Rapine') turns from life to death and good to evil as it takes root in the heart of man. There is nothing *idyllic* about man's relationship with nature: the Mediterranean is not the South Seas. The point is made more briefly at the start of *The Bride of Abydos*, where Byron stresses an ambiguity in nature herself:

Know ye the land where the cypress and myrtle
Are emblems of deeds that are done in their clime,
Where the rage of the vulture — the love of the turtle —
Now melt into sorrow — now madden to crime?
[lines 1–4]

And *The Corsair*, for all its heroic setting, contains a protagonist who is the very embodiment of self-division and self-contempt. The problems in Byron arise because man is seduced by the beauty of nature, and of women, into making demands *on the real*. Far from turning him into a mystic, his experience of the Mediterranean climate cured him of the naive idealisms and false moralisms of the conventionally educated society at home.

Islamic 'Costume'

Byron's 'realistic orientalism' extended to the communities that had the good fortune to live in those envied climes. He was very interested in what we call today 'local colour', but which he called, more suggestively, 'costume'. This term was a favourite with him. We have seen (page 222) that in his correspondence he reproves Murray for failing to do justice to the 'otherness' of Islamic culture with remarkable insistence in his letter of 14 November 1813 on 'my *costume*, and my *correctness*'. He returns to the theme in his correspondence with Dr Clarke (15 December 1813): '. . . *you* are one of ye very few who can pronounce how far my *costume* (to use an affected but expressive word) is correct . . . I am anxious to have an observer's — particularly a *famous* observer's testimony on yr. fidelity of my *manners* & *dresses*.'[35] Byron obviously placed very great importance on the accuracy of detail in the surfaces of life which only *travellers* would have access to. One reason is that he wished to distinguish himself from the rack of merely reading orientalists. But far more important was his desire to give full weight and dignity to an alternative social and religious reality. Much in the same way that the point of Mediterranean landscape was that it was not English, so the importance of Islamic civilization was that it was not Christian. His discovery of the East was the discovery of *other* realities.

To understand the implications of this, we could pass under review a few items of oriental 'costume' on show in the 'Turkish Tales'. In general, Byron records Islamic terms and idioms with great accuracy. Shouts of 'Allah Akbar', 'Salam Alaikum' and 'Laila ila Allah', for instance, are used in their proper religious contexts, and are appropriately expressive of Islamic identity. His terminology, in *The Giaour*, is equally accurate: 'tophaik' (line 225), 'jereed' (line 251) and 'ataghan' (line 354), all Turkish names of weapons (meaning musket, javelin and dagger, respectively). The same is to be found in his references to the 'Koran verse' (already encountered in Moore) decorating the Turk's scimitar blade, symbolizing the duty of waging a holy war against the unfaithful (*The Bride of Abydos*, line 671). He is equally precise in his reference to Turkish garments, for example, in *The Giaour* (lines 666, 717 and 1273, respectively): to 'palampore' (flowered shawl), 'calpac' (centre part of the headdress) and 'symar' (woman's robe, or shroud). A full survey would stretch from significant religious practices, like the festival of Ramazan, and Bairam, the feast-day marking the end of Ramazan (both described in *The Giaour*, lines 222–9 and 449–52); or the *Azan*, the five-fold call to prayer usually performed from the minaret (e.g. *The Giaour*, line 734, where Byron comments: 'On a still evening, when the Muezzin has a fine voice . . . the effect is solemn and beautiful beyond all the bells of Christendom'[36]); to the use of symbolic colours, such as the wearing of green, the privilege of the Prophet's numerous descendants (*The Giaour*, line 357); and the practice of formal hospitality, the blessing of the 'sacred bread and salt' (*The Giaour*, line 343), following the Koranic injunction, 'Serve God . . . and show kindness unto parents, and relations, and orphans, and the poor . . . and the traveller, and captives . . .' (Chapter IX). But rather than multiplying examples, I shall briefly consider only one cluster of practices, those associated with funerals, drawn from *The Giaour* and *The Bride of Abydos*.

As we have seen in his letter to Murray, Byron took special pride in the authenticity of his rendering of Muslim funerals. Canto II, stanza 27, of *The Bride of Abydos* offers a brief but telling glimpse of the funeral rites of Zuleika, which Giaffir comes upon after having killed his nephew Selim, whom Zuleika loves fatally:

By Helle's stream there is a voice of wail!
And woman's eye is wet — man's cheek is pale —
Zuleika! last of Giaffir's race,
Thy destin'd lord is come too late —
He sees not — ne'er shall see thy face! —
Can he not hear
The loud Wul-wulleh warn his distant ear?
Thy handmaids weeping at the gate,

The Koran-chaunters of the hymn of fate —
The silent slaves with folded arms that wait,
Sighs in the hall — and shrieks upon the gale,
Tell him thy tale!

[lines 621–32]

The 'Wul-wulleh' is the death-song of Turkish women, while the 'silent slaves' are the men whom decorum forbids to weep or grieve in public (the women's eyes are 'wet', but the men's cheeks are only 'pale'). The 'Hymn of Fate' is the so-called *Telkin*, a prayer offered by the imam after interment has taken place, following which, so Coleridge notes, the opening chapter of the Koran, known as the *Fatehah*, is recited ('in the name of the merciful and compassionate God. Praise belong to God, the Lord of the worlds, the Merciful, the Compassionate . . .'). Byron gives a high focus to the distinctiveness of these ceremonies, down to the burial itself:

Woe to thee, rash and unrelenting Chief!
Vainly thou heap'st the dust upon thy head . . .
Thy daughter's dead! . . .
Hark — to the hurried question of Despair!
'Where is my child?' — an Echo answers — 'Where?'

[lines 652–69]

Details that seem to be mere expressive rhetoric turn out, to judge from Byron's own remarks, to be a faithful representation of ritual practice. The strewing of earth on the head was a recognized mark of grief; the body of a dead Muslim had to be carried to the grave 'in haste, with hurried steps'. The last line Byron attributes to a 'familiar' quotation from 'an Arabic manuscript' cited in Samuel Rogers's *The Pleasure of Memory*: 'I came to the place of my birth and cried, "The friends of my Youth, where are they?" and an Echo answered, "Where are they?'" In fact, Byron's information on Islamic burial rites ultimately derives from Jonathan Scott's introduction to *The Arabian Nights*, an extract of which may be cited:

> At the instant of expiration, the women who may be present give the alarm, and are soon joined by all the females of the family in a loud chorus of lamentation, which is called wullwulleh: in this the men take no share, but assume a resigned silence, and retire to sorrow in private. Some of the near female relatives and friends, upon hearing of a death, repair to the house, and the wullwulleh is renewed upon the entrance of each visitant into the harem . . . A number of the officiators at the mosques, carrying tattered banners, walk first, incessantly repeating Allah, Allah! that is, God is God, in a sort of chaunt; next comes the bier, surrounded by others of the above description, who, in a loud voice, chaunt certain appropriate verses of the Koraun.[37]

It is striking that Byron was, in such instances, not content to rely on impressionistic memory, but sought, by the citing of evidence, to reinforce the authority and substantiality of his 'costumes'.

The cemetery in which Zuleika finally reposes is described too conventionally to warrant special attention. The inevitable cypress, the single white rose, the unseen bird (perhaps a houri), are the images Byron invokes as he winds up his poem. A much more striking example is that of Hassan's grave in *The Giaour*. In a sudden juxtaposition, the reception of the news of Hassan's death by his mother immediately yields to a description of a neglected graveyard after many years have passed:

> A Turban carv'd in coarsest stone,
> A pillar with rank weeds o'ergrown,

Whereon can now be scarcely read
The Koran verse that mourns the dead;
Point out the spot where Hassan fell
A victim in that lonely dell.
There sleeps as true an Osmanlie
As e'er at Mecca bent the knee;
As ever scorn'd forbidden wine,
Or pray'd with face towards the shrine,
In prisons resumed anew
At solemn sound of 'Alla Hu!'
[lines 723–34]

According to Byron's own notes to this passage, 'The turban — pillar — and inscriptive verse, decorate the tomb of the Osmanlies, whether in the cemetery or the wilderness. In the mountains you frequently pass similar mementos; and on inquiring you are informed that they record some victim of rebellion, plunder, or revenge.'[38] Byron notes elsewhere that 'a turban is carved in stone above the graves of *men* only'.[39] We are also told, '"Alla Hu" [are] the concluding words of the Muezzin's call to prayer from the highest gallery on the exterior of the Minaret.'[40] Such details bring home to the reader the density and distinctiveness of Hassan's religious environment. At this point in the narrative, the narrator is a Turkish fisherman, and therefore the perspective of his lines (180–797) is firmly Islamic, just as the Giaour's confession (lines 971–1334) later will be dominantly Christian, or at least 'Frankish'. In this view, the drowning of Leila, who had given herself to a 'Giaour', or 'infidel', is perfectly justified, and Hassan, who is killed by his Christian rival, becomes a Muslim martyr. Accordingly he is praised as a true worshipper of Mecca, and his soul is received by the houris or 'the maids of Paradise' (line 739), who wave their symbolic green kerchiefs to him — for

Who falls in battle 'gainst a Giaour,
Is worthiest an immortal bower.
[lines 745–6]

Indeed, this motif of Islamic burial produces two further oriental motifs: that of the curse and that of the evil eye. The Muslim narrator pronounces a curse on the surviving infidel:

But thou, false Infidel! shalt writhe
Beneath avenging Monkir's scythe;
And from its torment 'scape alone
To wander round lost Eblis' throne;
And fire unquench'd, unquenchable —
Around — within — thy heart shall dwell,
Nor ear can hear, nor tongue can tell
The tortures of that inward hell! —
[lines 747–54]

The Arabic word *lăna* (meaning 'curse') has much stronger implications than the corresponding western term, for it entails torment prolonged to eternity. In the Koran, the first person to be so cursed was Eblis, who was thereby expelled not only from God's paradise, but also from God's mercy. (In Arabic the name 'Eblis' means 'the one who has despaired, or lost hope of redemption'.) The fisherman's curse therefore extends to the next world — to 'Monkir', who, with his fellow angel 'Nakir', acts as the inquisitor of the dead, and who punishes unsatisfactory answers with torture by means of fiery scythes. In life (as opposed to the after-life), the torments will take the form of pursuit by a vampire ('The Vampire superstition is still general in the Levant,' writes Byron),[41] from which the victim's descendants will not be free. Thus, in *The Giaour*, the curse acquires a gothic colouring in addition to the Islamic one.

The second associated motif is that of the evil eye. This cursed gaze is reciprocal. The Giaour is recognized by it:

> ''Tis he — 'tis he — I know him now,
> I know him by his pallid brow;
> I know him by the evil eye . . .'
> [lines 610–12]

Byron says that the evil eye is 'a common superstition in the Levant, and of which the imaginary effects are yet very singular on those who conceive themselves affected'.[42] In fact, the Koran alludes to the evil eye as a sign of hatred and wicked jealousy. But the dead Hassan is equally capable of cursing through the eye. As he lies mutilated, his hand cut off by his rival:

> His back to earth, his face to heaven,
> Fall'n Hassan lies — his unclos'd eye
> Yet lowering on his enemy,
> As if the hour that seal'd his fate
> Surviving left his quenchless hate.
> [lines 668–72]

And this, in turn, infects the Giaour with a gaze filled with satanic suffering, by which even the friar to whom he confesses is disturbed:

> The flash of that dilating eye
> Reveals too much of times gone by . . .
> For in it lurks that nameless spell.
> [lines 834–5, 838]

These examples will suffice to demonstrate exactly why Byron was so concerned with authenticity of 'costume'.

He wrote his 'Turkish Tales' for many reasons; but prominent among them must be the refusal of the kind of perception of foreign nations that represents them only as deviants from one's own. Byron was not in the business of reinforcing English perspectives, that is, English complacency and supremacy. He wished the full reality of Islam to become perceptible — not because he was seeking an alternative authority to the West, but because, as a generous liberal who hated tyranny and believed in national independence, he took delight in racial, social, cultural and religious *variety* and *otherness*. The artistic effects of this position are brilliantly explored in *The Giaour*, where the multiple narrative technique, but particularly the contrasting points of view of the Turkish fisherman and the 'infidel' himself, expresses in the very structure of the poem the multiple perspective that constitutes its theme.

Islamic Figures

The 'orientalism' Byron brought to the oriental poetic narrative completely transformed this Romantic genre. The landscape is much more vivid, the local colour much more specific. The authenticity of the scenery and 'costumes' which the 'Turkish Tales' exhibit confer an altogether new degree of reality to Islam as a form of life. It assumes an independence from western values and perceptions which conventional orientalism could never attain, for it was, at least in part, expressive of a western dream, strengthened by moral and political allegories with their points of reference always in the West. In Byron, however, Islam has lost all traces of the allegorical as emblematical dependence: it plays its full part as *itself* in the moral, religious and political situations dramatized by the tales. This has already been developed through the motifs just examined. An examination of Byron's Islamic, that is, Turkish, figures will establish it fully.

Women

In his works dealing with the Orient, Byron recognizes the constraints imposed by the Turks on their women. This he does most explicitly in *Childe Harold*, Canto II, stanza 61, where, describing the festivity following 'Ramazani's fast', in the gallery and courtyard of Ali Pasha's palace, he adds:

Here woman's voice is never heard: apart
And scarce permitted, guarded, veil'd, to move,
She yields to one her person and her heart,
Tam'd to her cage, nor feels a wish to rove:
For, not unhappy in her master's love,
And joyful in a mother's gentlest cares,
Blest cares! all other feelings far above!
Herself more sweetly rears the babe she bears,
Who never quits the breast, no meaner passion shares.

This might seem a straightforward confirmation of English prejudice against the Islamic status of women: and it would of course be futile to deny Byron's liberal principles in this as in most other departments of life. But the fact remains that, even here, a turning of the tables against England can be perceived, for what Byron is saying is that Islamic restriction and discipline guarantees the *English* domestic ideal of wife and mother, so that a thoughtless condemnation of Turkish practices must necessarily be hypocritical.

As we quickly realize, however, even under conditions of male domination the Muslim woman scores over her English counterpart in sexual allure and luxury. We saw the extent to which Lady Mary Wortley Montagu savoured this atmosphere of feminine licentiousness. How readily Byron himself responded to this characteristic can be seen from his description of Zuleika's chamber in Canto II of *The Bride of Abydos*. This is the apartment in the tower from which she is preparing to elope with her lover Selim, and so escape the loveless marriage that her father, Giaffir Pasha, has arranged for her:

Yes there is light in that lone chamber,
And o'er her silken Ottoman
Are thrown the fragrant beads of amber,
O'er which her fairy fingers ran;
Near these, with emerald rays beset,
(How could she thus that gem forget?)
Her mother's sainted amulet,
Whereon engraved the Koorsee text,
Could smooth this life, and win the next;
And by her Comboloio lies
A Koran of illumin'd dyes;
And many a bright emblazon'd rhyme
By Persian scribes redeem'd from time;
And o'er those scrolls, not oft so mute,
Reclines her now neglected lute;
And round her lamp of fretted gold
Bloom flowers in urns of China's mould;
The richest work of Iran's loom,
And Sheeraz' tribute of perfume;
All that can eye or sense delight
Are gather'd in that gorgeous room —
But yet it hath an air of gloom —
She, of this Peri cell the sprite,
What does she hence, and on so rude a night?
[lines 63–86]

At first glance, this description may seem over-bejewelled. But the details are less conventional, and more effective, than they appear. The 'fairy fingers' rub the amber heads in order to produce perfume; the amulet contains a text from the 'Korsee', or 'throne verse' of the second chapter of the Koran, describing the perfection of God, and his providence, which has a protective function, like a St Christopher in the West; the 'Comboloio' is the Turkish rosary, which lies next to an exquisitely illuminated copy of the Koran, itself near to a lute, which in turn is placed alongside a golden lamp, a China vase and the perfume from 'Sheeraz' (the Persian city celebrated for its attar of roses). In short, this room combines religious purity with a banquet of the senses ('All that can eye or sense delight'). This extraordinary blend of innocence and sensuality, a sample of a Muslim paradise no doubt, is summarized in the image of the Peri — a beautiful feminine spirit — a sort of penultimate houri. It was indeed as a houri-image of heavenly licentiousness that Giaffir saw his daughter in Canto I:

> But hark! — I hear Zuleika's voice,
> Like Houris' hymn it meets mine ear.
> [lines 146–7]

And he goes on to spell out the full implications of this metaphor:

> My Peri! ever welcome here!
> Sweet, as the desart-fountain's wave
> To lips just cooled in time to save —
> Such to my longing sight art thou;
> Nor can they waft to Mecca's shrine
> More thanks for life, than I for thine . . .
> [lines 151–6]

The combination of purity and sexuality, religious yearning and sensual desire plainly follows the example of the Koran. Furthermore, Byron discovers in the figure of the Peri/houri a cultural image of Islamic femininity which Zuleika embodies in the purest form. His correspondence offers the most explicit corroboration of this idea. In his letter to Dr Clarke of 15 December 1813, he writes: 'I also wished to try my hand on a female character in Zuleika — & have endeavoured as far as ye. grossness of our masculine ideas will allow — to preserve her purity without impairing the ardour of her attachment.'[43]

The Muslim heroines of the other tales do not perfectly match this archetype, but they exhibit other variations. Leila, in *The Giaour*, is a Circassian, not a Turk like her husband, Hassan, or a Greek like her lover, the Giaour. These national distinctions allow Byron, as we shall see, to develop a suggestive political allegory. But, at the narrative level, Leila is a victim who has eloped, this time successfully, from Hassan's harem, with the hated infidel, and who pays the penalty reserved for such sins: drowning in a sack. She makes no direct appearance in the narrative; we learn about her mostly from her effect on the two men. From this we deduce that she possesses the same unity of the spiritual and sensual. For example:

> Her eye's dark charm 'twere vain to tell,
> But gaze on that of the Gazelle,
> It will assist thy fancy well,
> As large, as languishingly dark . . .
>
> [lines 473–6]

Yet, at the same time:

> But soul beamed forth in every spark
> That darted from beneath the lid . . .
>
> [lines 77–8]

On the other hand, Gulnare (a name which means 'the flower of the pomegranate') in *The Corsair*, also an inmate of a harem, is no victim. Indeed, she is 'the Haram queen' (line 830), who is freed by Conrad in the midst of his fight with Seyd, and transfers her allegiance from Seyd to Conrad, with a passionate gratitude in which it is impossible to disentangle natural instinct from social obligation. When Conrad therefore falls into the hands of Seyd, she does not hesitate to assassinate the Turkish pasha. But this act retains, in all its aggressiveness, the oriental mixture of sexual passion and fanatical fidelity. She, too, is no mere seductress — no over-sexed temptress such as Byron might have encountered in the London salons — but a creature compounded of fire and duty. (This, we remember, was an inspiration for Moore in 'The Fire-Worshippers'.) Henceforth, Gulnare's devotion to Conrad, prolonged to the point of disguise and death in *Lara*, remains absolute, like a religious faith. To that extent, she remains related to the archetype as defined by Zuleika. She makes no extravagant demands of reciprocity, as, for example, her Christian, or at least 'Frankish', rival, Medora, does; nor does she have Medora's intense inner life, nourished by sorrow, and even by guilt. She has a unity of self which seems beyond the reach of western woman, with her moral ambition and her mistrust of the senses.

There can be no doubt that, in his conception of the Muslim woman, Byron acknowledged their difference from the women of his own culture, and gave them an independent reality which he found intrinsically almost irresistible. How irresistible, a further consideration of Zuleika as archetype will demonstrate. When he began writing *The Bride of Abydos*, he proposed to represent Selim and Zuleika as brother and sister. But, as he explained in the letter to Dr Clarke already cited, he was forced to abandon this idea:

> I felt compelled to make my hero & heroine relatives — as you well know that none else could there obtain that degree of intercourse leading to genuine affection — I had nearly made them rather too much akin to each other . . . — yet the times & the *North*

> (not *Frederic* but our *Climate*) induced me to alter their consanguinity & confine them to cousinship.[44]

This statement makes it surely beyond argument that Byron found in Zuleika an indirect expression of his love for his own half-sister, Augusta. The combination of innocence and sensuality in the Muslim figure would offer a ready parallel for that mixture of fraternal affection and physical attraction that Byron must have offered Augusta. Whether or not this is true, the general point remains: that because Byron took his Islamic characters seriously, instead of merely making them part of a make-believe fantasy, he was able to use them to express his serious feelings.

Men

If Byron found in the East images of irresistible femininity, he also found examples of incorrigible masculinity. Traditional societies distinguish gender roles from public life to produce a male ideal of the commanding type that proves itself in war and government, and in its capacity to keep what it possesses, be it land or women. All Byron's Islamic 'heroes' possess this sort of virility. Hassan, in *The Giaour*, possesses an inflexible pride and sense of honour that punishes adultery by death, and meets death with unyielding defiance. Giaffir, in *The Bride of Abydos*, cannot tolerate disobedience in a daughter, and will not hesitate to pursue and kill her lover — or seducer, as he thinks of Selim — however sincere and honest her love for him, and at whatever risk to her happiness, and even her life. Seyd, in *The Giaour*, is an outstanding warrior, who will have no hesitation in exterminating his enemies. And although Alp, in *The Siege of Corinth*, is a convert to Islam and not a native Turk, his conversion drives him to adopting an even more extreme stance of virility as honour and consistency.

Undoubtedly, the whole of Byron's experience in the East lies behind these masculine ideals — but most important of all, perhaps, is his encounter with Ali Pasha, described in *Childe Harold*, Canto II, where the virtues that come from absolutism — dignity, confidence, generosity, courage — are appreciated and indeed extolled. This is Giaffir in Canto I of *The Bride of Abydos*:

Begirt with many a gallant slave,
Apparelled as becomes the brave,
Awaiting each his Lord's behest
To guide his steps, or guard his rest,
Old Giaffir sate in his Divan,
Deep thought was in his aged eye;
And though the face of a Mussulman
Not oft betrays to standers by
The mind within, well skill'd to hide
All but unconquerable pride,
His pensive cheek and pondering brow
[lines 20–30]

This pride is not merely a virtue of the mind, but a confidence drawn from possessions. In these figures of command, *honour* is not simply self-respect, but also *honours* — that is, wealth, slaves and instant obedience. This is why a warrior, before or after victory, must feast in plenty and luxury. Consider Seyd in *The Corsair* (Canto II):

High in his hall reclines the turbaned Seyd;
Around — the bearded chiefs he came to lead.
Removed the banquet, and the last pilaff —
Forbidden draughts, 'tis said, he dared to quaff,
Though to the rest the sober berry's juice,
The slaves bear round for rigid Moslem's use;
The long Chibouque's dissolving cloud supply,

While dance the Almahs to wild minstrelsy.
[lines 29–36]

We note again in passing the precision of Byron's orientalism — 'turbaned', 'bearded', 'pilaff' (a Turkish dish of rice and meat), 'forbidden draughts' (alluding to wine being forbidden by Islamic law), 'sober berry' (coffee), 'Chibouque' (pipe), 'Almahs' (dancing girls): Seyd is as completely in his milieu as Zuleika in hers. But it is these spectacular possessions which constitute his glory. The Muslim hero would not survive penury. Insofar as he has command over himself, he must also have command over others. The masculine ideal is an aggressive and dominating one.

That Byron takes it seriously is indicated, not only by his respect for it, but also by his criticism of it. It is undoubtedly a powerful and impressive conception, but it is also incomplete. The 'Turkish Tales' demonstrate that it is in their attitudes towards *women* that Muslim tyrants show their limitations. The Giaour is a far more complex figure than Hassan. Both are fighting for a woman, but Hassan is a much more rigid, unquestioning figure, who acts automatically in terms of the codes of his gender, class and culture. The criticism becomes more explicit in *The Bride of Abydos*, where Selim does not conform to the male ideal represented by Giaffir, but shows himself to be sensitive to Zuleika's wishes and feelings. He is a warrior, but he is also a 'hero' of sensitivity, whose feelings suggest that women are not only possessions and stereotypes, but have thoughts and feelings of their own. The pose that Selim strikes in Canto I when he learns that Giaffir has given Zuleika to another is that of the 'country' lover:

Still gazed he through the lattice grate,
Pale — mute and mournfully sedate —
[lines 255–6]

And later, the lover becomes still more audible:

> I would not wrong the slenderest hair
> That clusters round thy forehead fair,
> For all the treasures buried far
> Within the caves of Istakar.
>
> [lines 355–8]

This element undoubtedly qualifies the values embodied in Giaffir. *The Corsair* only confirms this pattern. It is Conrad's refusal to accept the slavery which Seyd imposes on Gulnare as a matter of course that awakens her love for him, and that saves his life. This attitude to the 'harem' is ideologically quite as much a challenge to Seyd's supremacy as the military attack itself.

In fact, in every case so far, a woman has left a Muslim despot for a figure who, whether Islamic or not, is sympathetic to the woman's desires and predicament. To that extent, the Muslim stereotype is seen to be wanting, even when it is militarily victorious, as in the case of Giaffir. This firm establishment of limitation is reinforced, in a more subtle way, by the last of the Turkish narratives — *The Siege of Corinth*. The subtlety of that situation comes from the fact that its protagonist, Alp, combines both the (Islamic) ideal of virility and the (Romantic) ideal of sensibility. As a Christian in Venice, he won Francesca's love in defiance of her father's commands (stanza 7):

> His hope would win, without consent
> Of that inexorable Sire,
> Whose heart refused him in his ire,
> When Alp, beneath his Christian name,
> Her virgin hand aspired to claim.
>
> [lines 181–6]

Before he had been accused of being a traitor (perhaps by that 'inexorable Sire' determined to get rid of him), he had been clearly the fashionable ('courtly') and responsive lover:

> Gayest in gondola or hall,
> He glittered through the Carnival;
> And tuned the softest serenade
> That e'er on Adria's waters played
> At midnight to Italian maid.
>
> [lines 144–8]

Driven away from Francesca, and Venice, and Christianity, he adopts the Islamic faith with a zeal that becomes fanaticism. And this includes, of course, the ideal of commanding masculinity that Byron has recognized in the East. This is plainly the point at issue at the climax of the narrative — the confrontation between Francesca and Alp by moonlight outside the walls of Corinth during the night preceding the assault and destruction of the city (stanzas 20–21). There she pleads with him to return to his 'fathers' creed' (line 576), if not to his role of a lover — 'if not for love of me be given' (line 628) — and his response is a reaffirmation of the inflexible masculine honour he has assumed:

> But his heart was swollen, and turned aside,
> By deep interminable pride . . .
> *He* sue for mercy! *He* dismayed
> By wild words of a timid maid!
>
> [lines 608–13]

This is the very voice of masculine arrogance. Alp's refusal, therefore, of the role of lover, and all it implies, in favour of the role of masculine self-sufficiency, is itself rejected, as it must be, by Francesca, and the destructive tragedy becomes inevitable. In none of the tales are the strengths and limitations of Islamic masculinity more brilliantly presented than in *The Siege of Corinth*. For Byron, Turkey represents part, and not the whole, of reality. Realistic orientalism cannot allow itself the simplifications and sentimentalities of conventional orientalism.

Imperialism and Liberty

Byron's experience of the East profoundly engaged his political principles and values, which were those of a post-revolutionary liberal. He set himself against the system of Europe inaugurated by the Congress of Vienna. This naturally led him to adopt a highly critical stance towards the British political establishment as represented by George III, Castlereagh and Wellington. Byron's liberalism began at home; and this capacity for national self-criticism made him particularly receptive to foreign nations. He had an absolutely unreserved contempt for any form of imperialism; this meant that he had a natural sympathy for subject nations. He was profoundly committed to national identity, independence and self-government, whether of Portugal against France, Italy against Austria, or Greece against Turkey. The most important of these was the latter; it is, in any case, the latter which concerns Byron's orientalism.

We should note here, too, the relevance of the concept of realistic orientalism which this chapter, as the culmination of these arguments, seeks to define. For Byron, the fall of Greece was *not* an *exemplum* to be turned into an occasion for moral meditation — as the theme of the fall of nations tends to be in Southey; or an *allegory*, covertly alluding to the British political scene, as in Moore. What it is is exactly what it is: the decline and subjection of a specific community of people who have a real historical existence. This means that the international interests, be they of the East (Constantinople) or the West (Venice,

France and even Britain for its plunder of the Parthenon marbles), that were engaged in the subjection of Greece were felt to be real rather than symbolic pressures. It is in this sense that Byron's diagnosis of the imperialism of Islam raises questions about the imperialism of the West. The West is implicated, one way or another, in the predicament of Greece. Once again, it is because of his capacity to take his own country seriously that Byron is able to take a foreign political culture like Islam seriously. He may condemn Turkish absolutism, but his condemnation is entirely free of English complacency.

In the 'Turkish Tales' Greece provides the occasion for and focus of Byron's political engagement. The theme of the subjection of Greece had long formed a leading preoccupation for Byron. The opening stanzas of Canto II of *Childe Harold's Pilgrimage*, addressed to 'Athena', had already broached it. He seeks 'the Warrior's weapons' and 'the Sophist's stole' of Athens' original greatness, but finds them 'gone . . . through the dream of things that were'.

Son of the morning, rise! approach you here!
Come — but almost not yon defenceless urn:
Look on this spot — a nation's sepulchre!
Abode of gods, whose shrines no longer burn.
Even gods must yield — religions take their turn:
'Twas Jove's — 'tis Mahomet's — and other creeds
Will rise with other years, till man shall learn
Vainly his incense soars, his victim bleeds;
Poor child of Doubt and Death, whose hope is built on reeds.
[lines 19–27]

Here the fate of Athens (the Parthenon became a Christian church in the sixth century, and a mosque in the 15th century) is moralized into a universal pessimism which roots the efforts and aspirations of mankind in doubt and death. This is the subject of the first 15 stanzas: 'That little urn saith more than a thousand Homilies' (line 36); and Athenian wisdom is summed up in the maxim: "All that we know is, nothing can be known"' (line 56). But this, the message of history, is inaudible to all except the poet. Harold sits alone 'upon this massy stone,/The marble column's yet unshaken base' (lines 82–3), and introduces the dimension of consciousness that has been up to this point absent from an indifferent present:

> Yet these proud Pillars claim no passing sigh,
> Unmov'd the Moslem sits, the light Greek carols by.
> [lines 89–90]

But Harold's awareness is not confined to Turkish inflexibility and Greek frivolity: it includes English — or rather Scottish ('Blush, Caledonia' — line 95) — cold-hearted greed: the depredations of 'the last, the worst, dull spoiler', Lord Elgin, who is, if anything, worse than the Turkish conqueror:

> But most the modern Pict's ignoble boast,
> To rive what Goth, the Turk, and Time hath spar'd,
> Cold as the crags upon his native coast,
> His mind as barren and his heart as hard,
> Is he whose head conceiv'd, whose hand prepar'd,
> Aught to displace Athena's poor remains:
> Her sons too weak the sacred shrine to guard,
> Yet felt some portion of their mother's pains,
> And never knew, till then, the weight of Despot's chains.
> [lines 100–108]

Islamic political tyranny is balanced by western cultural plundering. Harold alone shows himself aware of, and affected by, the realities of the existing political situation in Greece.

This perspective helps to define the structure of *The Giaour*, which presents itself as a series of disjointed fragmentary utterances by a variety of narrators, not all of whom can be reliably identified. The poem opens with an apparently irrelevant 167 lines of lament for the past greatness of Greece. But a closer reading quickly reveals that Byron's emphasis is no longer where it was in *Childe Harold*. He is no longer interested in the cliché of the fall of empires, but in the present condition of Greece, which he regards, literally, as a kind of death. The motif is introduced in the first six lines, which evoke the tomb of Themistocles overlooking the beautiful shores of the Aegean sea. The climate and landscape of Greece is as magical as it ever was; but the human content of the scene has changed utterly. The Greek fisherman's song is quenched by the pirate's brutality, and a 'paradise' is marred into a 'wilderness'. And the conclusion, drawn over 22 lines (68–89), is plain: the present is a corpse, still peaceful and even beautiful, but dead: ''Tis Greece, but living Greece no more!'; and her beauty has the 'fearful bloom' of the cadaver. The political implications are equally plain: part of the responsibility for this must be accepted by the modern descendant of the warriors of Thermopylae and Salamis: 'Thou craven crouching slave.' Byron's attempt to rouse this supine race are not very optimistic. 'What can he tell who treads thy shore?' he asks. And the answer does not inspire much hope:

> Now crawl from cradle to the Grave,
> Slaves — nay, the bondsman of a Slave,
> [lines 1501–2]

— for, as Byron notes, Athens is the property of Kislar Aga, who appoints the Waywode. And the former is a 'pandar and eunuch', who 'now *governs* the *governor* of

Athens!' Moreover, the subtlety of the ancient Greeks has evolved into the piratical 'wiles' and 'craft' of the moderns.

In the light of this 'introduction', *The Giaour* must, at least at one level, be interpreted as a diagnosis of modern Greece. And we are indeed given a cruel and vicious tale of private vengeance and counter-vengeance over an innocent woman destroyed by Islamic honour and Christian passion, and by male shame and guilt. It is a story of merely private violence, entirely unredeemed by any larger motive, whether moral or political; and as such it confirms the diagnosis just made. But, following the hint of Jerome McGann, we may hazard a further interpretation, in which Leila, herself not a Turk but a Circassian, 'represents the land over which the Turks and the Venetians have been fighting for centuries, and to which neither can have any complete claim'.[45] The plausibility of this reading rests on the identification of Leila with Greece, first of all as an emblem of the natural beauty of the country, then as the corpse over which Turk and Frank are fighting — for it is as such that she fixes the quarrel between the Muslim chief and the Giaour. The first point of Byron's political diagnosis is that the two antagonists are equally guilty of the destruction of Leila/Greece, presented in the tale wholly as a victim (the East has a different style, but it is not intrinsically more rapacious than the West). The second point is that, if an adequate political alternative is to emerge, it has to be independent of the sterile contest of imperialist powers.

The difficulties in the way of the emergence of such an alternative — a 'third way' — is explored in *The Corsair* and its sequel *Lara*. From a political point of view, the issue posed by *The Corsair* is quite plain: Conrad's pre-emptive strike against Seyd, who is on the point of mounting an assault on Conrad's island fortress, would seem to be justified in terms of self-defence and independence.

Furthermore, Seyd is a despot both politically and domestically, and Conrad is the western liberal in his attitudes both to subjects and to women. It would therefore seem that Turkey represents the oriental tyranny we have been taught to associate with Islam, and that it is politically vicious. But the matter is quickly complicated. First of all, Conrad is not the standard liberal at all, in that he seems haunted by a profound and mysterious guilt. Secondly, his destruction of Seyd, far from being a source of triumph, leaves him feeling still more guilt ridden. He triumphs over him by assassination. Admittedly, he does not strike the blow, but he benefits from it, and he is responsible for it in that it was his action which puts Gulnare, the assassin, on his side. The fact that this action was an act of liberal generosity (protectiveness towards women) only serves to entangle the web of good and evil more thoroughly. In fact, the paradoxes multiply: the paradise of loving fulfilment which his mistress Medora offers him, and which he is too tormented to accept, is completely destroyed by her death, itself the product of his need to protect his island, and herself at the centre of it. Whatever he does, he finds himself baffled. And this pattern is pursued in *Lara*, in a vague gothic context that suggests Spain and remembers Newstead Abbey, and where Conrad, now 'Lara', with Gulnare as his faithful page, 'Kaled', first finds himself involved in vicious quarrels with his peers, then identifies with a popular political rising of which he takes the leadership, and is finally killed by the army of the state. His political project thus seems to end in useless and pointless bloodshed.

It would not be impossible, in very general terms, to see the outlines of an autobiographical pattern here, in that we find a figure with whom Byron was popularly identified (to his secret gratification) in two locations roughly corresponding to Byron's own displacements: the eastern Mediterranean, and a western country. If this is so, then it is plain that in both he experiences a political impasse. Such a feeling he experienced increasingly upon his return to England after his 'grand tour'. A famous passage from his correspondence will have to suffice as an illustration. On 21 September 1813 he wrote to Lady Melbourne:

> At Bugden I blundered on a Bishop — the Bishop put me in mind of ye Government — the Government of the Governed — & the governed of their *indifference* towards their governors which you must have remarked as to all *parties* . . .[46]

His disillusionment with the right (the government) and — more significantly — also with the left (the governed) seems complete. The forces of reaction are corrupt, but the counter-forces of revolution are exhausted. This seems true of England, as it was true, more spectacularly, of Greece. The question then arises as to what role is left for such as Byron, who, like Childe Harold sitting among the ruins of the Parthenon, can *see* but cannot *do*, whose knowledge is in inverse proportion to his powers of action. In such contexts, any attempt to act must end in paradox and confusion.

Mistrusting both reaction and revolt, it is not surprising that Byron craved for the East, with its proud, uninhibited warriors and its opportunity for heroism. But the 'Turkish Tales' make it clear that the East merely reproduced the problem. Alienated in London, Byron was alienated in Athens. Every one of Byron's major figures turn out to be maladjusted to the point of having no country, indeed no community, they can call their own. The Giaour, as his very title indicates (significantly he remains nameless), is a foreigner in Greece who can never be assimilated. Conrad is not at ease on his island, and after his defeat of Seyd, he abandons it altogether. But he is no more at home than

Lara is in Spain (or wherever), where he has no social or political role, and is regarded by his peers, albeit with fascination, as an outsider.

But the most striking example must be that of Alp in *The Siege of Corinth*, for Alp is alienated twice. He is, in effect, driven out of Venice to become a convert to Islam and a leader of the Turkish forces. As such he gains an opportunity for heroic action. But this action is without political significance. Indeed, it returns to the original sterile antagonism of two imperialist powers fighting over the corpse of Greece — now in the form of Corinth:

> The Keystone of a land, which still,
> Though fall'en, looks proudly on that hill,
> The land-mark to the double tide
> That purpling rolls on either side,
> As if their waters chafed to meet,
> Yet pause and crouch beneath her feet.
> [lines 7–12]

The very setting of the city, on an isthmus dividing the eastern from western sea, is symbolic of her predicament. She is occupied by a small Venetian force. Surrounding her is a vast Turkish army, over which 'the crescent shines/Along the Moslem's leaguering lines;/ . . . and turban'd cohorts' (lines 30–31, 35). But even the control of such a mighty force brings Alp no real satisfaction. He remains tormented, self-divided and restless:

> Not his the loud fanatic boast
> To plant the crescent o'er the cross,
> Or risk a life with little loss,
> Secure in paradise to be
> By Houris loved immortally:
> Nor his, what burning patriots feel,
> The stern exaltedness of zeal,

Profuse of blood, untired in toil,
When battling on the parent soil.
He stood alone — a renegade
Against the country he betrayed.
[lines 252–62]

And although his Muslim followers obeyed him, for he had the success of courage and skill,

But still his Christian origin
With them was little less than Sin.
[lines 269–70]

His isolation in Islam is even greater than it was in Christianity, and his main motive for action — revenge against Venice, and the father of his original beloved, now the governor of Corinth — shows how deeply he is still implicated in the country he has betrayed and renounced, and how far he is from a true commitment to the Islamic alternative. It is not surprising, therefore, that his political struggle should be accompanied by nightmare images of sickness, perversion and death, such as those he sees by night under the walls of Corinth:

And he saw the lean dogs beneath the wall
Hold o'er the dead their carnival,
Gorging and growling o'er carcass and limb.
[lines 409–11]

— a veritable banquet of death. Nor is it surprising that the struggle should end in sterile futility, with the blowing up of the city's powder magazine that destroys Christian with Muslim, and half of Corinth with both. Here imperialist wars are presented as infectious of nature. It is Alp's tragedy that his renunciation of the Christian alternative can only leave for him the equally unacceptable

Muslim alternative. Politically, for Byron, Islam is at once a promise of release, and a recognition of impasse. Nowhere is his *orientalism* more *realistic* than in his refusal to turn Turkey into a sentimental oriental refuge.

The Byronic Hero

I cannot in this concluding section of my closing chapter on Romantic narrative orientalism pretend to offer a complete or even adequate account of the Byronic hero, a matter to which most critics of Byron have paid a good deal of attention, including Peter L. Thorslev, who has devoted an entire monograph to the subject.[47] What I propose is something more modest: to bring out the extent to which Byron's contact with the East played a part in the development and consolidation of a figure that has its roots in the literature of Western Europe — particularly the gothic villain, the Highland outlaw, and the Ossianic bard, together with such Romantic archetypes as Prometheus, Cain and Satan (especially the Miltonic Satan), and historical heroes like Napoleon.

While one cannot but welcome Peter Thorslev's warning against the oversimplifications of a single conception and his emphasis on the varieties of the heroic in the 'Turkish Tales' (the Giaour is a sympathetic gothic villain, Selim is a hero of sensibility, Conrad the noble outlaw, and Alp a composite figure); nevertheless these figures (with the exception of Selim) have enough in common to justify collective treatment. The 'Turkish Tales' were written at close intervals, and represent variations on a theme and re-exploration of a similar problem. Their heroes can therefore be presumed to be the expression of related preoccupations.

I have sought to establish that, in the imperialist conflict between East and West, Byron distances himself from both sides, but in so doing experiences considerable difficulty in defining a position of his own. Furthermore, this difficulty is seen as a personal predicament in that it implies that he belongs neither to the East nor to the West. He is, by definition almost, a homeless figure — to that extent, an alienated outcast. The Byronic hero shares this predicament to the fullest degree — as the narrative situations of the Giaour, Conrad and Alp amply confirm.

We should, however, examine this 'outsider' condition more closely. The Byronic hero is usually firmly distinguished from the typical English poet or politician. The classical statement by Byron against English conventional morality is recorded by Lady Blessington in her *Conversations of Lord Byron*:

> It is my *respect for morals that makes me so indignant against its vile substitute cant, with which I wage war*, and this the good-natured world chooses to consider as a sign of my *wickedness* . . . I am always lenient to crimes that have *brought their own punishment*, while I am little disposed to pity those who . . . add cant *and hypocrisy to the catalogue of their vices*.[48]

Why this quotation is so revealing is that it asserts that no one, least of all the conventional English, are innocent, or free from 'vices', and that the real difference between the admirable and the base is that the former know that they are 'wicked', whereas the latter pretend, or deceive themselves into believing, that they are blameless. Hence the real crime is *cant*, or 'affected language implying a goodness or piety that does not exist'.[49] Insofar as England is dominated by cant, it can offer Byron no self-respecting public role, except that of its satirist and scourge. But how does Byron's aggressiveness against moral and emotional hypocrisy express itself? We have already quoted his dark hints to his wife that he preferred Muslim beliefs and practices to Christian ones. Whatever truth these carried in them, they were basically designed to shock Annabella's conventional piety, as was his announcement to her that he was the avatar of a fallen angel. (He also told Dr Kennedy that he was impressed by the view that Satan was subject to God's power — a precisely Koranic notion.)

Byron's praise of the East and his declared identification with its spirit is therefore in part an expression of his contempt for western cant. From the point of view of his relations with England, it helps him to adopt a deliberately challenging stance, designed to discomfort and discountenance the complacent and the virtuous. The Orient contributes significantly to the satirical impulse in the Byronic hero. Among a number of critics, Jerome McGann has most explicitly defined the function of this figure as a threat to expose to the conventional observer his repressed knowledge of his own guilt and despair. Byron's hero fascinates precisely because he is able to shrug off the protective layer of cant which ordinary mortals wear, and live out the danger and extremes of human existence.[50] The monk in *The Giaour* is frightened to look at him; Lara has the same effect (*Lara*, Canto I):

> You could not penetrate his Soul, but found,
> Despite your wonder, to your own he wound;
> His presence haunted still; and from the breast
> He forced an all unwilling interest.
>
> [lines 377–80]

Similarly, in his earlier existence, Conrad's stern glance can 'quell', because it penetrates to the hidden weakness of ordinary men (*The Corsair*, Canto I):

> There breathe but few whose aspect might defy
> The full encounter of his searching eye;
> He had the skill, when Cunning's gaze would seek

To probe his heart and watch his changing cheek,
At one the observer's purpose to espy . . .
[lines 15–19]

But what McGann fails to note about these passages is that they could not have the desired effect if the hero was too closely associated with his conventional, timid or hypocritical compatriots. The Byronic hero may be a Christian, but he is also a *foreigner*, not only to England and the West, but also to ordinary piety and worship, just like Satan and like Cain. Like a fallen angel or demon, the hero embodies a truth at once applicable and terrifyingly alien to the conventional citizens of London and Paris. The Byronic hero must possess a tinge or taint of the Islamic, at a cultural level, and (virtually the same thing to such as Annabella Milbanke) of the demonic at the spiritual level (*Lara*, Canto I):

He stood a stranger in this breathing world,
An erring spirit from another hurled.
[lines 315–16]

If now we turn our attention directly to Byron's attitude to the *Islamic* side of the equation, we will discover another element in the Byronic hero owed to the East. Whereas it is perfectly true that Byron does not endorse oriental militarism and oriental masculinity, and does not identify with them, he nevertheless responds sufficiently to them to absorb some of their tone. Byron is not especially sympathetic to the morality of meekness, humility and self-denial that is characteristic of a certain aspect of Christianity, and even less to these qualities as they are reduced into salon sentimentalism and effeminacy. It is surely clear that in the 'Turkish Tales' the heroes — even Selim, in his readiness to fight — are infected by the dominating virility of their Muslim opponents. The

Byronic hero is aggressive, commanding, uncompromising — to the point of positive unpleasantness: above all, he is sustained by *pride*, the satanic vice/virtue *par excellence*. This pride is essentially an individual masculine quality rather than a social one; and it would not have had the force it had without Byron's contact with the Islamic East. Consider, as an example, the first entry of the Giaour as described by the Turkish fisherman. He suddenly appears on the scene: 'Who thundering comes on blackest steed,/With slackening bit and hoof of speed?' Passing 'like a Demon of the night', he pauses for a moment to look with hatred at the Bairam feast in Hassan's house, then spurs away out of sight:

> The spur hath lanced his courser's sides —
> Away — away — for life he rides —
> Swift as the hurled on high *jereed*,
> Springs to the touch his startled steed . . .
> The crag is won — no more is seen
> His *Christian* crest and *haughty* mien. —
> [lines 249–53, 255–6; my italics]

George Ellis, a contemporary critic, is responsive to the urgency and power of this passage, recognizing the passion, anxiety and agonizing impatience of the mysterious rider:

> Every gesture of the impetuous horseman is full of anxiety and passion. In the midst of his career, whilst in full view of the astonished spectator, he suddenly checks his steed, and rising on his stirrup, surveys, with a look of agonizing impatience, the distant city illuminated for the feast of Bairam; then pale with anger, raises his arm as if in menace of an invisible enemy; but awakened from his trance of passion by the neighing of his charger, again hurries forward, and disappears.[51]

But Ellis fails to do justice to the dependence of the Giaour's 'haughtiness' on the oriental context. For example, the horse is a main image of the horseman's character. Yet it is represented in terms of the 'jereed', a 'blunted Turkish javelin' employed in a Turkish sport which Byron's note shows he fully understands (the 'jereed' is 'darted from horseback with great force and precision'). Byron further notes, rather sardonically, that those most skilled at it are 'the black Eunuchs of Constantinople',[52] but this does not detract from the athletic masculinity demanded by the sport, and it imparts a special force to the Giaour's characterization of isolated Christian pride.

There is a further, most disturbing, connection between the western roots of the Byronic hero and his transplantation into eastern soil, hinted at by Annabella in the statement quoted earlier (page 224) where she claims Byron admired the Turks above all for 'their complete predestinarianism'. Byron's latent Calvinism, whose conception of God as an awesome rather than loving deity makes for a much more virile form of Christianity than, say, compromising Anglicanism, seems to find a profoundly sympathetic echo in Islamic fatalism. In both traditions, a real man is one who, like Prometheus or Satan, can endure the consequences of his fate, or his curse, without flinching or pleading, and above all, without seeking reassurance or comfort from others. The Byronic hero is essentially lonely in his confrontations with inevitable disaster. The Giaour feels himself responsible for the death of Leila, the woman he loves with inflexible fidelity, and who therefore becomes an inflexible reproach to him. Conrad similarly feels irrevocably cursed by being the indirect cause of two deaths — that of Seyd by murder and that of Medora by neglect. But most of all it is Alp of *The Siege of Corinth* who displays this trait in its purity. He is, of course, a Christian turned Muslim; but there is something in his native make-up that makes the oriental religion particularly acceptable: its virile and lonely stoicism before a fated future. This is especially evident in his one moment of weakness when, surrounded by the sound of dogs gorging themselves on the corpses of his warriors, he suddenly senses the underlying reality of 'honour':

> There is something of pride in the perilous hour,
> Whate'er be the shape in which death may lower;
> For Fame is there to say who bleeds,
> And Honour's eye on daring deeds!
> But when all is past, it is humbling to tread
> O'er the weltering field of the tombless dead . . .
> [lines 440–45]

It is a moment at which he is specially vulnerable to sympathy. But Francesca's sudden appearance has the effect of reawakening his inflexible acceptance of what he takes to be his inevitable destiny:

> . . . '*Whate'er my fate*,
> I am no changeling — 'tis too late:
> The reed in storms may bow and quiver,
> Then rise again: the tree must shiver.'
> [lines 622–5; my italics]

In short, he repudiates the invitation to return to the Christian fold, and he returns to the ranks of Islam. The ancient curse of Christian guilt (his betrayal of Venice and Francesca) is transmuted into a more endurable — certainly a more self-flattering — sense of Islamic fate. The Orient, then, may be said to affect significantly several aspects of the persona of the Byronic hero: his disturbing force as an outlaw, whether from England or from conventional Christianity, his masculine pride, and his sense of inevitable doom.

A final point, however, may prove to be the most significant. It involves a reconsideration of the first of the oriental characteristics analysed in this chapter: the Edenic beauty of the climate and landscape of the East. It is well known that the Byronic hero thinks of himself as a dark criminal, and he is certainly so regarded by his acquaintances, and indeed by his readers. That Byron encouraged this response is shown most spectacularly by the famous concluding couplet of *The Corsair* (Canto III):

> He left a Corsair's name to other times,
> Linked with one virtue, and a thousand crimes.
> [lines 695–6]

The one virtue, in the context, is plain enough: Conrad's love for Medora. But what are the thousand crimes? Presumably Byron must be referring to the crimes implicit in the life of a corsair, or pirate. Yet these are never given any reality in the poem: on the contrary, the Corsair's life is imagined at the outset in Canto I as involving daring energy and independent freedom:

> O'er the glad waters of the dark blue sea,
> Our thoughts as boundless, and our souls as free . . .
> [lines 1–2]

This opening couplet of the poem imparts a glamour over a form of life that persists to the closing couplet. We must therefore seek an explanation for this sense of criminality elsewhere. But we cannot really find it in the *private* life of the heroes: all the three major examples are caught in a snare of moral circumstance for which they cannot — except in the most abstract sense — be held responsible. The Giaour is not the *direct* cause of Leila's death, nor is Conrad of Medora's, nor is Alp of Francesca's. The one remaining alternative must therefore be in the human condition itself, and take the form of some original sin.

Original sin is, as we understand it, *banishment from paradise* as a consequence of free will and the thirst for knowledge of good and evil. There is no reason to assume that the experience of the East was in any way formative in awakening this sense in Byron. But the evidence of the 'Turkish Tales' decisively points to the East as a powerfully confirming factor. As Robert Gleckner has argued in *Byron and the Ruins of Paradise*, the 'Turkish Tales' dramatize a 'radical pessimism'.[53] All three major heroes live in an Edenic nature, but are profoundly cut off from it. That this vision of the perfect life is located in Greece, and so combines the natural beauty associated with the first garden with the grandeur that was Athens or Corinth, does not alter the position: it merely adds a political dimension to his metaphysical pessimism. The tales themselves implicate the Byronic hero through the woman he loves, who, unlike Eve, offers a promise of Edenic happiness that can never be secured. All the tales are stories of obsessive violence which Byron repeatedly identifies as *vengeance*. Revenge is in fact what excludes man from Eden (or, in the Islamic version, what has excluded Eblis from God's paradise as well as his mercy): it is at once the cause and the effect of his condition. Be that as it may, man is certainly at odds with the creation, as is the Giaour himself:

> Strange — that where all is peace beside
> There passion riots in her pride,
> And lust and rapine wildly reign,
> To darken o'er the fair domain.
> It is as though the fiends prevail'd
> Against the seraphs they assail'd . . .
>
> [lines 59–63]

Nature at its most exquisite takes the form of the Leilas, the Medoras and the Francescas of the narratives. This identification is easily established — in the case of Medora (in *The Corsair*, Canto I) by her song for Conrad and the speech that follows it:

'Then not for mine, but that far dearer life,
Which flies from love and languishes for strife —
How strange that heart, to me so tender still,
Should war with nature and its better will!'
[lines 394–7]

And in the case of Francesca, by her speeches to Alp in the brief lull in the assault on Corinth, where she offers, in her beauty and love, an alternative to the carnage under the city walls. But the best treatment of oriental beauty is applied in *The Giaour* to the character of Leila, who is identified with one of the most brilliant oriental images we have encountered in this exploration. In his note, Byron describes it as 'the blue-winged butterfly of Kashmeer, the most rare and beautiful of the species'. In his poem, he evokes it:

As rising on its purple wing
The insect-queen of eastern spring,
O'er emerald meadows of Kashmeer
Invites the young pursuer near . . .
So Beauty lures the full-grown child.
[lines 388–91, 396]

But this beauty, in a fallen world, exists to be destroyed: 'Woe waits the insect and the maid' (line 401). The Giaour cannot prevent the obliteration of his paradise, and has to endure the torment of original guilt. The emblem of this guilt, for which he is responsible and to which he is predestined, is represented in the last, and the most spectacular, oriental emblems we shall consider:

The Mind, that broods o'er guilty woes,
Is like the Scorpion girt by fire,
In circle narrowing as it glows
The flames around`their captive close,
Till inly search'd by thousand throes,
And maddening in her ire,
One sad and sole relief she knows,
The sting she nourish'd for her foes,
Whose venom never yet was vain,
Gives but one pang, and cures all pain,
And darts into her desperate brain. —
So do the dark in soul expire,
Or live like Scorpion girt by fire;
So writhes the mind Remorse hath riven,
Unfit for earth, undoom'd for heaven,
Darkness above, despair beneath,
Around it flame, within it death! —
[lines 422–38]

There is no doubt that Byron's contacts with the Orient influence the achievement most characteristic of his early poetry: the refashioning of the myth of the Fall. His version of this archetype includes two meaningful alterations. First, the damnation of man does not come from his being tempted by a woman already tempted by the serpent: it comes from his killing of a woman who is essentially innocent and beautiful. Manfred's famous confession could apply equally to our heroes in the tales: 'I loved her and destroyed her.'[54] Thus, in Byron's version, Adam is not seduced by Eve: he kills her. Secondly, hell or damnation is not a condition of the after-life, but is the state into which man finds himself falling here and now as a consequence of his original crime. Like the scorpion, he has only two alternatives: either to be burnt by the circle of guilty fire, or to poison himself by his own excess of remorse. So it is that the Giaours, the Conrads and the Alps of the 'Turkish Tales' are all, in some measure, satanic creatures. They are satanic less because of their power to do harm, than because of their power to torment themselves. Byron did not remain fixed in that position; but that was the position he found himself in after his return from the Islamic Orient, and out of which he fashioned the culminating texts in the tradition of Romantic narrative orientalism it has been our purpose to examine.

Notes

Introduction

1. Edward Said, *Orientalism* (New York: Vintage Books, 1978), p 3.
2. Said, *Orientalism*, p 23.
3. Said, *Orientalism*, p 96.
4. Ibid.
5. Said, *Orientalism*, p 59.
6. Ibid.
7. Said, *Orientalism*, p 60.
8. Said, *Orientalism*, p 153.
9. Said, *Orientalism*, p 5.
10. Said, *Orientalism*, p 63.
11. Said, *Orientalism*, p 5.
12. Marilyn Butler, 'Revising the canon', *The Times Literary Supplement* (4–6 December 1987), p 1349.
13. Butler, 'Revising the canon', p 1359.
14. 'Despotism', *Dictionary of the History of Ideas* (New York: Charles Scribner's Sons, 1973), p 13.
15. See Byron Smith, *Islam in English Literature* (Beirut: The American Press, 1939), p 121.
16. Edmund Burke, *The Works of the Honourable Edmund Burke*, ed by Walker King, 16 vols (London: C. and J. Revington, 1822), vol XIII, pp 75–6.

17. Burke, p 164.
18. Burke, pp 175–6.
19. *Byron's Letters and Journals*, ed by Leslie A. Marchand, 12 vols (London: John Murray, 1973–82), vol II, p 89.
20. James Bruce, *Travels to Discover the Source of the Nile* (Dublin: G. G. J. and J. Robinson, 1790–91), vol I, p 519.
21. 'An Essay on the Poetry of Eastern Nations', *The Works of Sir William Jones*, ed by Lord Teignmouth, 13 vols (London: Stockdale, 1807), vol VIII, pp 359–60.
22. *The Works of Sir William Jones*, vol I, pp 49–50.
23. *Lord Byron, The Complete Poetical Works*, ed by Jerome J. McGann, 4 vols (London: Oxford University Press), vol III, p 423.
24. See Martha Pike Conant, *The Oriental Tale in the Eighteenth Century* (1908; reprinted New York: Frank Cass, 1966).
25. William Beckford, *Vathek*, ed and introduced by Roger Lonsdale (London: Oxford University Press, 1983), p 105.
26. *Vathek*, p 86.

Chapter 1: Landor's *Gebir* and the Establishment of Romantic Orientalism

1. *The Poetical Works of Walter Savage Landor*, ed by Stephen Wheeler, 3 vols (London: Oxford University Press, 1937), vol I, p 474.
2. *Landor*, ed Wheeler, vol III, pp 480–81.
3. *Gebirus*, p 3n, quoted in R. H. Super, *Walter Savage Landor, a Biography* (London: John Calder, 1957), p 41.
4. *Landor*, ed Wheeler, vol III, p 474.
5. All subsequent quotations from *Gebir* or the notes refer to Wheeler's edition.
6. *The Koran, Commonly Called the AlKoran of Mohammed, Translated into English from the Original Arabic, with Explanatory Notes Taken from the most Approved Commentators, to which is prefixed A Preliminary Discourse*, by George Sale (London and New York: George Routledge & Sons, n.d.), p 445. Further quotations from the *Koran* or Sale's Notes and 'Preliminary Discourse' refer to this edition.
7. *Koran*, p 445.
8. *Koran*, pp 168–9.
9. Sale's Notes, p 169.
10. *Koran*, p 293.
11. Sale's Notes, p 293.
12. *Koran*, p 297.
13. Marmaduke William Pickthall, *The Meaning of the Glorious Koran* (Edinburgh: Knopf, 1930).
14. *Koran*, p 279.

15. *Landor*, ed Wheeler, vol III, p 474.
16. *Landor*, ed Wheeler, vol III, p 477.
17. *Koran*, p 252.
18. Ibid.
19. Sale, 'Preliminary Discourse', p 71.
20. Ibid.
21. *Koran*, p 430.
22. *Koran*, p 138.
23. Pierre Vitoux, '*Gebir* as an Heroic Poem', *The Wordsworth Circle*, vol vii (Winter 1976), p 53.
24. *Koran*, p 252.
25. *Koran*, p 433.
26. *Koran*, p 286.
27. Landor's note to Book II, line 111, in *Landor*, ed Wheeler, vol III, p 11.
28. 'Notes on Walter Savage Landor', in *De Quincey's Works*, author's edn, 16 vols, (Edinburgh: Adam and Charles Black, 1862–71), vol VII, p 293.
29. *Landor*, ed Wheeler, vol III, p 479.

Chapter 2: Southey's *Thalaba* and Christo-Islamic Ethics

1. Jack Simmons, *Southey* (London: Collins, 1945), p 64.
2. Simmons, *Southey*, pp 75–6.
3. *New Letters of Robert Southey*, ed by Kenneth Curry, 2 vols (New York and London: Columbia University Press, 1965), vol I, p 476.
4. *The Poetical Works of Robert Southey, Collected by Himself*, 10 vols (London: Longman, 1846), vol IV, p xii.
5. *The Correspondence of Robert Southey with Caroline Bowles*, ed by E. Dowden (Dublin: Hodges and Figgis, and London: Longmans and Green, 1881), p 52.
6. Quoted without reference in Simmons, *Southey*, p 91.
7. See Geoffrey Carnall, *Robert Southey and his Age: the Development of a Conservative Mind* (London: Oxford University Press, 1960), pp 25–6.
8. Samuel Taylor Coleridge, *Biographia Literaria*, ed by J. Shawcross, 2 vols (London: Oxford University Press, 1979), vol I, p 46; *The Letters of Charles Lamb*, ed by Ernest Rhys, 2 vols (1909; reprinted London: J. M. Dent, 1950), vol I, pp 362–3.
9. Simmons, *Southey*, p 212.
10. *Selections from the Letters of Robert Southey*, ed by J. W. Warter, 4 vols (London: Longman, Brown, Green & Longmans, 1856), vol I, p 77.
11. John Fryer, *A New Account of East-India and Persia, in Eight Letters, Being Nine Years' Travels, Begun 1672, and Finished 1681* (London: n.p., 1698); Sir John Chardin, *The Travels of Sir John Chardin into*

Persia and the East-Indies (London: var edns, trans from Dutch, from 1686).

12. *Poetical Works*, vol IV, p xv.
13. Ibid; see also Robert Southey, *The Common-place Book*, 4th series, ed by J. W. Warter (London: Reeves & Turner, 1876), pp 182–3.
14. *The Life and Correspondence of Robert Southey*, ed by C. C. Southey, 6 vols (London: Longman, 1849–50), vol III, p 45.
15. *Koran*, p 303.
16. Sale, 'Preliminary Discourse', p 5.
17. Sale, 'Preliminary Discourse', pp 30–33.
18. *Koran*, pp 445–6.
19. *Koran*, p 356.
20. *Koran*, p 422.
21. John Greaves, *Pyramidographia* (London: n.p., 1656).
22. *Koran*, p 287.
23. Sale, 'Preliminary Discourse', p 6.
24. Sale, 'Preliminary Discourse', p 18.
25. *Koran*, p 293.
26. *Koran*, p 352.
27. *Koran*, p 365; the underlined sentence is not Sale's, whose original ('took his people to light behaviour') does not maintain the meaning of the original Arabic which this translation does. See The Holy Qur'an. Text, Translation and commentary by Abdullah Yusuf Ali (1934; reprinted by Publications of the Presidency of the Islamic Courts and Affairs, State of Qatar), p 1335.
28. Robert Southey, *Thalaba*, 2 vols (London: Longman, Rees, 1801).
29. Robert Southey, *The Poetical Works of Robert Southey, Collected by Himself*, 10 vols (London: Longman, 1846), vol I, Book VII, stanza 18. All subsequent quotations from *Thalaba* refer to this edition.
30. *Thalaba*, vol I, p 440.
31. *Koran*, p 52.
32. *Koran*, p 192.
33. Southey was aware of this account, as the *Common-place Book*'s entry on 'Borag' indicates.
34. See *Koran*, Chapters 17 and 18, dealing with the Prophet's Nocturnal Journey.
35. Sale's Notes, pp 90–91.
36. Sale's Notes, p 90.
37. Sale's Notes, p 91.
38. *Thalaba*, vol I, p 35.
39. *Thalaba*, vol I, p 33.
40. Sale's Notes, p 192.
41. Sale's Notes, p 4.
42. Sale, 'Preliminary Discourse', p 5.

43. See *Life and Correspondence*, ed C. C. Southey, vol III, p 351, and *Selections*, ed Warter, vol I, p 214.
44. *Thalaba*, vol I, p 211.
45. *Thalaba*, vol I, pp 211–12.
46. See *Koran*, pp 313 and 290.
47. *Thalaba*, vol I, p 33.
48. *Thalaba*, vol I, p 36.
49. *Thalaba*, vol I, p 36. 'All' in the first sentence is a literal for 'Ali', as it correctly reads in his *Common-place Book*, 4th Series, p 136.
50. *Thalaba*, vol I, p 86.
51. *Thalaba*, vol I, p 108.
52. *Thalaba*, vol I, p 169.
53. *Koran*, pp 267–8.
54. Sale's Notes, p 268.
55. *Thalaba*, vol I, p 160.
56. *Thalaba*, vol I, p 160.
57. M. H. Abrams, *Natural Supernaturalism: Tradition and Revolution in Romantic Literature* (London: Oxford University Press, 1971), p 64.
58. Abrams, *Natural Supernaturalism*, p 64.
59. *Correspondence*, ed Dowden, p 52.
60. *Koran*, p 250.
61. *Thalaba*, vol I, pp 267–8.
62. *Koran*, p 250.
63. *Thalaba*, vol I, pp 32–3.
64. *Thalaba*, vol I, p 76.
65. *Thalaba*, vol I, p 76.
66. *Thalaba*, vol I, pp 175–6.
67. 'I thought it better to express a feeling of religion in that language with which our religious ideas are connected' — *Poetical Works*, vol IV, p 28.
68. *Thalaba*, vol I, p 28.
69. *Thalaba*, vol I, p 109.
70. *Thalaba*, vol I, p 109.
71. *Thalaba*, vol I, p 110.
72. *Thalaba*, vol I, p 161.
73. *Thalaba*, vol I, p 163.
74. *Thalaba*, vol I, p 163.
75. *Thalaba*, vol I, p 73.
76. *Thalaba*, vol I, p 121.
77. Sale's Notes, p 266.
78. Sale's Notes, p 266.
79. *Thalaba*, vol I, p 144.
80. See *Life and Correspondence*, ed C. C. Southey, vol III, p 351.
81. *Life and Correspondence*, ed C. C. Southey, vol III, p 7.
82. *Poetical Works*, p 180.

83. *Life and Correspondence*, ed C. C. Southey, vol IV, p 180.
84. *Life and Correspondence*, ed C. C. Southey, vol IV, p 180.

Chapter 3: Thomas Moore's *Lalla Rookh* and the Politics of Irony

1. *The Memoirs, Journal and Correspondence of Thomas Moore*, ed by Lord John Russell, 8 vols (London 1855–6), vol VIII, pp 92–3.
2. Thomas Moore, *The Poetical Works*, ed by Moore, 10 vols, (London: Longman, 1840–41), vol VI, p xvii.
3. *Memoirs*, vol VII, pp 255–6.
4. *British Review*, x (1817), pp 31–2.
5. *British Review*, p 22.
6. *Literary Panorama*, New Series (September 1817), vol vi, p 898.
7. *British Review*, p 35.
8. *Edinburgh Review* (November 1817), p 509.
9. Preface to *Lalla Rookh* in *Poetical Works*, p xvi.
10. Robert Welch, *Irish Poetry from Moore to Yeats*, Irish Literary Studies (Buckinghamshire: Colin Smyth, 1980), p 12.
11. *Byron's Letters and Journals*, ed by Leslie A. Marchand, 12 vols (London: John Murray, 1973–82), vol III, p 101.
12. Thomas Moore, *Lalla Rookh, an Oriental Romance*, 16th edn (London: Longman, 1828). All subsequent quotations of poetry and notes refer to this text.
13. *Koran*, p 102.
14. *Koran*, p 396.
15. *Koran*, p 192.
16. *Lalla Rookh*, notes, p 339.
17. *Koran*, p 47.
18. *Koran*, p 212.
19. *Lalla Rookh*, notes, p 339.
20. *Lalla Rookh*, notes, p 346.
21. *Lalla Rookh*, notes, p 95.
22. Cited in W. F. P. Stockley, 'Moore's Satirical Verse', *Queen's Quarterly*, vol xii, no 4 (April 1905), p 341.
23. Cited in Stockley, p 241.
24. Robert Birley, *Sunk Without Trace* (London: Rupert Hart-Davies, 1962), p 138.
25. *Poetical Works*, vol VI, p xvi.
26. *Lalla Rookh*, notes, p 358.
27. *Lalla Rookh*, notes, pp 353–4.
28. *Lalla Rookh*, notes, p 362.
29. *Lalla Rookh*, notes, p 245.
30. *Koran*, pp 245–6.
31. Sale's Notes, p 246.
32. *British Review*, p 33.

33. Quoted in Byron Smith, *Islam in English Literature*, p 197.
34. *British Review*, p 32.
35. *Lalla Rookh*, notes, p 162.
36. *Lalla Rookh*, notes, p 363.
37. *Lalla Rookh*, notes, p 146.

Chapter 4: Byron's 'Turkish Tales' and Realistic Orientalism

1. Isaac Disraeli, *Literary Characters*, 5th edn (London: Edward Moxon, 1834), pp 68f.
2. *Letters and Journals of Lord Byron with Notices on his Life*, ed by Thomas Moore, 10 vols (London: John Murray, 1830), vol I, p 95.
3. S. C. Chew, *The Crescent and the Rose: Islam and England during the Renaissance* (New York: Oxford University Press, 1938); vol I, W. C. Brown, 'Byron and English interest in the Near East', *Studies in Philology*, xxxiv (1937); H. S. C. Wiener, 'Byron and the East: literary sources of the "Turkish Tales"', in Herbert Davis *et al*, ed, *Nineteenth-Century Studies* (1940; reissued New York: Greenwood Press, 1968).
4. Bernard Blackstone, 'Byron and Islam: the triple Eros', *Journal of European Studies*, iv (1970).
5. *Letters and Journals*, ed Moore, p 100.
6. *Byron's Letters and Journals*, ed by Leslie A. Marchand, 12 vols (London: John Murray, 1974), vol I, p 250 (subsequently referred to as *BLJ*).
7. *BLJ*, vol I, p 250.
8. *The Complete Letters of Lady Mary Wortley Montagu*, ed by Robert Halsband, 3 vols (London: Oxford University Press, 1966), vol II, p 495.
9. *Montagu*, ed Halsband, vol II, p 386.
10. *Montagu*, ed Halsband, vol I, p 330.
11. *Montagu*, ed Halsband, vol I, p 368.
12. *Montagu*, ed Halsband, vol I, p 308.
13. *Montagu*, ed Halsband, vol I, pp 349–51.
14. This and subsequent references to Byron's poetry are taken from *Lord Byron, The Complete Poetical Works*, ed by Jerome McGann, 4 vols (London: Oxford University Press, 1981).
15. *Complete Poetical Works*, ed McGann, vol III, p 419.
16. Sales's Notes, p 80.
17. *Koran*, p 142.
18. *BLJ*, vol III, pp 190–91.
19. *BLJ*, vol III, p 191.
20. *BLJ*, vol III, p 164.
21. *BLJ*, vol III, p 165.

22. *BLJ*, vol III, p 200.
23. *BLJ*, vol III, p 195.
24. *BLJ*, vol III, p 205.
25. Blackstone, 'Byron and Islam'.
26. Cited by Malcom Elwin in *Lord Byron's Wife* (London: Macdonald, 1962), pp 270–71.
27. Disraeli, *Literary Characters*, p 64.
28. *BLJ*, vol III, p 227.
29. Blackstone, 'Byron and Islam', p 350.
30. *BLJ*, vol V, p 45.
31. *Complete Poetical Works*, ed McGann, vol III, p 436.
32. Thomas Moore, *Lalla Rookh* (London: Longman, 1856), p 423.
33. Jerome McGann, *Fiery Dust, Byron's Poetic Development* (Chicago: University of Chicago Press, 1980), p 163.
34. See McGann, *Fiery Dust*, p 163.
35. *BLJ*, vol III, p 199.
36. *Complete Poetical Works*, ed McGann, vol III, p 420.
37. Cited in Wiener, 'Byron and the East', p 89.
38. *Complete Poetical Works*, ed McGann, vol III, p 420.
39. *Complete Poetical Works*, ed McGann, vol III, p 424.
40. *Complete Poetical Works*, ed McGann, vol III, p 420.
41. Ibid.
42. *Complete Poetical Works*, ed McGann, vol III, p 419.
43. *BLJ*, vol III, p 199.
44. Ibid.
45. McGann, *Fiery Dust*, p 156.
46. *BLJ*, vol III, p 117.
47. Peter L. Thorslev, *The Byronic Hero: Types and Prototypes* (Minneapolis: University of Minnesota Press, 1962).
48. *Lady Blessington's Conversations with Lord Byron*, ed by Ernest J. Lovell (Princeton: Princeton University Press, 1969), pp 172–3. See other relevant passages in Byron's conversations with Dr Kennedy in Ernest J. Lovell, *His Very Self and Voice, Selected Conversations of Lord Byron* (New York: Octagon Books, 1980).
49. *Oxford English Dictionary*.
50. Jerome McGann, *'Don Juan' in Context* (London: John Murray, 1976), pp 27–30.
51. George Ellis, 'Lord Byron's "Giaour" and "Bride of Abydos"', *Quarterly Review*, x (October 1813–July 1814), pp 331–54.
52. *Complete Poetical Works*, ed McGann, vol III, p 417.
53. See Robert Gleckner, *Byron and the Ruins of Paradise* (Baltimore: Johns Hopkins University Press, 1967), Chapters 4 and 5.
54. *Manfred*, Act II, scene ii, line 117.

Bibliography

Abrams, M. H., *Natural Supernaturalism: Tradition and Revolution in Romantic Literature* (London: Oxford University Press, 1971)

Ahmed, Leila, *Edward William Lane: A Study of His Life and of British Ideas of the Middle East in the Nineteenth Century* (London: Longman, 1978)

Alexander, Boyd, *England's Wealthiest Son* (London: Centaur Press, 1962)

Arberry, A. J., *Oriental Essays: Portraits of Seven Scholars* (New York: Macmillan, 1960)

Asfour, M. H., 'The Crescent and the Cross. Islam and the Muslims in English Literature from Johnson to Byron' (dissertation, University of Indiana, 1973)

Asín y Palacios, Miguel, *Islam and the Divine Comedy*, trans by Harold Sunderland (London: Frank Cass, 1960)

Beckford, William, *The Episodes of Vathek* (London: Stephen Swift, 1912)

— *Vathek*, ed and introduced by Roger Lonsdale (London: Oxford University Press, 1983)

Bernhardt-Kabisch, Ernest, *Robert Southey* (Boston, MA: Twayne Publishers, 1977)

Birley, Robert, *Sunk Without Trace* (London: Rupert Hart-Davies, 1962)

Blackstone, Bernard, 'Byron and Islam: the triple Eros', *Journal of European Studies*, vol iv (1970), pp 325–63

— *Byron: A Survey* (London: Longman, 1975)

Brinton, Crane, *The Political Ideas of the English Romanticists* (New York: Russell and Russell, 1962)

Brombert, Victor, ed, *The Hero in Literature* (Greenwich, CT: Fawcett, 1969)

Brown, Wallace C., 'The Near East as Theme and Background in English Literature 1775–1825, with Special Emphasis on the Literature of Travel' (dissertation, University of Michigan, 1934)

— 'The popularity of English travel books about the Near East 1775–1825', *Philological Quarterly*, vol xv (1936), pp 70–80

— 'Byron and the English interest in the Near East', *Studies in Philology*, vol xxxiv (1937), pp 55–64

— 'English travel books and minor poetry about the Near East', *Philological Quarterly*, vol xvi (1937), pp 249–71

— 'Thomas Moore and English interest in the East', *Studies in Philology*, vol xxxiv (1937), pp 576–88

Bruce, James, *Travels to Discover the Source of the Nile* (Dublin: G. G. J. and J. Robinson, 1790–91)

Burke, Edmund, *The Works of the Honourable Edmund Burke*, ed by Walker King, 16 vols (London: C. and J. Revington, 1822)

Butler, Marilyn, 'Revising the canon', *The Times Literary Supplement*, 4–6 December 1987

Byron, Lord, *Letters and Journals of Lord Byron with Notices on his Life*, ed by Thomas Moore, 10 vols (London: John Murray, 1830)

— The Works of Lord Byron: Poetry, ed by Ernest Hartley Coleridge, 7 vols (London: John Murray, 1898–1903)

— *Lady Blessington's Conversations of Lord Byron*, ed by Ernest J. Lovell Jr (Princeton: Princeton University Press, 1969)

— *Byron's Letters and Journals*, ed by Leslie A. Marchand, 12 vols (London: John Murray, 1973–82)

— *His Very Self and Voice. Selected Conversations with Lord Byron*, ed by Ernest J. Lovell Jr (New York: Octagon Books, 1980)

— *Lord Byron, The Complete Poetical Works*, ed by Jerome J. McGann, 4 vols (London: Oxford University Press, 1981)

Carlyle, Thomas, *On Heroes, Hero-Worship and the Heroic in History* (1841; reprinted New York: Longmans, Green, 1906)

Carnall, Geoffrey, *Robert Southey and His Age: the Development of a Conservative Mind* (London: Oxford University Press, 1960)

— *Robert Southey*, Writers and Their Works series, no 176 (London: Longman, 1971)

Chapman, Malcolm, 'Ossian and the eighteenth century', in his *The Gaelic Vision in Scottish Culture* (London: Croom Helm, 1978), pp 29–52

Chardin, Sir John, *The Travels of Sir John Chardin into Persia and the East-Indies* (London: various edns, trans from Dutch, from 1686)

Chew, Samuel C., *The Crescent and the Rose: Islam and England during the Renaissance* (New York: Oxford University Press, 1938)

Chew, Samuel C., and Altick, Richard D., *Literary History of England: The Nineteenth Century and After, 1789–1939* (London: Routledge, 1967)

Cobban, Alfred, *Edmund Burke and the Revolt against the Eighteenth Century* (London: George Allen, 1960)

Coleridge, Samuel Taylor, *Biographia Literaria*, ed by J. Shawcross, 2 vols (London: Oxford University Press, 1979)

Conant, Martha Pike, *The Oriental Tale in England in the Eighteenth Century* (1908; reprinted New York: Frank Cass, 1966)

Daniel, Norman, *Islam and the West: the Making of an Image* (Edinburgh: Edinburgh University Press, 1960)

— *Islam, Europe and Empire* (Edinburgh: Edinburgh University Press, 1966)

De Quincey, Thomas, *De Quincey's Works*, author's edn, 16 vols (Edinburgh: Adam and Charles Black, 1862–71)

Disraeli, Isaac, *Literary Characters*, 5th edn (London: Edward Moxon, 1834)

Ellis, George, 'Lord Byron's "Giaour" and "Bride of Abydos"', *Quarterly Review*, vol x (October 1813–July 1814), pp 331–54

Elton, Oliver, *A Survey of English Literature*, 4 vols (London: Edward Arnold, 1965)

Elwin, Malcolm, *Landor, a Replevin* (London: Macdonald, 1958)

— *Lord Byron's Wife* (London: Macdonald, 1962)

Fitzgerald, Edward, *The Rubáiyat of Omar Khayyám* (London: Routledge, 1910)

Forster, John, *Walter Savage Landor, A Biography* (London: Chapman & Hall, 1869)

Fryer, John, *A New Account of East-India and Persia, in Eight Letters. Being Nine Years' Travels, Begun 1672, and Finished 1681* (London: n.p., 1698)

Gibbon, Edward, *The History of the Decline and Fall of the Roman Empire* (Boston, MA: Little, Brown, 1855)

Gleckner, Robert E., *Byron and the Ruins of Paradise* (Baltimore: Johns Hopkins University Press, 1967)

Grebnier, Bernard, *The Uninhibited Byron: An Account of Sexual Confusion* (London: Peter Owen, 1971)

Gwynn, Stephen, *Thomas Moore* (London: Macmillan, 1904)

Hobhouse, John Cam, *A Journey Through Albania*, 2 vols (London: J. Cawthorn, 1813)

Jones, Howard Mumford, *The Harp that Once: A Chronicle of the Life of Thomas Moore* (New York: Holt, 1937)

Jones, Sir William, *The Works of Sir William Jones*, ed by Lord Teignmouth, 13 vols (London: Stockdale, 1807)

Knight, G. Wilson, *Lord Byron: Christian Virtues* (London: Routledge & Kegan Paul, 1952)

Knipp, Charles C., 'Types of orientalism in eighteenth century England' (dissertation, University of California, Berkeley, 1974)

Lamb, Charles, *The Letters of Charles Lamb*, ed by Ernest Rhys, 2 vols (1909; reprinted London: J. M. Dent, 1950)

Landor, Walter Savage, *The Poetical Works of Walter Savage Landor*, ed by Stephen Wheeler, 3 vols (London: Oxford University Press, 1937)

Lane, Edward William, *An Account of the Manners and Customs of the Modern Egyptians* (London: J. M. Dent, 1936)

Lang, Andrew, ed, *The Arabian Nights Entertainments* (New York: Dover, 1969)

Lewis, John Livingston, *The Road to Xanadu* (London: Constable, 1927)

Le Yaouanc, Collette, *L'Orient dans la Poésie Anglaise de l'Epoque Romantique, 1798–1824* (dissertation, Haute Bretagne, 1973; Paris: Librairie Honoré Champion, 1975)

Lovell, Ernest J., Jr, *Byron: The Record of a Quest* (Austin: University of Texas Press, 1949)

McGann, Jerome J., '*Don Juan*' *in Context* (London: John Murray, 1976)

— *Fiery Dust: Byron's Poetic Development* (Chicago: University of Chicago Press, 1980)

Madden, Lionel, ed, *Robert Southey: the Critical Heritage* (London: Routledge & Kegan Paul, 1972)

Mahmoud, Fatma Moussa, ed, *William Beckford of Fonthill: Bicentenary Essays* (Port Washington, NY: Kennikat Press, 1972)

Maurois, André, *Byron*, trans and ed by Hamish Miles (London: Jonathan Cape, 1940)

Meester, Marie E. de, *Oriental Influences in the English Literature of the Nineteenth Century*, Anglistische Forschungen, no 46 (Heidelberg: C. Winter, 1915)

Melikian, Anahid, *Byron and the East* (Beirut: American University of Beirut, 1977)

Montagu, Lady Mary Wortley, *The Complete Letters of Lady Mary Wortley Montagu*, ed by Robert Halsband, 3 vols (London: Oxford University Press, 1966)

Moore, Thomas, *Lalla Rookh: an Oriental Romance*, 16th edn (London: Longman, 1828)

— *The Poetical Works of Thomas Moore*, ed by Moore, 10 vols (London: Longman, 1840–41)

— *The Memoirs, Journal and Correspondence of Thomas Moore*, ed by Lord John Russell, 8 vols (London: Longman, Brown, Green and Longmans, 1853–6)

Pickthall, Marmaduke William, *The Meaning of the Glorious Koran* (Edinburgh: Knopf, 1930)

Richardson, John, *Dissertation on the Languages, Literature and Manners of the Eastern Nations* (Oxford: n.p., 1777)

Said, Edward, *Orientalism* (New York: Vintage Books, 1978)

— *Culture and Imperialism* (New York: Knopf, 1993)

Sale, George, *The Koran, Commonly called the AlKoran of Mohammed, Translated into English from the Original Arabic, with Explanatory Notes Taken from the most Approved Commentators, to which is prefixed A Preliminary Discourse* (London and New York: George Routledge & Sons, n.d.)

Schneider, Elizabeth, *Coleridge, Opium, and Kubla Khan*, (Chicago: University of Chicago Press, 1953)

Schwab, Raymond, *La Renaissance Orientale* (Paris: Payot, 1950)

Shaffer, E. S., '*Kubla Khan*' *and the Fall of Paradise* (Cambridge: Cambridge University Press, 1975)

Shelley, Percy Bysshe, *The Complete Poetical Works of Shelley*, ed by Neville Rogers, 8 vols (London: Oxford University Press, 1972)

Simmons, Jack, *Southey* (London: Collins, 1945)

Smith, Byron Porter, *Islam in English Literature* (Beirut: The American Press, 1939)

Southey, C. C., ed, *The Life and Correspondence of Robert Southey*, 6 vols (London: Longman, 1849–50)

Southey, Robert, *Thalaba*, 2 vols (London: Longman, Rees, 1801)

— *The Poetical Works of Robert Southey, Collected by Himself*, 10 vols (London: Longman, 1846)

— *The Correspondence of Robert Southey with Caroline Bowles*, ed by E. Dowden (Dublin: Hodges and Figgis, and London: Longmans and Green, 1881)

— *Selections from the Letters of Robert Southey*, ed by J. W. Warter, 4 vols (London: Longman, Brown, Green & Longmans, 1856)

— *The Common-place Book*, 4th series, ed by John Wood Warter (London: Reeves and Turner, 1876)

— *New Letters of Robert Southey*, ed by Kenneth Curry, 2 vols (New York and London: Columbia University Press, 1965)

Stockley, W. F. P., 'Moore's satirical verse', *Queen's Quarterly*, vol xii (April 1905), no 4, pp 329–46; vol xiii (July 1905), no 1, pp 1–13

Super, R. H., *Walter Savage Landor, a Biography* (London: John Calder, 1957)

Thorslev, Peter L., *The Byronic Hero: Types and Prototypes* (Minneapolis: University of Minnesota Press, 1962)

Trench, Wilbraham F., *Tom Moore* (Dublin: Sign of the Three Candles, 1934)

Venturi, Franco, 'Oriental despotism', *Journal of the History of Ideas*, vol xxiv (1963), pp 133–42

Vitoux, Pierre, '*Gebir* as an heroic poem', *The Wordsworth Circle*, vol vii (Winter 1976), pp 51–62

Volney, Constantine François, *Les Ruines* (Paris: Chez Desenne, Volland, Plassan Librairies, 1791)

Wiener, Harold S., 'Byron and the East: literary sources of the "Turkish Tales"', in Herbert Davis et al, eds, *Nineteenth-Century Studies* (1940; reissued New York: Greenwood Press, 1968)

Welch, Robert, *Irish Poetry from Moore to Yeats*, Irish Literature Studies (Gerrards Cross, Bucks: Colin Smyth, 1980)

Index